OCLC
WorldCat

Advanced Search   Find a Library

Add to list   Add tags   Write a review   Rate this item   ☆☆☆☆☆

Linguistics manifesto : universal language & the super unified linguistic theory

Author:	Tienzen Gong
Publisher:	Diamond Bar, Calif. : PreBabel Institute, ©2010.
Edition/Format:	Print book : English
Database:	WorldCat

Find a copy in the library

Enter your location: 91745   [Find libraries]

Library

1. **University of Illinois at Urbana Champaign**
    Urbana, IL 61801 United States

2. **University of Wisconsin - Madison, General Library System**
    Madison, WI 53706 United States

3. **University of Chicago Library**
    Chicago, IL 60637 United States

4. **Georgia State University**
    Atlanta, GA 30303 United States

5. **Cornell University Library**
    Ithaca, NY 14853 United States

6. **Columbia University in the City of New York**
    Columbia University Libraries
    New York, NY 10027 United States

7. **Brown University**
    Brown University Library
    Providence, RI 02912 United States

8. **HCL Technical Services**
    Harvard College Library
    Cambridge, MA 02139 United States

« First ‹ Prev 1 2 Next › Last »

The Divine Constitution

Jeh-Tween Gong

Copyright © 1992 by Jeh-Tween Gong

Typesetting by Joseph Francis
(201) 798-5831

Library of Congress Catalog Card
Number 91-90780

International Standard Book Number
ISBN 0-916713-05-9

Printed in the United States of America

ADAMS PRESS

Preface

Since time immemorial, man has been astonished by and confronted with many mysteries. Why did I receive my life? What must I do with my life? Who created all this? Thus, man has always contemplated the mysteries of existence, of nonexistence, of life, of death, of suchness (that is, of why are things as they are rather than otherwise), of the creation of the world and even of the creation of the godhead.

The ancient people, in their search for explanations and solutions, invented gods. First, they deified ancestors. Then they animated nature. They used mythical language and symbolic expression. After the coming of Christianity, the mythology of the ancients was prohibited, and all mysteries were covered up with absurdities. The more absurd, the higher the divinity. Christianity sacrifices truths for the sake of dogmas, and dogmatism makes no distinction between degrees of knowability and equal certitude in all matters. Dogmatism does not search for truths but ordains them.

After the Renaissance, many scientists tried to eliminate the absurd Christian god in the interest of truth; in turn, they sacrificed the utmost truth for the sake of scientific methodology. Today, many of them find that they are facing a dead-end in their search for the ultimate truth. They have realized that this ultimate truth is nothing other than God Himself.

This book breaks out of all old methodological barriers and into the ranges of a total absoluteness where the godhead creates itself. It provides a remarkable explanation of the ultimate reality—the creation of the godhead, the essence of God, the language of God, providence and divination, the souls, and the triune universe. It also provides much insight into three major religions—Taoism, Buddhism and Christianity. In short, this book shows us God through understanding. It brings us to a new world that has never before been reached by either reasoning or faith. God is no longer shrouded in mysteries.

Jeh-Tween Gong

Bristol, Virginia
February 24, 1992

i

Contents

Chapter I
In Search of God

It was a very hot day. The west wall of the house was still releasing heat long after sunset. A small 60-watt light bulb baked our small living room to an intolerable warmth. We all went out to the front yard seeking a cool breath. My two elder sisters were arguing over which star was the brightest. On the contrary, I was trying to find the faintest one. My mind was expounding on what was behind this faintest star. What was it behind "that" still? Was "that" God? I was only five years old then.

At age six, I was baptized in a Lutheran church. The pastor sprinkled some holy water on the top of my head. This blessed water was supposed to cleanse my sins. He also drew a cross with his hand wetted with holy water. This cross was supposed to shield me from all harms, caused by either demons or evils. Indeed, I did know what I was doing. I was getting saved. I walked down the aisle between pews to the pulpit to receive my savior, Jesus Christ. I did all this by myself; nobody held my hand. I was saved. I had an admission ticket firmly in my hand for the future of going to heaven. I knew that, and my pastor told me so, too.

At the time, I did not really know what spiritual rapture means or is, but I was very happy, extremely happy. Although my body was still tiny, no doubt my spiritual body had matured. At sunset, my excitement slowly wore off, involuntarily. I was hoping I could stay at that spiritual summit forever, but my daily chores finally brought me back to earth. I was still obligated to set the dinner table just as before, to clean my bedroom just as before, and the worst of all still to take a bath. That day, I did go to heaven without knowing where and what heaven was. I did know that I was saved without knowing what it meant. In search of God, my journey began at age of six.

II

In Sunday school, there were always contests, seeing who could recite the most Bible verses. The winner always received a beautiful Christmas card, which was indeed a rare commodity in China then. In a few years, I won a big stack of those beautiful cards. Not only I was proud of my achievement but was sure that a clear understanding of God was indeed in hand. After all, I had spent at least twice as much study time reciting Bible verses as I had on all other books put together. But, to be honest to myself, I knew I did not know what God was, not just yet, at age of ten.

My pastor told me, "Jesus is the Son of God. He is God in a human form. God loves us, so He sent His only son to save us. So Jesus is God. God is love. What else do you want to know? Read the Holy Bible, then you will know it all."

I said, "But sir, I have already spent many years reading the Bible, and I do know every word you just said." I can recite them with my eyes closed. But those words are just words. They do not help me understand the essence of the true God. Love seems only to be an attribute or a character of God, not the essence of God. I already know that God is infinitely wise, infinitely loving and infinitely powerful. His grace is the driving force for the entire universe. His spirit is the soul of all lives. But wisdom, love, power and grace are only His attributes. Just look at this coin; this side is "heads," tails on the other side. Heads and tails are only the attributes, not the essence of this coin. The essence of this coin is a penny. The spirit of this penny is a buying power worth a penny. The penny itself is the "body essence" of this penny. The buying power is the "spirit essence" of this penny. The heads and tails are only the attributes that are associated with this penny. The essence is the core; the attributes are things associated with the core and are things dancing round about the core. Indeed, I can feel God's love. I can witness God's wisdom. I can sense God's power. But I cannot see and understand God's essence that is formless. I want to peek into this invisible spirit, to touch this untouchable area, to understand this incomprehensible nonbeing. Is there any other book that ought to be read along with Bible, which may help me more easily understand what the essence of God is?

"No. No. No," answered my pastor, "There is no other book and cannot be any other book. If you cannot get it from Bible, your faith is not strong enough to receive God. Therefore, you cannot understand what God is."

"But sir, what is faith?" I asked.

"You receive faith by accepting and believing in Jesus,"he answered with some impatience leaping out from his blinking eyes.

"But, I already accepted Jesus many years ago when I was six, and I still do," I said with a deep disappointment. My pastor had taught me many words—God, faith and many others. But they were mere words, meaningless words. I accepted Jesus because His teaching can be understood very easily. Everyone, even a ten year old kid like me, can understand that to forgive the transgressions of others is indeed a great human virtue. There is absolutely no reason to accept this teaching with dogmatic faith. Anyone who rejects this teaching is, for sure, either an idiot or an evil man by nature. An evil man's faith surely has no use and no value whatsoever. Jesus' teaching about God's love and grace is again a simple fact. Everyone, even an idiot, can see the beautiful creations around him, the beautiful creatures, the twinkling stars, the romantic moon, the forever shining sun and the gentle loving earth. If anyone enjoys making a fool out of himself by playing a doubting Thomas to doubt those so vividly self-evident God's attributes, he should slap his own cheeks 100 times on each side, very hard. He may then wake up to recognize and to love God's great creation, his own cheeks. Again, there is no reason whatsoever that anyone needs "dogmatic faith" to recognize God.

Faith, however, is a very important tool for building human knowledge. All sciences began with faith, by believing in some premises and axioms. All of those premises and axioms do not have proofs; we accept them mainly with faith. But this faith is not a blind action. All of these axioms are very much self-evident, just the same as God who is indeed the most self-evident existence. So, the foundation for any faith is those self-evident cornerstones. Often, between any two self-evident cornerstones, there is indeed an area of uncertainty.

Often, the only way to leap over those knowledge dividing canyons is by using "faith". Both faith and logic are not truth but vehicles for reaching truths. Nonetheless, there is a big difference between them. Logic is like two feet of human intellect. Every rational reality is the one that can be reached with these two intellectual logic feet. Every new logic step is the one that can be bridged, reached and connected with these two intellectual feet, from the previous logic step. On the other hand, only faith can bridge two known self-evident cornerstones that are separated with infinite logic steps. Therefore, a metaphysical jump without a stepping stone, without a landing land mark, without a guiding light on the yonder shore is not only stupid, but this foolish action cannot be justified in the name of faith.

We can never dive into the unknown with faith; groping is the only way for that. Anyone who hugs "faith" and shows it around to explain any mystery is either an idiot or a big liar. We have faith in our spouses that they will not betray us because we understand their love for us, their personality and their virtue. Having a faith in a stranger, in the same degree as in our spouses, not only is an insult to our spouses but a foolish act. Faith without understanding is stupidity, is superstition, is hypocrisy.

III

At age twelve, on a sunny morning, I got on my bicycle to begin a new journey. I stopped at a gate of a Buddhist's temple. The gate was halfway open, or halfway closed; I did not know which is correct. I went in. There was a big courtyard. Directly across the courtyard, two statues stood guarding the entrance. One was exceedingly beautiful, the another fearfully ugly. I was not afraid of them but felt uncomfortable nonetheless. Why were there two idols standing right in front of Buddha? Was Buddha not strong enough himself and needed two guarding idols? I did not know the answer and did not even care to know, then. Many years later, I finally understood what they mean; they are the two cornerstones of all true religions. These two idols represent two aspects of human nature, goodness and evil. They are not idols standing outside of us but reside in us all the time. We have to transcend them in order to recover or rediscover the Buddha nature which is our true self. These two idols remind us about this fact every time we go into Buddhist's temple.

On the right side of the temple, in a smaller room, a monk was reading a book, a Buddhist's sutra. I was sure that he knew that I was there, but he did not pay any attention to me, no greeting, no question. I sensed that he did not want to be disturbed. So, back I went into the temple, looked at Buddha's smiling face without receiving any inspiration, finally sat down in a corner of the temple and hoped to see some signs of God. I sat there for a long time, the entire morning. During this period, only one old lady came in. She was very old, very ghostly looking. She saw me but ignored me. She kneeled in front of Buddha and prayed. She prayed for long time, at least two hours or more. No doubt, she had a long lifestory, clearly imprinted on her ghostly face. She prayed, teared, prayed again and teared again. Buddha was listening patiently, smiling still. Finally, she got up, turned around and left. She left with a smile on her face and gave me a smiling glance. With a glimpse, I found she was at least 10 years younger, or at least she was much happier than when she first came in. I was confused. What had happened? That day, I did not see God, but it seemed she did. I did not find God but found a human heart who talked to Buddha and received inspiration and comfort from Buddha, a wooden idol!

Mother was much younger than this old lady. She was born in a Christian Church. Her father was a Lutheran bishop. I have never met and will never meet my grandfather. I was told that he was not only a well-respected Christian bishop but a well-loved person. Mother received God on her first birthday, and she loves Him ever since. She is a well-educated lady. She can write poems and short-stories. One day, I was aimlessly searching for something in her closet; I found some of her writing, mainly about her lifestory. In every story, God was right there with her either helping her to overcome the difficulty or joining her enjoying the happiness. But, she has never tried to preach to us children. She did not and still does not even demand us to pray before meals; she just prays for us. Every night she spends at least one hour or more kneeling on her bed praying. If we children did any bad deeds during the day, she simply prayed longer in the night to ask God to forgive our sins. She may not be the best theologian, but I am sure she is the best Christian. No doubt, God is always with her and in her, and she is always with God and in God. Indeed, I can still sense and feel God because of her, but I wanted much more, not just to sense and feel God's existence. I wanted to know how God comes to be, what God's essence really is and why God is God.

IV

I found more questions than answers during the first ten years of my search. At end of this period, I still did not understand what God's essence was, but I did find a human heart that is capable of receiving God. Indeed, the image of Jesus on the cross did and still do move my heart. The image of the smiling Buddha did and still do move my heart. As for me, having an inspired and peaceful heart was not good enough. I wanted to know what the essence of God is. I not only wanted to put the concretized God, Jesus Christ, in my heart but I also wanted to touch and feel the formless God Himself, the Father of Jesus, the true God.

At age seventeen, I went to college to study physics and hoped to find the essence of God in the sciences. I was taught that the concretized God, Jesus Christ, had really blocked all passage ways to the true God. Many sages before us must have realized this fact long ago, at least five centuries ago. Many of them risked their lives for trying tó push Jesus aside and to peek at what is behind Him. With a push by Galileo, out it came physics. With a push by biologists, out it came biology. I also found out that most of my classmates held disdain for us Christians. For them, the virgin Mary story was not only a super superstition but an outright lie. To believe in the virgin Mary story and the story of bodily resurrection was not only stupid but insane. They did not think that any intellectual person can believe in those stories without first murdering his own consciousness. For them, they viewed many claims in Bible as falsities and lies. Today, many educated Christians still try not to discuss anything associated with the claims that Jesus walked on water, raised Lazarus from the grave, resurrected in a bodily form. For those Christians educated in the sciences, they only see Jesus as a teacher — teaching the right way of life, and as a savior — saving them from their sins. These educated Christians try to separate the touchable reality from their spiritual life, to separate their heart from their mind, to separate truth from faith. What they have done, in the eyes of their adversaries, is only a cop-out, an escape from the hard truth.

The professional theologians did not help to defend Christianity any better. They defended the authority of the Bible with two arguments.

1) Jesus' claims that He Himself is God is too supreme for any man to say such a statement — unless it is true. Therefore, it must be true.

2) There is and always has been only one Book that speaks with the authority of God. No other book even comes close to revealing the answers as to how we got here, why we were born and where we are headed.

In the eyes of the opponents of Christianity, these two arguments are indeed stupid, coming from someone who is, no doubt, completely blind and completely deaf; they do not know what else is around in the world. Bhagavan Sri Krsna declared himself as God many centuries before Christ, and the book of Darwin revealed much better answers to the questions of how we got here and where we are headed. Therefore, these two arguments are not even worthy of a rebuttal.

The third Christian defense is to proclaim that man cannot prove the Bible or God's existence through his own reasoning ability. The Bible can only be understood by first accepting it with faith, and God must first reveal Himself to whomever He chooses. This argument uses the source of the argument in its own defense. In the view of any rational person, that many of us are, this defense is not only stupid, but sinful; man shall not lie about something that he does not know.

Today, many people believe that the Christian church has been degraded into a social club for the educated, and Christianity has become a religion for the uneducated. Today, there are not many good words about

Christianity coming from academic publications. "The Columbia history of the world" is a history book written and edited by many great historians of our time; at least they are the people occupying the honorable seats at the high place.

They wrote, "The material collected in Genesis to II Kings did not reach its present form until the end of the fifth century. Beside the legends, the collection contains fragments of law codes, historical works, imaginative literary compositions (notably the Joseph romance), borrowings early and late from Mesopotamian mythology, and many minor elements. Most of these have been worked over by three or four editors and cemented and augmented by editorial inventions. The collection now begins with the creation of the world, which it dates about 4000 B.C., and contains a history of mankind from creation to the building of 'the tower' of Babel, a genealogy of the Semites from the flood to Abraham, and finally a history of Abraham and his descendants down to 560 B.C. Of the elements which here concern us, the legends, there are six main groups: those dealing with the early history of mankind, the patriarchs, Moses, the 'judges,' Saul and David, and the prophets. Almost no one now claims historical value for creation stories and their like. The 'essential historicity' of the legends about Abraham, Isaac, and Jacob is still defended by determined believers, but a stronger case can be made for the view that these were legends about the founders of Palestinian shrines whom the Israelites, after their conquest of Palestine, adopted as ancestors. Jacob's children had to be driven by famine into Egypt so that the Israelites, arriving from Egypt '470 years' later, could be represented as his descendants. (Similarly, the children of Hercules had to be banished from the Peloponnese so that they could lead the later Dorian invasion.) Once Jacob and his children have settled in Egypt the Old Testament knows practically nothing of their stay — a clear indication that there was no continuous tradition connecting the pretended 'patriarchal period' of the 1700's with the exodus, which by Biblical chronology would have to be dated in the first half of the thirteenth century [B.C.]." (Page 140)

Again, they wrote, "For this account of the work of Jesus, his immediate disciples, and Paul, the sources are the four Gospels, written in the last quarter of the first century [A.D.]; the Acts of the Apostles, originally a sequel to the Gospel According to Luke; and the letters of Paul, dating mainly from the fifties. These sources disagree with one another, and sometimes with themselves, in many points — for instance, their stories of the resurrection. Further, they all represent Christian tradition as it was after one or two generation of reflection, controversy, exaggeration, and invention. Finally, they are full of incredible stories of which some — those of the resurrection will again serve as instances — may be of historical value as reflections of subjective experiences. Consequently, no more than the main outlines of the history can be ascertained with certainty. Of the events described above, Jesus' choice of the twelve and their role, his arguments with the Pharisees, and his teaching about himself are matters of particular dispute. The history given by Acts is full of riddles, and we know nothing of the history in areas Acts neglected, for instance, Alexandria and Rome." (ibid, Page 218)

V

I was deeply troubled not because I could not defend Christianity in an intellectual way but because I knew that the virgin birth for humans is indeed impossible although it is possible for some very humble cold-blood life forms, such as a special kind of lizard and some very primitive fish. This virgin birth process is called "partenogenesis". In fact, virgin birth represents not miracle but primitive, not honor but disgrace, not "high and mighty" but "low and humble". Talmud — a compendium of Jewish law, lore and commentary — describes Jesus as the illegitimate son of a Roman soldier. Confucius was also born out of wedlock. All Chinese still love and respect him for his teaching, wisdom and righteousness. We Christians can do the same to Jesus. Beyond this, I was urged to find a defense for all the Bible's claims, not only for defending Christianity but also for defending my roots — the honor of my Grandfather and Mother. Many years later, I did find the transcendental logic that can explain everything described in Bible without the dogmatism and without the blind faith required by dogmatism.

In order to rescue Christianity from the stupidity of dogmatism, firstly, we have to define the issues clearly. There are three stages or steps in order to reach the ultimate reality. The first stage, the era from one trillionth of a second or even a much shorter time after the Big Bang to today, is now 90% well-understood by the traditional physics. The second stage describes the creation before the Big Bang. How was the Big Bang created? Who did it? If we arbitrarily name this Creator God, then the third stage must describes how God creates Himself.

Without knowing exactly how God creates Himself, the word "God" is only a meaningless word, a null word. Today, the word "God" has been grossly misused and over used. Even my seven year old son, Jason, knows exactly who and what God is. As for Jason, the word "God" means "answers" for everything. My four year old son, Henry, asked me who made stars. Jason quickly answered, "God did." Not only for seven year old Jason but for all churchgoers, God is "the answer" for all incomprehensible questions. Although this is indeed a correct answer, it is nonetheless a cop-out answer, an irresponsible act to avoid the responsibility of searching for the answers and of understanding the questions. Thus, my task is to show you step by step exactly what the word "God" is and means. Before all those steps are completed, the word "God" is only a null word, a meaningless word.

Secondly, a starting point of this searching journey must be clearly defined. I start the search for God with and from one and only one principle — the inclusive principle, that all facts (such as: physics, mathematics, social science, religious concepts etc.) must be included in God.

Regardless of how truth or knowledge was obtained, too much knowledge has won the name and title of truth, and nothing (dogmatism or blind faith) can deny them. Anyone who denies or ignores known facts in the name of dogmatism or blind faith has lost all rights to be a reasoning being. Darwin's evolution theory is indeed incomplete. Although it is unable to fill in many missing links that exist in the framework of evolution theory itself, there are many known facts as its foundation; furthermore, it does not rule out the creation theory. Anyone who denies these facts is immediately violating the inclusive principle.

Thirdly, a methodology must be clearly defined. What is knowledge? How many different paths are valid paths for obtaining knowledge? How many different kinds of vehicle are available for obtaining knowledge? These issues are discussed in Chapter II.

VI

Demanded by the inclusive principle, the second step has no other choice but to be some known facts. Among all known facts, physics is more universal than all other knowledge. In fact, all other physical knowledge must obey the laws of physics. Thus, the second step will begin with the facts of Physics.

Physics has a history of unifying many diversified physical forces. Coulomb force is symmetrical for both time and space. But, when an electron moves, its symmetry breaks down, and a magnetic force is created.

By understanding this symmetry breaking, Maxwell unified electric force and magnetic force into electromagnetism. Electromagnetism has a much higher symmetry. But, its symmetry breaks down at Beta decay, and a weak force is created. By understanding this symmetry breaking, three physicists unified electromagnetic force and weak force into the Electroweak theory, and they received a Nobel prize in 1979. Then, an even higher symmetry, quark color symmetry, was constructed. The breaking down of quark color symmetry generates strong force. By unifying this broken symmetry, Grand Unification Theory (GUT) is constructed.

Eighty years ago, Einstein tried to unify electric force and gravitational force but failed. Obviously, by looking at the above unification hierarchy, Einstein had no chance to succeed. The gravitational force is not the immediate symmetry partner of electromagnetic force but a partner of GUT force that is the grandmother of electromagnetic force. By unifying GUT force and gravitational force, Super Unified Theory (SUT) is constructed. Then, my book — Truth, Faith, and Life — presented the first TOE (Theory of Everything).

This process of unification in physics shows us a "path" to the ultimate reality. At this point, we need to pause and ask the following questions.

A) Can this unification process go beyond the notion of TOE? If yes, then what is it?

B) Is this unification process an infinite progressive process? If this process is indeed an infinite progressive process, then there is no way to reach or to conceptualize the last consequence. Using the word "God" to represent this limit point will neither help conceptualize the last consequence nor concretize the meaning of the word "God" itself. In other words, if there is meaning for the word "God," this unification process must stop in a finite number of unification steps.

C) But, why shall this unification process stop in a finite number of steps? How can it stop? Where does it stop? The word "God" can have meaning if and only if the above questions can be answered.

D) In order to answer the above questions, we first need to know what symmetry and symmetry breaking are and mean.

VII

Almost everyone has some fuzzy ideas of what symmetry is and means, but this fuzzy understanding is not good enough for our task — in search of

God. In our journey of searching for God, symmetry is defined precisely in terms of physics and mathematics.

Every morning when you look at yourself in a mirror, you realize that your face is symmetrical along the center line of your face. But, if you rotate that center line with an angle, your face will no longer be symmetrical along this new line. So, your face has a very low degree of symmetry.

If you fill up a square with 20 columns and 20 rows of the letter A, this square has a much higher symmetry than your face has because we can move our reference point or line from place to place in a certain way, and the same symmetry remains around its neighborhood. This kind of neighborhood symmetry is called gauge symmetry in Physics. When we change the letter A to the letter o (perfect circle), the new square has an even higher symmetry because the reference point or line for this new square has much more freedom.

In the above examples, the order of symmetry is measured in terms of transformation, by moving the reference point or line. For a square filled with letter A, the reference line has much freedom to move in parallel, and its neighborhood symmetry is not effected. For a square filled with letter o (perfect circle), the reference line not only can move in parallel but also rotate along many axes without effecting the neighborhood symmetry. This kind of linear movement or rotation of any given reference line or point is called "transformation" in physics. Any attribute of a system, which is unchanged under this kind of transformation, is called invariant. Every invariant always connotes a conservation law. Since "Space" is homogeneous and symmetrical for all linear translation operations, the linear momentum conservation law is manifested. Since "Time" is homogeneous and symmetrical under all transformations (linear, non-linear or rotation), energy conservation law is the result of this symmetry. The isotropic property of Space insures the invariant to rotation; in turn, there is angular momentum conservation law.

So, every symmetry property insures the existence of a conservation law. By the same token, every conservation law insures the existence of a symmetry.

Symmetry has another very important property — degrees of freedom. For example, an identical triplet is three identical kids. If we mark A, B and C on their back in order to distinguish them, we then can identify them from the back but are still unable to distinguish them from the front. The observer who observes them from their backs while they are sitting in a row of three seats can distinguish six different ways of sitting — ABC, ACB, BAC, BCA, CBA and CAB. But, any observer who observes these kids from the front is unable to distinguish these six different combinations. In other words, the degrees of freedom of these triplets is six for the observer in the front.

In general, the degrees of freedom of any system is equal to the number of variables needed to describe the system minus the number of confining equation in the system. This is the precise definition for degrees of freedom in physics or mathematics, but it may not be understood easily by everyone. Fortunately, degrees of freedom can be described precisely in terms of symmetry. The higher the symmetry a system has, the smaller the number of confining equation. Thus, the degrees of freedom of any system can be measured in terms of the "order" of symmetry of that system.

All philosophers and all theologians mumble about the notion of free will and free choice. They will never be able to know the true meaning of free will and free choice unless they first understand the meaning of degrees of freedom and the meaning of symmetry. Symmetry connotes conservation laws and degrees of freedom.

All known symmetries, from electromagnetism to Super Unified force or even to TOE, are not perfect symmetries; they all are broken in one way or another. So, why and how does any symmetry break? What is symmetry breaking? What is the consequence of a symmetry breaking?

When you use your index finger on your left hand to push your nose to the right side of your face, you have broken your face symmetry. Can you see now how to break your face symmetry? Repeat as many times the above procedure as needed to discover the meaning of this symmetry breaking.

All symmetries can only be broken by force. By the same token, any symmetry that breaks by itself always generates force. In other words, symmetry breaking connotes the generation of force in the physical world. When Super Unified symmetry breaks, it generates gravitational force and grand unified force. When grand unified symmetry breaks, it generates strong force and electroweak force. When electroweak symmetry breaks, it generates electromagnetic force and weak force.

VIII

With this clear understanding of the meaning of symmetry and symmetry breaking, we are now able to begin the third step on our journey of searching for God.

Is the super unified symmetry the last consequence on our journey? Obviously, it is not. The super unified symmetry is only the last consequence "after" the creation of the Big Bang in terms of physics. Many realities and notions — such as: love, consciousness, providence, etc. — are clearly not included in this super unified symmetry, at least not in its present form.

Is the TOE (Theory of Everything) symmetry the last consequence of our journey? This will really depend on the definition and the meaning of TOE. In its present form, "everything" connotes every mortal existence; if so, TOE is not the last consequence. We all have some fuzzy ideas of what mortal and immortal are. The meaning of these two words, mortal and immortal, will be clearly defined in Chapter III and IV respectively. Nonetheless, this fuzzy idea of these two words is good enough here for our discussion. If TOE only connotes all mortal realities (physics, lives, universe, etc.), then obviously there is a higher symmetry that consists of TOE and its symmetry partner.

What is this higher symmetry then? Is it the last consequence on our searching journey? Why shall it be the last? If it indeed is, how does it stop the progressive trend? What is its difference from all other known symmetries?

If we give this highest symmetry a name "God," the word "God" at this point is meaningless because we do not have the slightest idea of what it is. Nonetheless, we do know three requirements it must meet.

A) It has to be a symmetry.

B) It must be able to stop the process of infinite progression and to stop the question as to who created God if God created the universe. In short, this symmetry must be a "perfect" symmetry, not breakable upward.

C) While it cannot be broken upward to a higher symmetry, it must break downward into lower symmetries. In other words, this perfect symmetry cannot take an eternal nap; it must break into TOE and its symmetry partner.

Indeed, God has no intention of making our search any easier. The two requirements above (B and C) are no doubt contradictory. On the other hand, this "perfect-broken" paradox becomes a guiding light for our search. With this guiding light on hand, we are now able to find the meaning of the word "God" step by step. In Chapter II, a new methodology is introduced for our task. In Chapter III, a paradox axiom, some attributes of God and the meaning of the word "mortal" are discussed. In Chapter IV, the essence of this highest symmetry is found, and at this point the word "God" is no longer a null word.

With the clear understanding of the meaning and the essence of God, many philosophical and religious issues can be addressed. Chapter V — The Language of God — discusses how the two broken symmetries, TOE (mortal universe) and its symmetry partner (immortal sphere), are represented. Chapter VI discusses the moral truths. Chapter VII discusses the origin and the rise of consciousness.

Chapter II
Knowledge and Truth

Buddha showed us God by denying and denouncing logic, the objective world and even God Himself. This methodology of Buddhism is discussed in detail in Chapter VIII.

Jesus showed us God by proclaiming that he himself was God. His claim cannot be proved by either himself or his followers. Since his claim cannot be accepted by intuition of every reasoning being, thus, this methodology of Christianity is dogmatism. Dogmatism demands a "blind faith" from all followers. Dogmatism classifies mankind into two categories — one group having blind faith, the other having intuitive faith. Dogmatism does not search for truths but ordains them.

On the other hand, science shows us God by expelling God from its domain. In science, the question of God is outside the realm of physical experiments, and any experiment needs to have control and variable parts, but God cannot be excluded or included from either of these; thus, science discusses those aspects of the world which are free from detailed divine intervention. Although science is the only discipline found many concrete facts about both God's laws and His nature, science by definition can never reach the ultimate reality nor even formulate the concept of the ultimate reality because the ultimate reality is much more and beyond the physical realities. Thus, we must transcend scientific methodology in order to reach the ultimate reality. Our task of searching for a true understanding of the essence of God must take two actions — developing a theology which includes all known scientific facts which are God's laws and developing a new methodology to transcend the barrier that has imprisoned all sciences. This new methodology will not contradict the scientific methodology but includes it and goes well beyond it. In fact, to include the scientific methodology as the foundation is the prerequisite for the construction of this new methodology.

In this chapter, we will first examine the meaning of "knowledge and truth" and then distinguish the differences between them. We will then discuss the two paths and the two vehicles for travelling the journey to the ultimate truth. Finally, these paths and vehicles will be organized into three parts to form the ultimate problem solving tool box.

15

II

For many people, science represents truth. Does it really? Not entirely! Science is a sincere effort of searching for truth. Science itself is not truth but a vehicle that is trying to approach truth. Thus, a scientific finding is only an approximation of truth. Today, because of this self-restrained definition, science has won a very high reputation as a truth finder. Often, science has been perceived as truth itself. Today, all other truth seekers — by using some meaningless words such as inspiration, revelation, etc. — have been viewed as fiction tellers by all rational people. If these meaningless words cannot be clearly defined and if there is no clear process to show how inspiration begins, proceeds and concludes, then these inspiration truth seekers are indeed fiction tellers. In Chapter VII — The Origin and the Rise of Consciousness, I will provide a clear definition of what inspiration means and a clear defined process of how inspiration proceeds and works. Now, we shall first try to understand what is truth, how to approach it and what are the results that have already been found by our predecessors.

What has been found by our predecessors? Not truth, but a path to truth, a way to understanding. Truth itself is too obvious, too self-evident. A thing is "self-evident" if it can be conceived by all conscious minds without any contemplation, reasoning or faith. Or if it is denied, then all conscious minds will fall into a state of confusion. There is absolutely no need to prove that we are alive. We do need to know how lives begin, to understand how lives function. There is absolutely no need to prove the existence of God, but how God functions and how God comes to be. Thus, it is very clear that truth itself is quite different from the truth we perceive. Truth itself is immutable, eternal, and independent of all transient existence — a bubble, a consciousness or the entire universe.

Einstein was trying to describe the same truth that Newton described. Not surprisingly, their views of this same truth are quite different. Newton believed that all bodies, either earthly or heavenly, with mass were governed by a thing called "force," gravitational force. Amazingly, he even came up with a very simple mathematical equation to describe this thing (gravitational force) that he invented. Force was a word that had some fuzzy meanings long before Newton borrowed it for explaining the universal order. Before Newton, force implied a physical influence with a physical means. But Newton's force is an invisible dog leash that ties a planet to the sun or a moon to a planet. Amazingly, his simple equation proved to be quite accurate. Not only do all observable planets obey his equation, but we discovered two new planets from the prediction of his equation. It seems that Newton indeed found the truth. But, Einstein disagreed.

As for Einstein, he believed that the conception of force, especially the concept of an invisible dog leash, is nothing but a mistaken notion, a result of Newton's near-sightedness. He used a thought-experiment to explain his argument.

When two kids were playing marbles in an empty lot beside the Empire State Building, a marble often curves when it runs up to and down from a small hump. It is very obvious that the curvature of the marble movement is caused by the hump, the geometry of the ground surface. But, "Newton" was standing on the top of Empire State Building, looking down. He was unable to see the hump, the uneven ground surface. No doubt, he was puzzled as to why this marble changed direction. After long contemplation, he finally dreamed up a notion of an invisible dog leash, which he called gravitation, that must exist to cause this marble to change its direction so suddenly. For Einstein, Newton was no doubt only seeing an illusion. The universe is not controlled by any force that is only a dreamed up illusion but controlled by its own internal geometrical structure.

But surprisingly, the refined Einstein's equation does not provide a better portrait of our universe. If you can imagine that this page you are reading is the portrait of the entire universe according to Newton's idea, the portrait of the universe according to Einstein is exactly the same as this page with one additional small ink drop that sits at the margin of this page.

Surprise! Surprise! There is not much difference between Newton's illusion and Einstein's reality. This is the "Newton and Einstein paradox". But, why? Are they both only opinions of the same absolute truth? Does this absolute truth have many different faces? Is this absolute truth independent of our perception? Or, is there no such thing as the absolute truth?

Unfortunately, Einstein and his followers believe that there is no such thing as the absolute truth in the name of "Relativity Theory". This relativity theory ended an old civilization and started a modern world. During the short 80 years after its appearance, the knowledge we generated accounts for 90% of all knowledge accumulated since the beginning of mankind. This relativity theory also ended three millennia of wisdom, the recognition of God by Confucius, Buddha and Jesus. Indeed, the relativity theory is both a triumph and a tragedy of the twentieth century. God is so absolute, so self-evident, and all sages of mankind recognized Him except the modern scientists, although many of them may still go to church every Sunday but expel God from their intellectual thinking.

Is the relativity theory wrong? It has been verified in laboratories all around the world many, many times. But God is much more evident than all those laboratory tests that cover only a finite domain. Furthermore, Einstein and his followers' interpretation of the relativity theory, indicating that there is no absolute reference point in the entire universe and all frames are relative among one another, is indeed contradictory even to his own postulates and has no logic connection with all test results that proved his theory. In other words, his equations are correct but his interpretation is wrong. To understand this point, we shall first briefly discuss what the relativity theory is.

Many people believe that the relativity theory is way over their heads before they even try to understand it, and thus there is no reason even to try. In fact, the relativity theory is amazingly simple. It says that our watches will slow down when we travel at high speed. For many people, this statement is incomprehensible. How can a mechanical watch slow down when it is on a high speed train? Indeed, this statement is misleading. A mechanical watch will not slow down by itself; only time slows down, and therefore we have to slow down the watch. The watch and time are two different things. The watch itself is not time but an instrument for measuring time. If a watch is not synchronized with all other watches in the world, it obvious cannot provide the right time. Therefore, all watches have to be calibrated again and again. Let us assume that all watches in all train stations have been calibrated. Now we are on a high speed train and want to know what time it is and whether my watch is correct or not. The only way to find out the correct time is by checking with the nearest train station. So, we turn on our ham radio and ask what time it is. One second later, the train station receives our request and reports back to us that now the time is 1:00 p.m.. Since we are on a high speed train that is running away from the train station with a near light speed velocity, it takes a while for the radio signal to catch up to our train, for example : 10 minutes. When we receive this signal, "Now it is 1:00 p.m.," we adjust (slow down) our watch to 1:00 p.m., but the watch in the train station is now pointing to 1:10 p.m.. So, our watches slow down when we are on a high speed train.

Does the above phenomenon happen only to humans who have a perceptive mind, a conception of time and a watch? No! This phenomenon happens to all things, mindless electrons, protons, etc., and it was proven in laboratories around the world many, many times. I will discuss this electron consciousness in Chapter VII — "The Origin and the Rise of Consciousness".

Today, many scientists do believe that no truth can exist independent of an observing mind. Even a mindless electron has an observing mind! In other words, God cannot exist without an observing mind, the universe. Many people also believe that God is the final stage of a cosmic process. God exists wholly within the world, which is His body, but does not yet exist as an infinite, transcendent reality. He is only a goal to which the world continually strives but which is unattainable. Therefore, there is no such thing as the absolute truth. In other words, there is no God in the same sense as all sages recognized. This is the interpretation of Einstein and all of his followers for the relativity theory.

This interpretation of Einstein is the most ridiculous notion that ever dreamed up in human history, although his equations are, no doubt, correct. In fact, special relativity theory is indeed describing the facts that represents half of the ultimate reality which will be understood completely in the next few chapters. Nonetheless, his interpretation is even contradictory to his own postulates. He developed his theory with two postulates.

1) All reference points (inertial frames) are completely equivalent.

2) The velocity of light is independent of the motion of its source.

Both of these postulates point out the notion of absoluteness. When a south bound car and a north bound car are both driving 50 miles per hour, the relative speed between them is 100 miles per hour. But if they are both driving at light speed, the relative speed between them, according to the 2nd postulate, is still one light speed, not two light speed. Light speed plus light speed equals light speed still. Light speed is so "absolute," and nothing can be added on to it. Only infinity has the same kind of characteristic as light speed does. Indeed, light speed is the incarnation of infinity in this material world.

That all reference points are completely equivalent (the 1st postulate) is also pointing to absoluteness. It means that all laws are the same in all reference points (earth, solar system, or the entire universe), despite the fact that these points may be in uniform translation with respect to each other. What else can be more absolute than this postulate?

I do not know why the relativity theory was named the relativity theory. It should have been named the "Absoluteness Theory". His equations are indeed correct, but his interpretation is no doubt wrong. Often, a wrong theory or a wrong interpretation can indeed provide a right prediction. For example, the existence of Neptune was predicted by Newton's theory. After the discovery of Neptune it was found that there were still residual perturbations in the orbit of Uranus which could not be accounted for on the basis of Neptune's gravitational attraction. This led Lowell to postulate a trans-Neptunian planet, Pluto, and to calculate the orbit and mass of this planet using the same techniques that had let to the successful prediction of Neptune. Pluto was eventually found quite close to where it had been predicted to be, but it is now known that the actual mass of Pluto is much smaller than the mass that Lowell calculated, and that in fact there were no residual perturbations that required an account in the first place. In short, Pluto is discovered because of a wrong observation and a wrong calculation. A wrong theory or a wrong interpretation can indeed often provide a correct prediction.

III

From the examples above, truth very obviously is not only different from knowledge but independent of it. Knowledge is the pursuit of truth by consciousness. Both truth and consciousness are realities. Unfortunately, Einstein and his followers believed that consciousness is the master of truth; the truth (our Almighty God) is only the subject of consciousness. What kind of mistake can be more tragic than this one?

Consciousness is indeed a living reality, but it emanates from the ultimate reality. It pursues truth through two and only two ways, knowing and knowing of not knowing. Both Confucius and Socrates knew this. Confucius said, "knowing is knowledge, knowing of not knowing is also knowledge." In fact, knowing of not knowing is often a much more powerful way to obtain knowledge than the knowing is.

Newton realized that we do not really know how to measure a varying velocity, that we do not really know how to measure the gravitational force between two irregular shaped objects and that we do not even know how to analyze a curve. The only things we can handle are straight lines and constant velocity. Therefore, Newton cut all curves into an infinite number of pieces. These small pieces will be straight enough for us to handle. He invented Calculus. He turned the "not knowing" into a wonderful tool to analyze this complex universe.

Heisenberg realized that we are unable to locate a quantum particle's position exactly and to know where it is really going at the same time. The human ability seems so small and so helpless. But as soon as he realized his "not knowing," he discovered the uncertainty principle, and in turn he realized immediately that electrons are unable to stay in nucleus. And then, he developed quantum mechanics. The uncertainty principle is trying to prevent us to see through the secret of micro-world. But as soon as we accepted the uncertainty principle, we conquered micro-world.

The "uncertain knowledge" was viewed as a self-contradictory phrase by the ancients. Today, quantum physics is 100% certain that we are quite uncertain about the micro-world. By knowing of this uncertainty, quantum physics is able to predict the uncertainty of mirco-world with a great certainty. Quantum physics is not only a certain knowledge about the uncertain reality but itself is indeed an uncertain knowledge (especially the quantum perturbation theory for many particles) about the certain uncertainty.

We have not only seen the "Newton and Einstein paradox" already, but the ways of obtaining knowledge is also sort of a paradox in nature. Either knowledge itself has a paradoxical nature or the truth itself is a paradox. Nonetheless, there are two paths to truth, knowing and knowing of not knowing.

IV

Traditionally, truth is defined in two ways, in agreement with reality or in agreement with intent.

William James wrote, "Working successfully is the sign of its truth.... To agree in the widest sense with reality, ... Any idea that helps us to deal, whether practically or intellectually, with either the reality or its belongings... that fits, in fact, and adapts our life to the reality's whole setting, will agree sufficiently to meet the requirement. It will be true of that reality. ...

"A house is said to be true that fulfills the likeness of the form in the architect's minds."

But, there are two kinds of reality, subjective realities and objective ones. Freud wrote, "Science aims to arrive at correspondence with reality, that is to say with what exists outside of us and independently of us. ... This correspondence with the real external world we call truth."

But, the objective universe, being a finitude, is very small compared with the subjective world. The universe before and the universe after have no physical reference at this moment, but no doubt they are realities. I can even predict how they will be born, evolve and die. Furthermore, the truths of mathematics are no doubt realities although they are purely formal or lacking of direct reference to physical existence; they always act as languages to represent the physical realities. In short, there is in general no way of separating out what is made true by our linguistic conventions or subjective minds and what is made true by the facts of the world.

If we define truth as an agreement with reality, then we must first know what reality is and where the boundary of reality is. In Chapter IV — God's Essence, the ultimate reality is defined as God Space. If we define truth as an agreement with intent, then we must first know what intent is and how many different kinds of intent are out there.

There are three kinds of intent — intent of self, of others and of God. The intent of self is quite different from the intent of others. The intent of a cow is to be a cow and to have a long and meaningful cow-life, but the intent of man about a cow is to fatten it up and then to devour it. Therefore, the truth perceived by a cow is quite different from the truth beheld in men's hand.

From the above analysis, the truths of realities or of intent are only limited truth. In my book (Truth, Faith, and Life), I classified truths into three categories, utmost truth, limited truth and empty truth. The utmost truth is the union of all truths derived from all realities and intents. In other words, the utmost truth is the utmost reality and is God's intent. Aquinas wrote, "Natural things are said to be true in so far as they express the likeness of the ideas that are in the divine mind; for a stone is called true, which possesses the nature proper to a stone, according to the preconception in the divine intellect."

V

Now, our problem is how to obtain or to discover the truth. Many people classify knowledge into three classes, intuitive knowledge, demonstrative knowledge and sensitive knowledge. But there are only two paths available for pursuing knowledge, knowing and knowing of not knowing. There are also only two vehicles available for traveling on these two paths to knowledge. One vehicle is the sensing and reasoning-mind, its perceptions, experiences and logic. The other is the intuitive-mind, its faith and belief.

The sensing and reasoning-mind can often be deceived by illusions, hallucinations and dreams. Therefore, no doubt, this type of knowledge often has some degrees of uncertainty. But we do not have a big problem in finding truths with this vehicle. Often, we simply throw away the old knowledge when a new light appears and when our sense travels into a new territory.

Both science and philosophy is driven by the reasoning vehicle. The only valid methodology in science is the interplay between hypothesis and verification. The most important methodology in philosophy is the interplay between reflection and speculation. But, both hypothesis and speculation can be generated or come alive if and only if there is "free will". Furthermore, all transient reflections and inductive verifications can become lasting truths if and only if the "immortality" is a reality, not just a possibility. In Kant's time, it was indeed impossible to prove, not merely to speculate, or to derive these two concepts, free will and immortality, from anything more fundamental. The only easy way out is by accepting God as a necessary Being by "Faith" and by accepting God as the source of both free will and immortality, again by faith. Therefore, the vehicle of reasoning is powered by the energy of "Faith" and is constructed with three postulates — God, immortality and free will.

Kant simply accepted that God is the source of all truths by faith. Therefore, faith is the foundation of all knowledge. Unfortunately, the word "faith" has been misused by many people for thousands of years. First, they view "faith" as the opposite of "reason," not knowing that the vehicle of reason is indeed powered by the energy of faith. It is by faith that all scientific axioms are accepted. Furthermore, even demonstrative knowledge relies upon intellectual judgement to verify its steps of logic. Again, it is by faith that this judgement is accepted. Too many people have mistaken the discursive steps and the logic steps to have lives of their own that they can reveal truth all by themselves without any external support. This is another very unfortunate mistake. The gap between two logic steps is often small enough; therefore, human minds can·bridge it easily because of some preexisting intuitive and practical knowledge. But they often forget that the preexisting knowledge are built on some axioms that are initially revealed with and accepted by faith alone. Not only the demonstration process of all demonstrative knowledge depends upon indemonstrable truths, but also the connection between all reasoning steps (deduction or induction) is also indemonstrable and must be intuitively perceived. Not only intuition and belief supply the first principles or ultimate premises of reason, but they also certify each step in the process. There is never at any stage of the reasoning process independent of belief and intuition. Although there are many formal reasoning structures — such as: deduction, induction, proof, inference, syllogism, comparison, judgement, prior and posterior analysis, etc. — reasoning is only a fancy name for faith and belief. Reasoning is and involves the rooted beliefs that all people have taken for granted. Reasoning has become the intellectual feet of all people, which they use to walk through and bridge over all their intellectual thoughts, from one thought to the next. If the gap between two thoughts is too wide and cannot be bridged over by their intellectual feet, then faith is needed. Reasoning is miniature faith.

For any paradox, the gap between two opposite sides is great, often infinite and far apart. Thus, there is always no practical knowledge that is able to bridge this gap. It can only be bridged by faith. Only faith can reveal the unifying principle that reconciles every paradox. There is always a unified principle that is associated with each paradox. This "paradox axiom" is discussed in the next chapter. So, faith and belief is only a vehicle to connect two known facts. Faith and reasoning are only different in degree, not in kind. In fact, faith contains an infinite number of logic steps or an infinite number of reasoning steps.

Secondly, too many people have mistaken "belief" to be knowledge. I sincerely believe that Einstein and his followers do not intentionally deceive us with their wrong interpretation. They are simply ignorant of the truth. They claim, with complete sincerity, to know things which turn out to be false in the end. They do believe that they know the truth. Often, we can believe what is indeed false. Belief is not knowledge.

In the vehicle of faith, there are two tools, intuition and revelation. Revelation operates as an irrational factor in problem solving, such as when the solution is reached suddenly by a leap of imagination, by a dream, by a sign which is not related to the problem, or by the divine inspiration which comes out of blue. For example, a person was very sad and mad because he had a flat tire and therefore missed his air flight. Soon after, he found out that that air plane he was supposed to be on had crashed, and there were no survivors. He "suddenly" understood not only the existence of God but also His love and providence, although the event he just experienced may not be all clearly related to the truth he just comprehended. Nonetheless, this reveled truth can be not only verified with both intuition and reasons by the individual but also by the public. Intuition does not oppose logic but transcends it. Intuition does not depend on the thin thread of reasoning, inductive or deductive, but has a broader basis.

Spinoza wrote, "He who has a true idea knows at the same time that he has a true idea. ... It is impossible to have a true idea without at the same time knowing that is true."

Aristotle wrote, "Axioms, or self-evident and indisputable truth are those propositions immediately known to be true, and necessarily true, because their contradictory are impossible statements."

Augustine wrote, "Within me, in the inner retreat of my mind, the Truth, which is neither Hebrew nor Greek, nor Latin nor Barbarian, would tell me, without lips or tongue or sounded syllables: 'He speaks truth.'"

No doubt, the intuition is an intrinsic criterion of truth and is the inner voice which is guaranteed by God's embodiment and which plainly signifies the truth. Unfortunately, too many people have mistaken "hallucination" to be intuition or revelation, and therefore have severely destroyed the word "faith".

Faith can only bridge two truths, which may stand infinitely far apart. Faith can never reveal anything that is unknown, which lacks at least two guiding lights. Faith can never reach the unknown. Believing anything unknown in the name of faith is superstition. Believing anything untrue in the name of faith is stupid. Asking anyone to believe anything unknown and untrue in the name of faith is evil.

Today, faith is an over used and misused word. To overcome this misfortune, the true faith will be called "intuitive faith" which is the driving force for reasoning. The dogmatic faith will be called "blind faith" which is superstition and stupidity.

Thirdly, too many people have mistaken "faith" as a "state" or as a dogma instead of as a tool or a vehicle for pursuing truth. Only "understanding" is a state, a state that is reached by the combined effort of both vehicles — reason and faith. Aquinas wrote, "When anyone in the endeavor to prove what belongs to faith, brings forward arguments which are not cogent, he fall under the ridicule of the unbelievers; since they suppose that we base ourselves upon such arguments, and that we believe on their account. Therefore, we must not attempt to establish what is of faith, except by authority alone." In this statement, Aquinas first mistook "belief" as the foundation of faith, then mistook faith as dogma, then worst yet placed faith in the hand of an institution. In other words, Saint Thomas Aquinas, as brilliant as he was, did not truly understand what "faith" is and means. Faith is a vehicle or a tool for pursuing truth; faith is neither a dogma nor an institution. Faith is the inner voice of every individual, the third eye of every human.

Dogmatism makes no distinction between degrees of knowability and equal certitude in all matter. It knows everything because it is dogmatism. The top lip of the authority of a dogma is "dog," the bottom lip "ma," and any noise they uttered is "dogma". Dogmatism is only hypocrisy, only superstition, only stupidity.

VI

Knowledge always involves a relationship between a knower and a known. From the view point of human, truth always consists of some kind of correspondence between what the mind thinks or understands and the reality it tries to know. No doubt, this is how we human beings perceive and attain truth, but it is not the definition of truth.

Plotinus wrote, "The object known must be identical with the knowing act. If this identity does not exist, neither does truth." This is a terrible mistaken notion. Without the knowing act, we human beings will be ignorant beings, but truth will remain to be truth.

In fact, this is a many thousand years old debate between objectivism and subjectivism. Phenomenalism reduces all material objects (of distinct, external physical entities perceptible by different persons at once) to sensa (private, transitory, probably mental existents that many also be called sensations, sense data, ideas, representations or impressions). Hence, if material objects are reduced to actual sensa and consist only of them, they must cease to exist when unobserved, and those never observed must never have existed. Worse still, the material objects in a room must apparently come into and go out of existence as one looks at or away from them—the blinking of human eye can destroy or create them. Seemingly, this ridiculous notion of phenomenalism is wrong, but with some deeper investigations the subjectivism always comes back to play a central role in epistemology. Which one, objectivism or subjectivism, is right? How can we obtain objective knowledge of the physical world?

In order to answer this, we must first understand the meanings of veridical perception, nonveridical perception and objectivity. Traditionally, nonveridical perception includes misperception, illusion and hallucination. Misperception is caused by misidentification and can be corrected as a result of further perceptual examination. Hallucinations are cases of perceptual experience that occur without the usual causal process originating in the physical world. Although both misperception and hallucination are realities, they themselves are not knowledge but are objects that can be investigated.

Traditionally, illusion is classified as nonveridical perception, such as a straight stick looks bent when it is partially submerged and a white rose looks blue under blue light. In fact, these illusions are not results of a malfunction of the perceptual system (eyes, brain and mind); they are objective facts. According to objective physics laws, a white rose must look blue under blue light, and a straight stick must look bent when it is partially submerged.

Then, what is veridical perception? Can veridical perception indeed obtain objective knowledge of the objective world? Can veridical perception guarantee the items I perceive indeed existing in the physical world?

After Lowell predicted the existence of Pluto, astronomers looked for it for some twenty-five years, and thousands of photographs were taken, but they all failed because the area in question is so densely populated with stars that there were some 300,000 images on each photograph. Pluto was finally observed after the blink microscope was invented. In other words, many astronomers looked at the same photographs for twenty-five years but were unable to observe the existence of Pluto. Thus, veridical perception can only be accomplished by proper capabilities.

There are two kinds of perceptual capabilities, seeing and epistemic observing. When I look at a watch, I am seeing 'a watch' and am epistemically observing 'time.' When I look at a thermometer, I am seeing a thermometer but am epistemically observing temperature. Seeing relies on instruments, such as: eyes, microscope, camera, etc. Epistemic observing depends on beliefs and theories. Two individuals, operating from different conceptual frameworks, may be observing the same physical object and still be perceiving different, even incompatible, items.

At this point, the difference between objectivity and subjectivity appears. Every object not only has an infinite number of objective attributes but also have many subjective ones. The chair I am sitting on can be seen as a chair, but a botanist might be epistemically observing it as only the remain of an oak tree. Thus, the subjective perceptual identification of any external object not only can differ in an infinite number of ways but can never be identical with the object itself. In short, the subjective image of an object has no physical reference. Many philosophers have confused the subjective object with the external object and thus claim that the external object is not a reality.

Furthermore, this chair (an external object) also has many subjective attributes. For me, it carries many good memories; I sit on it to study for many years. For Gloria, it means chores, cleaning it and putting it away. For Henry, it is an obstacle; he tripped over it many times. In short, when we perceive the external objects, on the one hand our perception brings only a friction information of the objects to our subjective mind, and on the other hand our mind perceives information that goes much beyond that carried by sensory stimulation.

With the great entanglement of this subjective and objective nature of every external object, how can we obtain objective knowledge from this big mess. In fact, it is very simple. First, the external objects imprint their primary qualities onto our subjective mind through our sense organs. Then, our subjective mind constructs beliefs and theories and uses them to perform epistemic observation. Although the epistemic observation is subjective and theory-dependent, it not only must be consistent with the original object but it itself becomes a new object which subjects to public investigation. This process forms an infinite recursion, from objective object to subjective belief, then to objective object(s), and the objectivity of scientific knowledge is thus obtained.

The discovery of neutrino is one good example of the above process. Neutrino can never be seen and was originally postulated to account for the continuous energy spectrum of the electrons emitted in beta decay. With this postulate, the subjective theoretical work about neutrino thus began. Then, the neutrino theory predicted the interaction between neutrinos and other particles. Thus, the observation of neutrinos became possible and was in fact achieved. Physicists built a causal-chain to extend their epistemic senses. The neutrino interaction happened in bubble chamber, and the images of the products of the interaction (not neutrino itself) were captured on photographs. With this causal-chain, physicists indeed epistemically observed neutrinos. Then, the status of neutrino was transformed from a postulated particle to an objective entity, and the neutrino theory became the genuine knowledge, and they were used to be as foundation for postulating new particles and new theories.

In fact, this infinite recursive process (from external object to subjective object, back to objective objects) contains two inductive processes, the scientific induction and the historical induction. On the one hand, every scientific truth is reached with inductive proof. On the other hand, the history of science consists largely of a sequence of theories that were highly successful as judged by scientists in the relevant period, but which were nevertheless eventually rejected and replaced by very different theories, such as Einstein's theory replaces Newton's and my Super Unified Theory is replacing Einstein's. The infinite interplay between these two inductive processes on the one hand guarantees the objectivity of knowledge and on the other hand guarantees that knowledge is always the slave of truth.

VII

The difference between knowledge and truth is now very clear. Truth is independent of knowledge. Truth is the ultimate reality that is pursued by knowledge (consciousness). Knowledge is obtained with two vehicles, reason and faith. Although knowledge is indeed a reality, it does depend upon truth to be alive. Truth is the master, knowledge the slave. We humans are mortals and are trapped in "Time and Space". We have to move our thoughts from one point to another, whether by using reasoning, believing, dreaming, imagining or with intuition. Only immortal, the ultimate truth, can see all knowledge even without the effort of seeing, because the whole knowledge is only Himself. Aquinas wrote, "In the divine knowledge, there is no discursiveness, no succession, neither the turning from one thought to another, nor the advance from the known to the unknown by reasoning from principles to conclusion. God sees all things in one thing alone, which is Himself."

God is the source of all truths. In fact, God Himself is the ultimate truth. At this point, the word "God" is still a non-defined word, a meaningless null word. It will be defined clearly in the next two chapters. All concepts that are described in this book are clearly understood simultaneously by the author but can only be written out in a sequential order. Often, a concept that is introduced in the early part of the book can only be understood with the concepts that are described in the later part of the book. Furthermore, I have no desire to prove to you that God is the source of all truths or that God is indeed a reality. I hate the word "prove" or "proof". All scientific proofs, excluding mathematical proofs, are only inductive proofs which are confined in both time and space, meaning transient and limited. Their universal and lasting true value, if any, is guaranteed by Kant's three postulates, God, immortality and free will. In Kant's view, it is indeed stupid to try to prove the postulates. On the contrary, I can help you to reach a true "understanding" of what God is without placing Him as a postulate.

Two cornerstones are needed in order to accomplish this. The first one is the inclusive principle — that all facts (such as: physics, mathematics, social science, religious concepts, etc.) have to be included in the ultimate truth.

The second cornerstone is a new methodology. This new methodology consists of three tool boxes — intuitive faith, scientific methods and transcendental faith. The intuitive faith is the primal energy that turns on the reasoning vehicle. The scientific methods consists of the interplay between hypothesis and verification and of the interplay between reflection and speculation. Although the transcendental faith is the most powerful problem solving tool, it must be supported by the other two tools. Without the support of intuitive faith and scientific facts, there is no valid transcendental faith but blind faith, superstition and stupidity.

In my book (Truth, Faith, and Life), "intuitive faith" is called "the principle of conviction-in-common"; "Transcendental faith" is called "the principle of example-in-kinds". The intuitive faith is the intelligence embodied from God. The scientific methods are powered initially with the energy of intuitive faith, then guaranteed by the realities of free will and immortality. The transcendental faith (the principle of example-in-kinds) is much more than the methodology of induction, which attains a general truth with an inductive leap, from only some observed particulars that are the same kind. The principle of example-in-kinds leaps over the boundaries of different kinds, science, philosophy, and religion. It is also much more than the methodology of analogy, which depends on exact similarity and resemblance, and when the similarity is less than perfect, the analogy is less than conclusive.

This transcendental faith is the direct consequence of the demand of the inclusive principle. Since relativity is only transient reality, all different "kinds" must unite into a harmonic Oneness. For example, the ancient Chinese developed Taoism because of the belief that human body is a Microcosm that is exactly identical in operation as the Macrocosm which is the entire universe. Although this belief is supported by some very primitive observations, it is the result of transcendental faith. Even some modern thinkers, Whitehead or Hartshorne, used the same method (the principle of example-in-kinds) to construct an organismic model for the God-world relationship by comparing it with the human mind with respect to its bodily organs.

Many more examples in the following chapters will show you exactly how this transcendental tool is used. It is a method capable of reconciling all paradoxes. In fact, it is not only a problem solving tool but a transcending eye which is able to see all paradoxes simultaneously, in a single glance. In fact, the validity of symbolism or mythology is guaranteed by this tool — the transcendental faith, and metaphor and myth are its language. This tool in general is not used to analyze the relationship between realities but used to reconcile all paradoxes and to analyze the transcendental relationship between reality and its apparent contradiction — the non-reality. For example, science finds many facts, which are indeed God's law, but it pursues truths by expelling God from its domain. Nonetheless, science is the only discipline that has almost reached and understood God. The only way to reach a true understanding about God is by following the path of science, although the scientific methodology is also the only barrier that prevents us from reaching a true understanding of God. This is indeed not only a great mystery but also a great paradox. The transcendental faith is the only vehicle that can transcend this barrier.

Obviously, there is a danger that someone will use this method of transcendental faith in an abusive manner to promote some absurd opinions just as dogmatism has done. Fortunately, the interplay of all these three tools keeps this kind of nonsense out of the domain of true knowledge.

In summary, truth is independent of knowledge. Truth is the master, knowledge the slave. There are three categories of truth — empty truth, limited truth and utmost truth. Empty truth is a statement defined by itself, a reiterative definition — such as the statement "I am I" in Bible. Limited truth is a fact that is true only in a finite domain; it may not be true any more outside of the defined domain. The utmost truth is the Absolute Totality which is the direct consequence of the inclusive principle. The utmost truth is immutable and eternal.

Knowledge is the result of pursing the truths by consciousness. Thus, there are two type of knowledge — immortal knowledge and mortal knowledge. The immortal knowledge is the result of conceiving either the empty truth or the utmost truth by consciousness, and it is called immortal because it is immutable in terms of "time". In general, mathematics does not depend on any physical reference for its validity; thus, mathematics is immortal knowledge. On the other hand, physics does depend on physical reference. When the physical reality evolves, the physics laws also change; thus, physics is only mortal knowledge. So far, the terms of mortal and immortal are not clearly defined, but everyone has a fuzzy idea of what they mean, and this fuzzy idea is good enough for now. The meaning of "mortal" will be clearly defined in Chapter III, "immortal" in Chapter IV.

There are three criteria for truths — intuition, agreement with reality or intent, and the inclusive principle. With these three criteria, three problem solving tools are developed — intuitive faith, scientific methods (reasoning) and transcendental faith.

Chapter III
Paradox axioms and God's attributes

Descartes said,"I think; therefore, I exist." My twelve year old daughter strongly believes that the opposite - I exist; therefore, I think - is a much better postulate. This example demonstrates two very important points. On the one hand, the meaning of existence can be easily conceived by any ten-year old kid. On the other hand, it is so difficult that even a well-educated philosopher cannot easily grasp its true meaning. This is indeed a paradox, the existence paradox. But, there is always a unified principle that reconciles each paradox.

Many philosophers and theologians have discussed the meaning of existence from a subjective view, such as: "whatever is thought of must exist in order to be thought of," or, "a public object that exists outside the mind as well as in it is a greater existence than to exist in the mind only." This type of argument often falls into the same trap that caught Einstein, taking and mistaking human consciousness as the ultimate reality. I will discuss this issue from a different angle.

II

Every two-year old baby recognizes his own existence. He even knows that there are two hands and two feet that belong to him. Soon, he will also learn that he even has eyes, ears, etc. He recognizes his own existence and the existence of his mother and others mainly by instinct (his consciousness), no philosophy involved. It is as simple as 1, 2 or 3. But, in science and in philosophy, the meaning of existence is very complicated. The boy's consciousness not only recognizes the existence of his body but also the existence of his own consciousness. Which one, the body or the consciousness, is the higher existence? There are many, many different kinds of existence.

The first one is called "independent existence". It can be identified as a unit, a whole thing. Every life is an independent existence. Every whole item — furniture, an appliance, etc. — is also an independent existence. No doubt, an eye ball is also an existence, but it is not really independent. If we remove an eye from its socket, it becomes a piece of dead cells and cannot perform its designated function. A detached eye is not an eye any more functionally, but a pile of dead cells. Therefore, the existence of the eye has a

33

somewhat lower existence rank. It cannot continue its existence after leaving its master. This kind of existence can be called component existence, attached existence or confined existence. The eyes, the ears and the heart are indeed only having a confined existence. They are permanently confined to their host.

Is independent existence immortal existence? Everyone knows it is not. If we remove a life from its habitat - food, water and air - for a long period of time, it also will lose its existence. Every life is indeed also confined in its environment. The independent existence and confined existence of a component are only different in degree, not in kind. Even the pyramids will crumble. This kind of existence, both independent and confined, can be called "Mortal existence" or transient existence.

There is another kind of existence, virtual existence. Many philosophers call "confined existence" virtual existence. I choose not to follow their definition because every independent existence is also always the constituent of something greater. For me, the virtual existence has quite a different meaning, a new meaning. When an acorn is in my hand, I can virtually see the existence of an oak tree. It seems to be that the independent existence can be verified at present. It connotes "now". The virtual existence implies the existence of "future". We all know that "now" is transient, therefore, is mortal, by definition. Does virtual existence imply the existence of immortality, the absolute existence? No doubt, the future seems to have no end. An oak tree has a virtual existence in an acorn. Then, an acorn can virtually exist in an oak tree. Indeed, there seems to be no end to this virtual cycle. But, this cycle is time-dependent. It can exist only if time has meaning. Later, I will prove to you that even "Time" is not immortal. Therefore, virtual existence is also only a mortal existence.

Not only an oak tree is virtually existing in an acorn, but all independent existences are also virtual existences. "Today's I" is no doubt different from "Yesterday's me" and will surely be different from "tomorrow's me". I am moving from one virtual existence into another virtual existence. Every independent existence is a virtual existence. Again, virtual existence is also a mortal existence.

After the death of a life, its material body will decompose into atoms. According to mass conservation law, no atom will be lost with any death process. But, the atom is not an absolute existence; it can be broken up in the nuclear reaction. So, even the atom still has only a transient existence, the mortal existence. Today, almost all physicists believe that even the proton will eventually die.

III

We have defined many different kinds of existence, but so far all their differences differ only in degree, not in kind. No wonder for thousands of years, philosophers do not understand the meaning of existence much more than a ten-year old kid. Is anything existing absolutely, the immortal existence? Is space immortal? First, what is space? Every two-year old kid knows what space is. He can place one peg at one place and another peg another place, and he can sit between them. There is something that he sits on. Soon, he will learn that something is space. The existence of space is too self-evident to be denied. He learns from common sense.

Can common sense always perceive truth? The desk that I am using for writing this book seems to be very solid from my common sense perception. But, physicists indicate that this solid desk is really a big void. The amount of void in this solid desk is just about the same proportion as the void in the solar system. Is my common sense of the solidness only an illusion? Which is right, common sense or physics?

They both cannot be wrong. The solidness of the desk is too obvious, too self-evident to be denied. The emptiness of this desk has also been proved in laboratories many times. Again, we have a paradox. For every paradox, there is always a unified, simple principle that is associated with it. This paradox is caused by scale difference. This "Scale Paradox" is indeed the scientific and philosophic definition of space. Space is the unified, simple principle of this scale paradox. So, space indeed exists. It can be perceived with common sense and is supported by a paradox.

Everyone also has the concept of "Time". What is time? Does time really exist? Gwen, my wife, is very sure that time exists. She always makes breakfast before lunch. As for her, it is impossible to do something before something else without the existence of time. In fact, it is downright stupid to ask this kind of question. Time is too obvious, too self-evident to be denied. Time is clearly perceived by common sense from the sequence of events. Then, is time immortal or absolute? Einstein said NO! He said that time will slow down when we travel in a fast moving train. Theoretically, time will stop and stand still as if dead, when we travel at light speed. For the reason of preventing the death of "Time," he concluded that we can never travel at light speed. Again, his conclusion is misleading, although not completely wrong. But time can be dead by definition in another situation.

Using your wristwatch, you will have a difficult time to measure how long a sound 'yah' lasts. If the lifetime of the sound is only in the range of hundredth-seconds, and you can only guess in tenth of seconds with your watch, then your measuring error is much larger than the true measurement you try to get. For example, your first measurement is one-tenth of second. Your 2nd measurement is two-tenths of a second because you realized that you did not catch the beginning point accurately for the first measurement. Your third measurement is nine-tenths of a second because you realized that you might miss the end point for the first two measurements. With these three measurements, the measured average life of the sound 'yah' is four-tenths of a second and the measuring error is thirteen-tenths of a second, which is three times over the average life. By following the statistics calculation, the true life time of this sound 'yah' can be anywhere between two points.

Point one: the average plus the error (.4 + 1.3 =1.7 seconds).

Point two: the average minus the error (.4 - 1.3 = -.9 seconds).

So, the true lifetime of sound 'yah' can be between -.9 to +1.7 seconds. What does the negative lifetime mean? It means that the 'yah' sound we heard and measured has not yet happened. This possibility is too absurd to be accepted by common sense, and we simply discredit it completely. But, our common sense is unable to probe the micro-world. To determine whether an event in the micro-world has indeed happened or not is not an easy matter. No common sense is there to help us make this judgement. Therefore, we have lost the obvious evidence for discrediting the negative lifetime of an event. It means we have lost the sense for time. Often, the sequence of events in the micro-world cannot be determined. The past, the present and the future cannot be distinguished. Time is dead by definition. Time is not immortal. Which is right? Our common sense tells us that time is real, a real existence. The sequence of events is clearly distinguishable. But, both the relativity theory and the quantum mechanics tell us differently that time can die in two ways, standing still or that the sequence of events cannot be distinguished in the micro-world. This is the "Sequence paradox". Again, from this sequence paradox, time is manifested from it. Time is the unifying principle to unify this paradox.

With the same logic, we can easily prove that energy, mass and space all have mortal existence only. All existences associated with time are mortals. Therefore, time itself is also mortal, by definition. All mortals must die eventually. Death is defined with the conception of time. If there is no time, there is no death. If an existence will not die, it is immortal. The immortal does not sense the existence of time, therefore no death.

Today, almost all physicists believe that even the universe will eventually collapse. We all know that a bubble has only transient existence, a mortal existence. An insect can live a few days or a few weeks. We, human beings, can live eighty years more or less. A turtle can live a few hundred years. A tree can often live a few thousand years. The solar system will last for a few billion years. Space has no boundary but is still finite. Time has no end but is still a mortal as we just proved. The existences of all these — a bubble, a life, the solar system, time and space — are different only in degree, not in kind.

Then, is there an immortal existence? What is immortal? Can mortal existences come to existence without the existence of an immortal existence? The meaning of immortality is discussed in the next chapter. The existence of God is not only very self-evident but also has been proved by many philosophers and theologians. I have no desire to prove to you that God is indeed a reality. I will, however, show you the meaning, the attributes and the essence of this ultimate reality by showing you the meanings of many paradoxes.

IV

All God's attributes and essence always show up in the form of paradoxes. Every paradox always contains two truths, but they are directly opposite of each other both in their meaning and in its internal reasoning process. For two contradictory parts, if one is true and the other is false, there is no paradox. Therefore, every paradox points out a higher truth which transcends the paradox itself. This fact can be expressed in three axioms.

Axiom A: Every paradox is the result of a symmetry breaking from a higher symmetry structure in which a higher truth (or principle) resides.

Axiom B: Every paradox can be reconciled in two ways: a) A further symmetry breaking, b) The recovery of a higher symmetry.

Axiom C: Every genuine paradox created by breaking the perfect symmetry (the absolute totality) always points out an attribute of God.

The first two axioms point out two very important realities, symmetry and symmetry breaking. In fact, all paradoxes come out of the interplay between these two realities. Furthermore, the union of these two realities is the essence of God, and all God's attributes, the axiom C, manifest from the interplay of them.

For example, proposition A states "All propositions are true," and proposition B states "Proposition A is false". Obviously, proposition B has to be true if proposition A is true. But, if B is true then A has to be false. Now, we have a very simple paradox on our hands. Now, there are two ways to solve this problem. The easiest way is by burying our heads in the sand and by ignoring or denying the problem. This is a cop-out which, in fact, is the solution of the majority of people.

The other way is by finding out the root cause of the problem. The problem is caused by the attempt of categorizing the world with a definition, "what is true?" This categorizing and defining procedure is a symmetry breaking process. This paradox is created by breaking a symmetry, the totality. When the null term " " is replaced by "true," the symmetry of the null proposition (All propositions are " ") is broken, and the new proposition (All propositions are "true") creates a paradox. This paradox can be removed in two ways, downward or upward solution. The downward solution is obtained by a further downward symmetry breaking, with a new proposition such as: All propositions "except proposition B" are "true". The upward solution is obtained by removing the first symmetry breaking which causes the problem, and the null symmetry is regained. With this new understanding, all traditionally unsolvable paradoxes can be reconciled.

In 1908, Kurt Grelling presented a paradox, that of "heterologicality". A word is said to be "autological" if and only if it applies to itself. For example, the word "English" means English, and it is indeed an English word; therefore, it is an autological word. On the contrary, the word "French" means French but is an English word instead of being a French word; therefore, it is not an autological word; instead, it is called a "heterological" word. Now, is the word "heterological" heterological? If we assume that "heterological" is heterological, then by definition, "heterological" is autological; on the other hand, if we assume that "heterological" is autological, then by definition again, "heterological" has to be heterological.

Obviously, Grelling got himself into this predicament by inventing a definition for autological and heterological. Every definition always acts as a symmetry breaking procedure, separating a totality into categories.

The above two paradoxes precisely point out the vivid existence of the Absolute Totality. In this Absolute Totality, there is neither truth nor falsity. Any attempt to break the perfect symmetry of this Absolute Totality will inevitably face the problem of a traditionally unsolvable paradox. This Absolute Totality is indeed the Almighty God Himself. I have no desire to prove to you that this Absolute Totality is indeed God Himself. I, however, will show you the meaning, the attributes and the essence of this Absolute Totality.

V

Any "final" theological system has to account for all self-evident attributes of God, such as: forces for physics, love for religions, creations, infinities and the reality of "Self". Indeed, each of these attributes corresponds to a well-known paradox. Most of these paradoxes are discussed in mathematics, such as the Number Theory, Set Theory and Group Theory. I am listing only two of them as examples.

The first one is the Cantor's paradox. In Cantor's Set Theory, there is a cardinal number for every set. For any two sets A and B, the cardinal number of A is less than the cardinal number of B if and only if A is equivalent to a subset of B and B is not equivalent to a subset of A. The power set of A, PA, is defined as the set of subsets of A. If set A contains two elements (a, b), then set A has four subsets — (a), (b), (a, b) and the empty set. Therefore, the power set of A, PA, has four elements. If set A contains three elements, then the power set PA contains eight elements. Therefore, if set A has "n" (a finite number) as its cardinal number, then the power set of A, PA, has a cardinal number equal to the "nth power of 2". For all finite numbers "n", set PA always contains more elements than set A. But, if now we let S be the set of "All" sets, then its power set PS has a greater cardinal number and contains more sets than set S, whereas, on the other hand, "All" sets are in S, by definition. So, on the one hand, PS is larger than S; on the other hand, S is larger than PS. This is the Cantor's paradox.

In the Number Theory, two transfinite numbers were discovered; $N(0)$ as countable infinity and $N(1)$ the uncountable. The countable infinity is the limit point of the countable numbers, such as: 1, 2, 3, ..., n, ..., countable infinity. This countable infinity can be comprehended by every ten year old kid. On the other hand, the uncountable infinity is a very difficult mathematical concept, and it is infinitely larger than the countable infinity. It is indeed very hard to imagine that one infinity can be larger than the other, but this is a well-known mathematical fact.

For trying to solve his paradox, Cantor arbitrarily assigned N(1), the uncountable infinity, as the cardinal number for power set PS, while the cardinal number of set S is indeed equal to N(0). In other words, he arbitrarily assumed that N(1) is equal to the "N(0)th power of 2". This arbitrarily arbitrary assumption is the well-known Cantor's Continuum Hypothesis. One hundred years after the appearance of this ridiculous hypothesis, mathematicians today finally admit that this hypothesis can be both right and wrong.

In fact, this Cantor's paradox precisely points out a very important reality, the "Self". In my book (Super Unified Theory), I listed four "Self". These two transfinite numbers, N(0) and N(1), are two "Self" of the four. If there are N(0) numbers of element in a set, there are N(0) numbers of subset for it because "N(0)th power of 2" is not larger than N(0) but is equal to N(0), N(0) being a "Self," and no operation can transform N(0) to anything but to itself. In the same way, if there are N(1) numbers of elements in a set; there are N(1) numbers of subsets, N(1) being a "Self," too. Cantor wrongly concluded that "N(0)th power of 2" is larger than N(0), then again wrongly guessed that "N(0)th power of 2" is equal to N(1). The Cantor's Continuum Hypothesis is no doubt wrong.

There is no way that N(0) can be transformed into N(1) in the Number Theory until an even higher symmetry structure is introduced. The Russell's paradox is indeed the guiding light precisely pointing out this higher symmetry structure. The Russell's paradox is the second one I am going to discuss.

Russell defined "Russell Set," R, as the set of all sets that do not contain themselves as elements. In mathematical terms, R is defined as "for every set A, A belongs to R if and only if A does not belong to A." It can be rewritten as "R belongs to R if and only if R does not belong to R." In common language, set R is the totality. If set R is an element of any set, it violates its definition of being a totality. Therefore, set R cannot be an element of any other set. But, since set R is totality, it has to contain its power set PR, too. But in the Set Theory, set R is an element of set PR, by definition. Therefore, set R is an element of itself, and it violates its original definition.

The Russell set is defined in accordance with all the rules in the Set Theory. The contradiction is not caused by any violation of either the definitions or the logic of the Set Theory. In fact, it is caused by breaking a symmetry, the Absolute Totality.

This Russell's paradox exists in a much higher symmetry structure than Cantor's. The Cantor's paradox exists in a structure that consists of four concepts — set, element, subset and cardinal number, and it reveals the realities of two "Self". On the other hand, the Russell's paradox involves only two concepts — set and element, and it reveals the highest reality, the Absolute Totality. This Absolute Totality is the highest "Self," the Almighty God. God, the highest "Self," creates many self-beings with a process of symmetry breaking. These self-beings try to reverse this symmetry breaking process and smooth out the self-nonself boundary, in turn find "love". That the self-nonself boundary reduced by blood-relation creates family love, reduced by compassion creates religious love.

In fact, I have pointed out three very important concepts — a) the perfect symmetry revealed by the Russell's paradox, b) the process of symmetry breaking which creates the Russell's paradox from the perfect symmetry, and c) the recovery of the perfect symmetry by reconciling the paradox. In this process, the perfect symmetry (the Creator) creates many self-beings; then, they discover the "love" of the Creator by trying to return to the perfect symmetry. In this process, the transcendence and the immanence cannot be distinguished and are unified.

VI

The three paradox axioms can be understood in a general sense without the aid of any special example, by only introducing the concepts of symmetry and symmetry breaking. For example, the statement of "Men are mortal, Jesus is immortal" is somewhat paradoxical. At first glance, this paradox seemingly could be solved by the concept of inductive probability. Since the inductive probability of men being mortal is always less than 1, therefore, Jesus being immortal is always a possibility. But, this argument quickly runs into trouble when the second order of probability of this possibility is calculated. The probability of all men before Jesus being mortal, then Jesus alone is immortal, then all dead men after Jesus were also mortal, can be calculated with binomial probability, at least theoretically.

This probability will approach to zero so fast even "Eternity" cannot rescue it because time moves to eternity with a much slower speed than this probability approaches zero.

On the other hand, not only can this paradox be reconciled with the concepts of symmetry and symmetry breaking, but even a self-contradictory paradox can also be reconciled. For example, that "Jesus is mortal and Jesus is immortal," can be reconciled two ways. First, with a downward approach, Jesus (body) is mortal and Jesus (teaching and spirit) is immortal. This paradox is reconciled by a symmetry breaking process which distinguishes two "Jesus" in a lower symmetry structure. Second, with a upward approach, Jesus (body and death) is Jesus (teaching and spirit); they cannot be distinguished because not only is Jesus the Son of God and his dead body has been resurrected, but also his dead body itself is the teaching of God. This paradox is reconciled by ascending into a higher symmetry structure.

Furthermore, this self-contradictory paradox can be reconciled even without the help of the special personality of Jesus, being the Son of God. It can be reconciled while we replace Jesus with a common man, Mr. Smith, in the above paradox, if this paradox exists in a symmetry structure that "mortal" and "immortal" cannot be distinguished. Does this kind of symmetry structure indeed exist? This is beside the point. This self-contradictory paradox can be reconciled on the conceptual level at least; even if it might not have a real reference.

In general, every genuine paradox can be resolved in two ways, upward or downward solution. The Cantor and Russell paradoxes are avoided by axiomatizing the set theory. In 1905, Zermelo changed the definition of "set," and it becomes an object satisfying certain axioms. By doing so, "the set" of "all" sets is illegitimated. In fact, this illegitimating or axiomatizing procedure is a symmetry breaking process. This is a downward solution, and indeed all paradoxes vanish in a lower symmetry structure.

Therefore, from this point of view, those paradoxes are not problems but manifestations of some properties of a higher symmetry structure. In other words, every genuine paradox is in fact the guiding light pointing out a higher symmetry property. By understanding this higher symmetry property, the paradox will not be a paradox any more. This is the upward solution for a paradox.

VII

Now, I have "proved" all three paradox axioms either by using special examples or by using a more general argument. Every paradox is the manifestation of a symmetry breaking from a higher symmetry space in which a higher truth resides. Every paradox can be reconciled in two ways — a further symmetry breaking or the recovery of a higher symmetry. And, every genuine paradox created by breaking the perfect symmetry (the totality) always points out an attribute of God. The Cantor's paradox points out the meaning of "Self". The Russell's paradox points out the vivid existence of the Absolute Totality. From the symmetry breaking and the symmetry recovery processes, we also have learned the meanings of creation and of love. We have understood many of God's attributes by investigating paradoxes. In the next chapter (God's Essence), we will reach a final understanding of God's essence by investigating some more very difficult paradoxes.

28 June 1991

Dr. Jeh-Tween Gong
P.O. Box 1753
Bristol, VA 24203

Dear Dr. Gong:

It was with great interest that I read your book <u>Truth, Faith, and Life</u>. I also received your keen commentary about my work <u>The Possible Universe</u>.

As with your paper 'In Search of God', I was astonished by the ultimateness of your concept of final unification in chaos. This is an idea that breaks out of old methodological barriers and into the ranges of a total absoluteness where the godhead creates itself.

Then, downward from this pure domain, your notion of symmetry breaking and ghost partner is a remarkable explanation of our universe's diversity in every realm— from conceptual counterpoints like science and religion, to categorical manifestations of space and time, to quantum phenomena of matter-energy and virtuality.

I confess that my thesis does not reach that level where you have found harmony even in paradox. My theory is still limited by the demands of formal logic, within which I am glad to see in your commentary that you have detected a useful philosophical method.

In any case, even from the self-doubting position that makes me view my own thesis just as the vision of a hypothesis, I deeply empathize with your exalted quest and answer. What else could a person do who has been smitten by Philosophy?

Sincerely yours,

J. A. Tallet

Chapter IV
God's Essence

By believing in God, it will not help us understand what God is, not one bit. Almost all philosophers and theologians believe in one form or another of agnosticism that God is incomprehensible. Instead of believing in agnosticism with free will, they all are really forced into accepting it because of no other choice. Pascal wrote, "if there is a God, He is infinitely incomprehensible."

Some do claim that humans can obtain a certain knowledge of God's existence and nature. Aquinas proved the existence of God by using five different ways, but still he did not know what God is. He wrote, "we cannot know what God is, but rather what He is not." Maimonides wrote, "we comprehend only the fact that He exists, not His essence."

The existence of God is intrinsically self-evident, regardless of the different views of the different doctrines, ontological argument or practical reason. Kant wrote, "it is morally necessary to assume the existence of God." So, the existence of God can be conceived by human with reason alone. Therefore, the agnostic look upon dogmatic faith either as blind faith and superstition or as hypocrisy.

On the other hand, Aquinas did not believe that the existence of God is self-evident because he did not know the essence of God. For him, the essence of God is different from the existence of God; that He is is different from what He is. For a tree, the leaves, the branches, the trunk and the roots are all attributes of this tree. The essence of this tree is the seed that this tree grew out of. For this seed, the hard shell, the soft skin and the nut are all attributes of this seed; the genetic DNA is the essence. For this DNA, the four building blocks and sequential order of these building blocks are the attributes; God's spirit is the essence.

God also has many very self-evident attributes: all loving, all powerful, infinitely wise, infinite in space, infinite in time, also immutable and eternal. All these attributes can be conceived by us easily without any difficulty. But, they are not the essence of God. Many theologians and even many philosophers do, therefore, believe that God's essence is incomprehensible. Montaigne wrote, "it is faith alone that vividly and certainly comprehends the deep mysteries of our religion." Without a clear understanding the essence of God, the word "God" remains to be a meaningless null word because all of the attributes of God are also possessed by many beings who are not God.

II

In the past, no one is able to describe what the essence of God is in a comprehensible way. Traditionally, there are two methods to formulate the conception of God. The first one is dogmatism which is gross nonsense; thus it will not be discussed here. The second method is "reduction" or "negation" which is an act, a movement that seeks to pass through the different levels of consciousness in order to secure, step by step, their foundation. In Husserl's three steps of reduction, the first step (psychological intentionality) sorts the factual given from signification: eidetic reduction. The second step (noetic intentionality) brings into view the Cogito and its correlate, the world: transcendental reduction. The third step (productive intentionality) discloses that intuition creates essences: constitutive reduction. At this level, Husserl specified that man is the creator of all determinations. This reduction method is similar to the negation method in Buddhism but is inferior to it. This reduction method can only specify God in a negative sense; such as: 1) God is not an order; he is that by which order can exist. 2) God is beyond being; he is not less, but more, infinitely more; he is its source. 3) God could not be attained by a simple regression that would put him into an objective series or place him at the summit, making him an order, whereas he is the source of all orders.

Often, this reduction method does not find God but pantheism that makes the structures of human analysis absolute. Although the negation method of Buddhism is much more powerful than this reduction method, it is still not possible to understand the essence of God without losing Him completely. Both the reduction and negation methods violate the inclusive principle. Although everything that is reduced or negated indeed cannot be the totality of God, it nonetheless must be part of God according to the inclusive principle. Thus, the only way to understand the essence of God is neither by reduction nor by negation but by studying the paradoxes which are manifested from God's essence. There are three important paradoxes.

The first is the transcendence and immanence paradox. In Judaism and Christianity, God is unquestionably transcendent. This means that God exists apart, infinitely removed from the world He created. But even more people, including Christians themselves, also believe in the opposite view, the immanent nature of God. God's spirit does not exist apart from the human spirits. Plotinus wrote, "God is present through all. We cannot think of something of God here and something else there, nor is all of God gathered at one spot: there is an instantaneous presence everywhere, nothing containing and nothing left void." Aquinas wrote, "God is in all things, and intimately." Spinoza wrote, "outside God there can be no substance, that is to say, outside Him nothing can exist which is in itself."

The second is the omniscience and impassibility paradox. Almost everyone believes that God is omniscient and omnipotent, that He knows the future regardless of the random acts performed by the human's free will and that He is the ruler of all things and all beings. Then why does God permit suffering? Why does evil exist in this world that is created by God who is both infinitely powerful and infinitely good? There are many answers to these questions. In Christianity, Satan is accused as the creator of all evil. In this view, God is not the only creator and did not create the entire world but only the good part. Satan created the other half of the world, the evil half. Another answer for these questions is the conception of impassibility that God cannot experience pain. God does neither intervene in the order of nature nor concern Himself with human affairs. Lucretius wrote, "the nature of God must ever in Himself of necessity enjoy immortality together with supreme repose, far removed and withdrawn from our concerns; since exempt from every pain, exempt from all dangers, strong in His own resources, not wanting aught of us, He is neither gained by favors nor moved by anger."

The third is the infinity and nothingness paradox. God has to be unborn. If God is born by anyone else beside Himself, then this 'anyone else' shall be God by definition. God also has to be an infinity. Not only both time and space are unbounded, but there are indeed two known infinities in mathematics. Obviously, these two infinities cannot exist outside of God nor come to be before God, by definition. Therefore, God has to be the utmost infinity.

III

At this point, I find no way to tackle the first two paradoxes. Fortunately, the third one (the infinity and nothingness paradox) might possibly be analyzed in terms of mathematics. With the transcendental faith, I hope all these three paradoxes are only different expressions of the same puzzle, and by unifying and reconciling only one of them, especially the last one, all of them will be unified and reconciled automatically. This hope turns out to be true. The transcendence and immanence paradox will be reconciled after the concept of God Space is introduced, and I will discuss this reconciliation in much more detail in Chapter VII — The Origin and The Rise of Consciousness. The omniscience and impassibility paradox also will be reconciled and will be discussed in detail in Chapter XII — Providence and Divination. As for now, I am going to show you how the infinity and nothingness paradox is reconciled.

Here, unborn means nothingness and can be represented as '0,' zero. We all know that zero cannot be the same as infinity, at least we all think we know. Are we sure that we really know?

Mathematicians tell us that zero is the inverse of infinity and vice versa. So, in mathematics, there is indeed a relationship between zero and infinity, but they are not the same. Now, both common sense and mathematicians tell us that zero is not the same as infinity. Therefore, God must either have a split personality or not be in existence in first place. But this is not the case. So far, we accept the existence of God only with our intuitive faith. But we can never be sure until we can unify this zero-infinity paradox, the Immortal Paradox.

Surprisingly, it is amazingly easy to unify and to reconcile this zero-infinity paradox. We look at the answer many times a day. For any two points, A and B, the distance from A to B usually does not equal the distance from B to A. This statement seems to contradict Euclidean geometry, but Euclidean geometry is valid only in a very small region of this vast universe. For example, you (point A) love a famous movie star deeply, but she (point B) does not care for you the slightest bit. Then the distance from A (you) to B (she) is almost 0 (you want to be as close to her as possible), but from B to A is almost infinite (she wants nothing to do with you). So, AB does not always equal to BA. I am sure you are not convinced with this example. For many people, geometrical points are quite different from 'you' and 'she.' Furthermore, how can I unify zero and infinity by dividing the sameness, AB and BA? But this is the only way. If the sameness can be divided, then the difference can be reconciled.

I am going to show you another example, a much more convincing example. Just look at your watch, the ₍point A is 12 o'clock, point B 11 o'clock. Then AB equals 11 units and BA equals one unit. Again, AB does not equal BA. If we move B approaching to A and finally overlaps with A, then AB equals 12 units, and BA is zero. If we increase the radius of our watch to infinity, then AB is an infinity, and BA is still zero.

In the above example, the difference is caused by the direction of time that time cannot run backwards, at least not that we know of. But, if the direction can be reversed, then AB and BA cannot be distinguished. In other words, at this circumstance, zero and infinity cannot be distinguished.

I proved to you in Chapter III that time is only a mortal existence, not an absolute existence. Almost all physicists believe that protons will eventually die and the entire universe will also eventually collapse. Therefore, the direction of time does not have to be absolute, although it seems to be absolute for all mortals. So, at the point of timelessness which is the immortal sphere and the perfect symmetry, zero and infinity are indeed the same. In other words, the immortal does not sense the existence of time. God creates the universe without any effort, without sensing the very act He is acting. Almost all theologians believe that God created this world with His free will. Indeed, only God has an absolute free will. But, the creation act is definitely not the result of His free will. The very act of creation is His essence. Even God cannot freely alter His own essence. I will describe what God's free will is in chapter VI — "The Moral Truths".

IV

By finding this infinity and nothingness symmetry (the perfect symmetry), the word "God" is now no longer a meaningless null word, but we still cannot say that we have understood God's essence because many questions remain. Why shall this infinity and nothingness symmetry be the last consequence? How can it stop the infinite progression?

The only way to stop the process of infinite progression is by using the process of infinite recursion, such as: to represent an infinite sequence A1, A2, A3, ..., An, ... with ABABABAB.... This means that the perfect symmetry must break down into three parts. The immortal nothingness (A) must go through the mortal sphere (B, the creation) and then reunite with the immortal infinity (A, which cannot be distinguished from the immortal nothingness, A). In other words, the perfect symmetry (the immortal sphere) must be broken down by a symmetry breaking process, and this process creates the mortal universe and its symmetry (ghost) partner. In short, God has no free choice of not creating. "Creation" is God's essence. Even God Himself cannot be not of Himself.

The perfect symmetry denotes the absoluteness. The mortal universe is governed by relativity, just as described in Einstein's relativity theory. This relative universe then moves through "time" and enters into infinity — the eternity, and this process regains the perfect symmetry and brings the relative universe back to absoluteness. In fact, God is this infinite recursion, from absoluteness (the immortal sphere) to relativity (the mortal universe) then back to absoluteness. This infinite recursion is a process. Therefore, God is a process, neither a state nor a being. Being always connotes with "time," but process can be associated with both time or timelessness. Being can never enter the domain of timelessness, but a process can bring or transform the state of timelessness into the domain of "time". In fact, "a process" is synonymous with "a spirit," "a life," and "a will". Therefore, the perfect symmetry (the immortal sphere) itself is not God. God is the union of the perfect symmetry and its creations — the mortal universe and the ghost partner. God is both transcendent and immanent.

Therefore, the whole world, which is finite and mortal, is God's material body and exists in Him. Nothing can exist outside of God. The whole world is only a transient part of God's existence. God creates the mortal world out of His own essence, the nothingness. Many philosophers do speculate the process of creation out of nothing. But, none of them reaches a comprehensive understanding. Almost all of them in the end turn against the idea of creation out of nothing. One of their arguments is as follows: "That to be created out of nothing is simply not to be created out of anything, and God Himself is created out of nothing in this sense. But to be created (as God of course is not), yet not created out of anything, is to be given existence; and to what is existence given if there is literally nothing there to give it to? To give existence to nothing, surely, is just not to give existence to anything, and thus not to create at all." Obviously, all those theologians and philosophers do not understand what the true meaning of "Nothingness" is, not at all. They further claim that the only thing which cannot be an object of knowledge, which cannot be thought about in any way except negatively, is that which has no being of any sort — the nothingness. On the contrary of their understanding, the true fact is that the nothingness contains an infinite numbers of possibility. The nothingness is as rich in possibilities as the infinity, just as I have described. A detailed mechanism of how God creates this mortal world out of His essence, nothingness, is clearly described in my book — Truth, Faith, and Life.

But, why? Why shall this infinity and nothingness symmetry break down into the immortal sphere and the mortal world instead of taking an eternal nap? What force breaks it? By definition, there cannot be any external force; thus, this perfect symmetry itself must also be an infinite violent force. Surprise! Surprise! Not only symmetry breaking connotes force, but symmetry itself always produces force. In fact, symmetry connotes chaos.

But, why? There are two reasons. Firstly, symmetry always connotes degrees of freedom, which in turn means chaos. A square peg can go into its mating hole in four ways, a hexagon peg into its mating hole in six ways. The higher the symmetry, the higher the chaos. In turn, the highest symmetry (perfect symmetry) has the utmost chaos.

Secondly, not only every symmetry is always a broken symmetry, but the perfect symmetry is also a broken one. In order to understand this symmetry paradox, we must first reexamine the meaning of symmetry breaking. In fact, there are two kinds of symmetry breaking — the spontaneous symmetry breaking and the simultaneous symmetry breaking. The spontaneous symmetry breaking process always breaks a higher symmetry into a lower one. For example, the road convention (adopted by different countries — driving on the left in England, the right in the USA) is symmetrical between right and left, which means that no difference can be detected by adopting the right or the left convention, but once a particular convention is adopted as a solution, the left-right symmetry is "spontaneously" broken. On the other hand, the simultaneous symmetry breaking process does not break a higher symmetry into a lower one. For example, a square peg is a four-sided symmetry; thus it is simultaneously broken to be not a five- or a six-sided symmetry. A square matrix filled with the letter "o" no doubt has a good symmetry, but it is simultaneously a broken symmetry at its boundary. If we extend its boundary to infinity, it is still a broken symmetry in view of the points that are between any two letters. The simultaneous symmetry breaking is not caused by any external force but is the intrinsic nature of any symmetry. In fact, every symmetry is a simultaneously broken symmetry. Even the perfect symmetry (the infinity and nothingness symmetry) must simultaneously break into the infinite recursion symmetry in order to stop the infinite progression.

Thus, nothingness, infinity and the utmost chaos are indeed three in one, and the one is three. I have unified nothingness and infinity, two into one. But, we need three into one. As I have showed in that book, the nothingness can never become "something" unless the nothingness is also the utmost chaos.

In fact, the proof of that that "Three" is indistinguishable is amazingly simple. We can reach zero, the nothingness, by building a sequence, 1, 1/2, 1/4, ... After an infinite number of steps, we will reach zero. In fact, we will reach the nothingness and the infinity at the same time, at the exact same time. In other words, we are unable to know what we have got — the nothingness or the infinity — with this process. It is indeed very chaotic when the nothingness and the infinity cannot be distinguished, isn't it? Not only does this strange phenomenon paint a very chaotic picture, but it is because both nothingness and infinity are the utmost chaos. In fact, we will reach the nothingness, the infinity and the utmost chaos at the exact same time from the example above.

The above proof seems to be too easy to be true. The essence of God is a very deep subject. No one in the past was able even to begin to tackle it. An eight-line proof simply does not have enough credibility, does it? So, I am going to show you another proof, which may twist your brain a bit, but in a delightfully wacky way. Besides, this proof will show us much more about the essence of God than the short proof will.

I will start by asking the question: what is the shape of our universe? Many people have told me that our universe looks like a ball because all known planets and stars have a ball-shaped configurations. Even Einstein believed that the universe has to be a ball-shaped object because of his gravity theory, the theory of General Relativity. But soon, many cosmologists disagreed with Einstein because, from every point of observation in the universe, the universe is expanding outward. In other words, every point in the universe seems to be the center of the universe. How can that be? But, it is a fact. Also, this universe cannot have edges. If there is an edge, then what is outside of this edge? Restrained by these two facts, some physicists came up with a rubber beach ball scenario. "This universe is on the 'Surface' of the beach ball," they said. All galaxies are laid on the surface of this beach ball, nothing inside the ball. Inside the surface of this beach ball is a big void, absolutely nothing. Can you imagine that our universe exists in this way. It is sort of wacky, isn't it? But surprisingly, this wacky model is indeed able to meet the requirements of both restraints.

First, when this rubber beach ball is inflated, all other points move away from any given point. This phenomenon can be demonstrated very easily. Use a red ink pen to mark a point on the surface as the given point, then use a black ink pen to mark three or four points to represent the rest of points. When this rubber beach ball is inflated, you can see easily that the distance between any black point to the red point is increasing. All black points are running away from the red point. In other words, every point on this surface is the center of the rest of points that are also laid on the surface.

Second, we indeed are unable to find the edge of this universe that is laid on this surface. Can you?

Unfortunately, this is not the true picture, not yet, although it is very close to it. If all other physicists know the true picture, they will surely know what the essence of God is, instead of still expelling God from all physics theories.

I need to introduce a new concept, the space, before I can show you the true picture. Everyone knows what space is. We walk in it every day. The space you know is indeed a subset of the space, an abstract space, that I am going to introduce. The distance in this abstract space does not have to be in inches. It can be measured with time, with relationship, with anything that you dream up. For example, a family can be a space. The members of the family are also the members (points) of this family space. The distance between members in this family space can be measured with love, trust, compassion, etc.

Now, I am going to introduce a very special space with a very wacky definition. I give it a name — the impossible space. For any given point (member) of this impossible space, the distance from this given point to each of the rest of points is exactly the same. For example, a space has four points (members), A, B, C and D. If we arbitrarily choose B as the given point, then BA = BC = BD. If we arbitrarily choose D as the given point, then DA = DB = DC. Can you think of a space that has an infinite number of points and still obeys this definition? There are infinite points on the surface of the beach ball. If a space is the union between the surface of the beach ball and the center of the ball, nothing else, then the center of the ball obeys the definition. Let's call this space Jay Space. The distance between this center point to any point on the surface is the same. When we choose any point on the surface of this beach ball as the given point, can it become the center of the rest of points while having the same distance to each one of them? This requirement has to be met for this Jay Space to be an "Impossible Space". It is very hard to imagine that it is possible, isn't it? Can you imagine what kind of shape this space is? Maybe, the easiest way is to deny the existence of this kind of space. It is simply too wacky to be real, isn't it? But, I can show you a few good examples.

The equilateral triangle, which is identified with ABC, is the first example. This space has three points (members) A, B and C. Obviously, for A, AB = AC; for B, BA = BC; for C, CA = CB.

The stranger space is the second example. When fifty strangers are in a room, they form a stranger space. None of them knows one another. If the distance between each member is measured by the amount of knowledge known about one another, then the distance between any one to the rest of members is the same, knowing nothing. If the people in this world are all strangers to one another, then this stranger space not only is an Impossible Space but also quite large.

If we assume that human relations are only earthly attributes and they will vanish when the soul departs from the body, then the Soul Space, which is made of all souls that have a deceased body, is also an Impossible Space. The Soul Space has many members now and can become infinitely large in the future.

The nothingness is a true Impossible Space, with an infinite number of members. There are infinite number of sequences that converge into nothingness, such as : $(1, 1/2, 1/4, 1/8, ...)$ or $(1, 1/3, 1/9, 1/27, ...)$, etc. Each of these sequences is a member of the nothingness. Again, the nothingness and the infinity cannot be distinguished. Furthermore, there are infinite number of ways to define the term "Distance" in this Nothingness Space. Therefore, I will let you dream up some definitions or find any definition that will prove that the Nothingness Space is not an Impossible Space.

No doubt, infinity is also a true Impossible Space. There are infinite number of sequences that diverge into infinity. Again there are also infinite number of ways to define the term "Distance" in this Infinity Space.

V

Now, I will call the true Impossible Space, that has an infinite number of members, the God Space. For God Space, every point is the center of the rest of points, and the rest of these points all lay on its ball surface.

At first glance, this definition seems contradictory, but it is indeed a genuine mathematical space. If you are not a mathematician, please ask one of your mathematician friends to help you. The important issue now is to understand what God Space means. In fact, it means "Everything" because it is the mathematical representation of God. I will only list several important ones here.

1) God Space is the highest (perfect) symmetry. There is no way to distinguish one member from another in God Space, by definition. Furthermore, there is no way to distinguish members from subspace or from God Space itself.

2) God Space is the utmost Chaos. Why? What if all the people in the world had the same social security number, the same look and the same of everything? Don't you think that this situation would be very chaotic? The more members a space has, the more chaotic it will be. The God Space has an infinite number of members, therefore, infinitely chaotic. The God Space is the utmost chaos. The nothingness, the infinity and the utmost chaos are indeed three in one. Chaos denotes both symmetry and symmetry breaking, also denotes the creation, the intelligence and the creativity (See Chapter V & X).

3) God Space is the Absolute Totality. Firstly, it is an infinity, by having an infinite number of member. Secondly, it is mathematically identical with the "infinity and nothingness symmetry". Thirdly, God Space is a Russell Set which is the set of "all" sets that do not contain themselves as elements, Such as: God Space is the set of "all" center points which are transcended from the rest. The Russell set indeed points out the reality of the Absolute Totality (see Chapter III).

4) God Space is the source of relativity. Exactly the same as Einstein's first postulate that "all reference points (inertial frames) are completely equivalent, every member in God Space is completely equivalent with the rest. Indeed, this is what Einstein tried to say in his interpretation, but he did not say it correctly. He did not realize that only God Space, which is absolute, can have this relativity property. God Space is both absolute and relative. Relativity can only come out of absoluteness.

5) God Space contains an infinite number of universe in two ways: a) At any instant, there are an infinite number of ego-centered subjective universes, and it is also the basis for equal right, thus the basis of moral truth (see Chapter VI). b) On a very large time scale (cosmic time), there are also an infinite number of universes, the infinite recursion of the Big Bang and the Big Crunch.

6) God is God Space; therefore, God is transcendent. The model of universe, that I mentioned before and was invented by some physicists, is almost correct, but they missed the center point that is the Almighty God. With this model, the entire universe is laid on the surface of the ball. God, the infinite void or the absolute nothingness, resides in the center of the ball. The surface of the ball, the entire material universe, is only skin thick. The nothingness, our Almighty God, in the center is not empty space but infinitely solid. The empty space is something, not the nothingness. The surface is transient; the center is eternal. In this picture, God is infinitely transcended from the world He created. This is only a still picture of God's portrait, a snap shot. The dynamic picture of God's portrait will be discussed in detail in Chapter XII —"Providence and Divination". The God Space contains an infinite number of mortal universes.

7) God has immanent nature. Not only is God Space infinitely larger and richer than the material universe, but each point in the universe is also a point in the God Space. Therefore, every point in the universe is also the center of God Space. In other words, God is in every point of the universe. God is in each of us, the embodiment. Only with the embodiment, the spiritual communion (the mutual in-dwelling) becomes possible and makes sense. The transcendence and immanence paradox is therefore resolved.

8) God Space is a simultaneous broken symmetry. By definition, God Space itself is its own element. Being a subset, every element is intrinsically different from any other element although it can never be distinguished from all the rest of elements. This contradiction is reconciled in Chapter V, because they are identical in reality (ontological possibility) but differ in potentiality (quantum possibility).

9) There is only one God (Infinite) but many infinity(ies). Any difference in finite (being, that associates with time and is mortal) causes difference in essence, but difference in 'Infinite' will not change the essence of the Infinite (God). Infinite minus infinite is still Infinite. Because the essence of the Infinite is immutable, an infinite number of finites (beings) can be pulled out (creation) of the Infinite without changing the essence of the Infinite (God). Thus, creation is the inevitable consequence of the characteristic of God Space.

10) God Space is an ego-centered space. In fact, God Space is a process, moving from ego-selfishness to human love (altruism), then to asceticism, then to religious compassion and finally to the divine love. Love is neither a

state nor a quality but a process, a series of acts. On the one hand, love builds up boundaries or psychic walls to protect the beloved. On the other hand, love eventually transforms into compassion and thus breaks down all walls and brings souls together.

11) Not only are both subjective universe (phenomena) and objective universe (noumena) realities, but the bridge (intelligence) that links the two is also a reality. Not only are both ego and other-ego realities, but the bridge (love and compassion) that links the two is also a reality. These facts are the inevitable consequence of the characteristic of God Space. The moral truths demand the existence of possible universe(s), and God Space contains an infinite number of possible worlds.

12) God Space is a self-cause that the cause is the effect and that the effect is the cause (See Chapter X).

VI

With a clear understanding of the concept of God Space, the word "God" now not only is no longer a meaningless null word but is filled with infinite rich meaning. Very obviously, nothingness is eternal and immutable because there is nothing that can be lost or changed from nothingness. Infinity is also eternal and immutable because no amount of loss or change can alter infinity one bit. Now, I have unified and reconciled two opposite conceptions, nothingness and infinity, under the condition of timelessness, which is in the immortal sphere. In the mortal sphere, the infinity is unable to be defined in the material sense. Therefore, nothingness and infinity show up in an inverse relationship in mathematics. In the material world, the distance AB of all physical processes is guaranteed to be different from BA by the 2nd law of thermodynamics.

Since God is nothingness, He is immutable. Being immutable, He neither intervenes nature nor concerns Himself with human affairs. Being immutable, God cannot even be changed by the very creating act He is acting. God is transcendent and impassible.

God is the creator of this mortal world. Being a creator, His image permeates throughout the entire world. His spirit exists in every mortal existence. His divine consciousness becomes the consciousness of all mortals. This is why Einstein and all his followers have mistaken that the mortal consciousness (The relativity theory, the awareness of the existence of time) is the only reality. God has an immanent nature.

God is also infinity. Being infinite, He is eternal and omnipotent. Being omnipotent, He is all-loving, all-wise, with infinite power and infinite grace. In the mortal world, every material thing is finite. Only love — the love of Confucius, the love of Buddha and the love of Jesus — can be infinite. God's essence of infinity is manifested in the form of love and providence in this mortal world.

Being both nothingness and infinity, God is indivisible. Being indivisible, whenever reason is created, a paradox is also created at the same time. Wherever orderliness is created, chaos is also appears right beside it. Wherever goodness appears, evil comes along with it.

In summary, God is both transcendent and immanent, both impassible and provident, and is both orderliness and chaos. God's essence — nothingness, infinity and the utmost chaos — is the only unifying principle for all paradoxes. In His essence, there is no paradox. In the mortal world, the phrase "round square" is self-contradictory by definition, and therefore no such an item can exist. But, round square does exist in both nothingness and infinity. When the radius of a circle is reduced to zero, the roundness and squareness cannot be distinguished; therefore, both round square and square circle are not only identical in the nothingness but are both realities. Also, when the radius of a circle is increased to infinity, we again find the true existence of both square circle and round square. All self-contradiction and paradoxes disappear in the immortal sphere, the essence of God. God Himself is the proof of the paradox axioms.

VII

I was taught that God is "perfect" before I learned how to speak. But, what does "perfect" mean? What is perfect? My parents were unable to give me a satisfactory answer, neither the preachers nor anybody else. I had not the slightest idea about these issues until I completed my book — Super Unified Theory.

In Super Unified Theory, "perfect" means perfect symmetry. The perfect symmetry means the utmost chaos. The perfect symmetry is synonymous with "the utmost chaos". The utmost chaos means the "infinite violent force". The infinite violent force means that the perfect symmetry will and must break. The perfect symmetry can never be a "still state" because it is an infinite violent force. The perfect symmetry has to break down into a mortal universe and its ghost partner.

Without symmetry breaking, the diverse mortal universe cannot be created. Without symmetry breaking, the meaning of the absoluteness itself cannot manifest; even the absoluteness cannot provide a reference to itself without creating a relative universe. The most important of all, without symmetry breaking, the perfect symmetry cannot be maintained.

The only way to maintain the perfect symmetry is by breaking it. Only the infinite recursion, the symmetry breaking to create the relativity and the regeneration of the absoluteness from relativity by expanding it into infinity, can maintain the perfect symmetry. God is this infinite recursion, the union of the perfect symmetry and its creations — the mortal universe and its ghost partner. The creation of the godhead is thus complete.

In the immortal sphere (the perfect symmetry), time has no direction, meaning the perfect symmetry. In this perfect symmetry, the nothingness and the infinity cannot be distinguished. The mathematical representation of this union, between the perfect symmetry (the immortal sphere) and the mortal sphere (the relative universe and its ghost partner), is by using the concept of God Space. Within and with this God Space, the difference between transcendence and immanence is reconciled. This God Space is also the foundation of moral truth, of the rise of consciousness, of embodiment, of providence and of divination.

God the Spirit, who creates relativity by the process of symmetry breaking and then by reconciling all paradoxes to regain the absoluteness, is an Absolute Totality. Not only is truth true, but all falsities are also true realities (see Chapter V — The Language of God). William James wrote, "falsity means their disagreement with reality." Plato wrote, "A false proposition is one which asserts the nonexistence of things which are, and the existence of things which are not." Obviously, both of them did not comprehend the meaning of the Absolute Totality. The unicorn is no doubt a reality although it does not have a physical reference. The issue of fictitious reality will be discussed in detail in Chapter V — The Language of God. In short, truth is truth and falsity is also truth. In fact, this truth-falsity paradox precisely points out the existence and the meaning of the Absolute Totality. Many preachers say that God creates men and men create false gods; they obviously do not know what and who God is. Man can never create or imagine anything outside of or not of God, the Absolute Totality. In fact, the false God (the image or idol) is indeed the Almighty God Himself that He manifests and concretizes Himself as an image or an idol through the minds of men. In other words, the notion of no God or of a dead God is just as true as the notion of a living God. The Almighty God is vividly alive even inside of the notion of no God or of a dead God. The Absolute Totality is so powerful even the contradictory notions of God and of no God cannot divide Him but be reconciled by Him.

The Absolute Totality (the Almighty God) is an eternal process, the infinite recursion, from absoluteness to relativity, then back to absoluteness. The Absolute Totality is the perfect symmetry. The perfect symmetry must be a simultaneous broken symmetry. In fact, the term of symmetry denotes both the symmetry breaking and chaos. The first symmetry breaking separates the Immortal Sphere (without time, meaning Eternity) from the mortal universe (time was created, as the carrier of th gravitational force). The second one is the color symmetry breaking, from colorless to quark colors and genecolors; in turn, strong force manifests itself. The third one is the parity symmetry breaking which distinguishes weak force from an electromagnetic force. Then, magnetic force is created by the symmetry breaking of an electromagnetic force. Then, there are ... galaxies, lives, consciousness, and then, and then,....

Many can never conceive the essence of God. But everyone is no doubt able to recognize God because His attributes — love, wisdom, power and grace — are permeating all around the world. We can see them, smell them, feel them and imagine them. We can sense God without knowing any philosophical proof, any scientific proof or any theological proof. God is too obvious and too self-evident. Even atheists have to recognize God. When they deny the existence of God, they firstly have to know exactly what they are trying to deny. It means that they have to affirm and to construct the conception of God in their understanding and in their minds. Only when God has become a reality in their minds, can they expel God from their belief; in turn, God is indeed existing outside of their understanding. Again, God reveals Himself in this atheist paradox. God reveals Himself to all mortals — electrons, lives and the entire universe — in the form of paradoxes, but the essence of God is the unifying principle for all these paradoxes.

Chapter V
The Language of God

All prophets and all oracles spoke in the name of God while they did not and still do not have any idea of what God is and what the language of God is. They used miracles and signs as the language of God. But, the true miracles are not anything out of the ordinary, not the things that cannot happen in nature, not the events that are prohibited by the laws of nature. The true miracles are things that happen everyday, are events that follow the laws of nature. Everything around us is a miracle created by God. God expresses Himself with God's language. The laws of nature are a small part of God's vocabularies. The language of God will describe as to who and what God is to the precise point, no more, no less. The only way to understand what God is is by learning the language of God. On the other hand, the only way to understand what the language of God is is by understanding what God is.

God is the union of the immortal sphere and the mortal universe. God is the infinite recursion, from immortal sphere to mortal universe, then back to immortal. Therefore, there must be two kinds of languages to express these two different parts of God.

II

Indeed, the mortal universe can be expressed in terms of mathematics and science. Mathematics and theoretical science are God's language. The experimental science has no value whatsoever in the eyes of God. The Electrodynamics was developed with mathematics after four basic laws were discovered. Experiments did not add any new knowledge and insight into the already well-understood Electrodynamics. Einstein's theory was also developed by using only pencils and paper. Experiments only helped other physicists to accept his theory, but it did not add anything new to his theory. The experimental science is only a tool to show and to prove already known knowledge to those ignorant humans and to help them to build up their faith. Mathematicians and theorists can see inside of a black box without opening it, but experimentalists cannot understand any simple truth with intellect and faith if the box of truth is closed. One thing I am absolutely sure is that those experimentalists will never understand God because we are already inside the box of God. God can never be placed in

61

any kind of laboratory. The essence of God can never be proved experimentally. The portrait of God can only be understood by understanding God's language.

There is no experimental mathematics. The development of mathematics is very amazing. Mathematicians simply dream up some definitions and collect some axioms, and out comes a new mathematics. Surprisingly and amazingly, those dreamed up notions always turn out to be good language and tools for physicists to use for describing nature. The vector analysis was invented long before Maxwell developed Electrodynamics, but nobody today can tell the difference between the two. The matrix analysis also was invented long before Heisenberg developed Quantum Mechanics, but I had to use matrix analysis to solve the problems of Quantum Mechanics. Why? Why do all these coincidences exist? No doubt, the mathematics itself is the truth, the language of God. It is now employed as a tool for physicists to describe nature, but it contains much more truths than physicists can ever discover. It contains the complete truth.

III

Are we indeed so privileged to understand God's language? How can we be sure that those dreamed up mathematics are indeed God's language? There are two proofs. I have discussed the first one that all physical phenomena can be expressed in terms of mathematics. The second is that our mind-space is also a God Space. This is why the ancient people were able to conceive God, while not knowing any of the modern knowledge, either mathematics or nature science. The language of God is imbedded in our minds.

Before looking into how the mind works, we shall understand how a modern computer works first. In every computer memory location, it contains two pieces of information. One is its address, the other its content. For every computer memory spot, it can never be connected to another spot without the help of an external program. It has no life of its own. It can only be a stepping stone for a train of procedures. Sometimes, it can be a key word to invoke an external search program. It does not include an index file internally itself. It is impossible for it to jump to a new spot that is outside the train of procedure. So, the computer-mind is confined by a property of "continuity".

On the contrary, the human mind works quite differently from the computer-mind. The human mind does follow the train of thought sometimes. It does have the property of continuity. But, the human mind can randomly jump from one memory spot to another without any help from an external program. This can never be done by any computer program, at least not yet.

For example, on Christmas Eve last year, I was thinking of a Christmas gift, a watch that I received a year before. Then, I thought about the train set I brought for the kids this year. Then, I contemplated Einstein's theory of how to adjust time on a high speed train. Then, I thought that this Einstein phenomenon has to involve an observer who is conscious of what is happening, but an eyeless and mindless electron is also having this same kind of consciousness. Then, I was trying to understand the electron consciousness. Then, I knew that I have to understand what the definition of consciousness is first. So, I was thinking about the definitions for conception, self, time and space. Then, I remembered the turkey that is still in oven and, then, the duty to be a Santa Clause. Then, I contemplated who shall get what gift.

No doubt, my thought was jumping from one topic to many new subjects that have no logical connection at all among one another. Moreover, I learned those topics at different times of my life. I experienced those events at different places. Amazingly, my thoughts can jump from a childhood memory to a far away future and return to present without any difficulty. I can think of an event that happened twenty years ago as easily as an event that happened yesterday. The distance from my mind to these two events are the same. I can also dream about the future forty years from now as easily as I can recollect the past. The different lengths of "time or space" show no difference in my mind space. My perception can experience the real Time only one at a time, from past to present to future. In my mind space, I can see them simultaneously, whether it is a long ago past or a far away future. My mind space can also envision the entire space, from my own body to the edge of the universe, with a single glance. The mind space is not governed or controlled by physics laws. The light speed limitation of the relativity theory for this material world is no longer valid in this mind space.

The memory spot in the computer comes alive only if an external program invokes it. The memory spot in the mind space contains a living program of its own. In fact, every memory spot in the mind space acts as the center of the universe and can reach any point in the rest of universe with an equal effort. In short, the mind space is a God Space.

Today, neuroscience indeed discovers that the major difference between the human brain and a super computer is that the brain acts and reacts in a very chaotic fashion. In fact, the two major issues in neuroscience, the classic problem of separating foreground from background and the problem of generalization-over-equivalent receptors, can only be resolved by a Chaos brain model. The only way that brain can respond to a very small external signal and forms perception is because the steady state of brain is chaotic; thus, a very small external stimulus can abruptly and spontaneously shift this chaotic state to an orderly one. The chaotic activities of the brain is the source of intelligence. In short, chaos denotes intelligence and creativity (See Chapter X — The Triune Universe).

We can analyze our mind space from another angle. We can organize our mind space as a book. All the same subjects are written on the same page. The information on each page can be written from different time periods. Every new page contains a new subject. For the sake of discussion, let us assume that our mind space is composed of 100 pages; on every page, there are 100 memory spots. For any thought (memory) spot in page one, it can connect to any other spot either in the same page or in a new page all by its own choosing, and no external index file nor a searching program is needed. Every thought-spot contains a searching program and an index file of its own. Therefore, any thought-spot can jump to any of the rest of the spots with the same ease. In other words, the distance from any spot to each of the rest of thought-spots in the entire book is the same. Again, we can easily see that the mind space is a God Space. In fact, I discovered the God Space by analyzing our mind space. Only because our mind space is also a God Space, are we therefore able to understand our Almighty God. We are indeed privileged to understand God's language. It is imbedded in our mind. Thus, that the freely dreamed up mathematical notions by us humans are "always" suitable as tools for describing nature.

Thus, not only the ancient people were able to conceive God while not knowing any of the modern knowledge, but we are able to understand the essence of God while the box of God can never be opened. It is impossible for any computer program to simulate my train of thoughts. My train of thoughts on that Christmas Eve jumped tracks many, many times.

Our minds have two different properties: the continuity which is the train of thought and the random jumps which are the quantum tunneling effects. When we are learning a new subject, we always try to understand it by using old and known knowledge. This can be called "a process of attachment," to attach the new subject to the old knowledge. If the attachment cannot be accomplished, then the new subject cannot be memorized easily. But, the ability of randomly jumping from thought to thought is the only key to our ability to understand both nature and God, and it is the only key for imagination. Many fictitious objects that cannot exist in nature, which are confined in Space and Time, can thus exist in mind space. In fact, all fictitious objects are as real as any physical reality. I will prove this fact from two directions. Firstly, the physical world is only a small part of the total reality. Moreover, the Galilean view of this physical world is terribly wrong. Secondly, the conceptual world is not only as real as the physical world but is much more superior to the physical world.

Schrodinger, a cofounder of quantum mechanics, pointed out that our scientific theories must contain no evidence of the consciousness of the observer. Since Galileo, science has insisted that all scientific observers have to deliberately ignore the existence of themselves. For them, the observing mind has no place in either truth or nature. This is as if we were wondering the cause of the death of an animal that was shot dead by our own gun, but our rules have prohibited us to admit and to recognize the existence of the gun. No doubt, we can find out a lot of information about this event, including the cause of the death — a bullet, but we will never know from where this bullet came.

When Both Einstein and Heisenberg discovered that the observing mind is indeed the essence for both Relativity Theory and Quantum Mechanics, they both still had no courage to denounce the Galilean position but simply rejected the notion of an absolute existence. Thus, anything transcends from Time can never be understood by science. Science is, therefore, trapped and confined in Space and Time, the mortal sphere. Thus many religious stories are labeled as superstition and falsity by science.

All fictitious objects are indeed realities. They are not only truly existing in mind space, which is a subset of the ultimate reality — the God Space, but they can be concretized in the forms of idols and symbols. Not only are these concretized forms themselves real, the messages and principles they try to project are also real. They both can be perceived and conceived. Idols are concretized human virtues, principles and imaginations. Jesus is the greatest idol of mankind because he is the Word that became flesh. His image is worshipped all around the world. All realities and principles in the immortal sphere often are much easier described with fictitious objects and idols. The moral principles and human virtues, which are unable to be described in scientific terms, can be expressed in fictitious stories. The following is one example extracted from a very famous Chinese book — Strange Tales of Liaozhai.

IV

Fang Dong of Chang'an, though a scholar well reputed for his talent, was wild and negligent in the rules of good behavior. Each time he saw a girl walking in the open country, he would tag after her in a frivolous manner.

Once, the day before the Qingming Festival, he was taking a stroll on the outskirts when a light carriage with red curtains and an embroidered awning moved up. Riding closely behind were several servant girls, one of whom, sitting astride a pony, was exceedingly beautiful. Fang drew a little nearer to take a look and found that the front window was not draped with curtains. In the carriage sat a finely dressed girl of sweet sixteen, a raving beauty such as he had never before seen in his life. Dazzled and bewitched by her beauty, Fang could not take his eyes off the object of his admiration. He followed the carriage for several miles, now running in front, now trailing behind.

"Let down the curtain," the young lady in the coach said, summoning her maid to her side. "Who is that rude young man that dares to peep in all the time?"

The maid dropped the curtain and turned on Fang angrily, "You know the seventh son of the Lord of Hibiscus City? This is his bride on her way to her parents' home. She is not a country wife that you can stare at with impunity." So saying, she scooped up a handful of dust and threw it at Fang. The dirt got into his eyes so that he could not open them. By the time he rubbed his eyes and looked again, the carriage and the horses had already vanished.

Fang returned home in great wonder, yet the dirt kept troubling his eyes. He asked someone to turn up his eyelids and examine them. It was found that a tiny film had grown on the cornea of each eye. The following day things became worse: tears began streaming down without stopping, and the film grew bigger. In a few days it was as thick as a copper coin, with a spiral forming on the right eye. All drugs administered proved ineffective. Extremely remorseful, Fang bitterly repented his folly. He was then told that the Sutra of Brightness could relieve him of his misfortune. So he procured a copy and asked someone to instruct him in chanting it. At first he could not easily calm down, but gradually he began to secure peace of mind. When he had nothing to do , he would cross his legs and sit quietly counting his worry beads. This went on for a year, and he became completely devoid of desires and vexations.

Then one day he heard a small voice within his left eye say: "Such darkness is really unbearable!" A response came from the right eye: "Let us go for a stroll and cheer ourselves up." Fang began to feel his nose tickling as if something were wriggling out of the nostrils. Quite some time afterwards, the things returned, making their way to the eye sockets through the nose.

Fang told his wife what he had just experienced and heard. Greatly amazed, she quietly hid herself in the room and watched. Soon two tiny men, less than the size of a bean, came out of her husband's nose and went outdoors. She lost sight of them as they went off into the distance. But soon afterwards they came back arm in arm, flying up to Fang's face just like bees or ants seeking their homes. This recurred during th next few days. Then one day the left eye was heard saying, "The passage twists and turns; it is not convenient for us to go around. Why not make an opening ourselves?"

"The wall here is rather thick. It will be no easy job for me to break it," replied the right eye.

"I will try to cut a path. If we do that, we can stay together."

Fang then faintly felt something tearing at the nebula within his left eye. When he opened his eyes a moment later, he suddenly saw light and the things around. Exhilarated, he told this to his wife. In examining the left eye, she saw a tiny hole in its nebula and that much of a dark shining pupil about the size of half a pepper corn. The next day the film on the left eye disappeared completely. A careful inspection found that it had a double - pupil, but the spiral on the right eye remained. So the two pupils must have begun sharing the same eye.

Although he had definitely lost one eye, Fang could see much better than any normal person. From then on, he was all the more discreet and restrained in his behavior. And all the local people praised him for his excellent conduct.

Regardless of whether this story ever happened or not, of whether it is true or false, it is true in three aspects. Firstly, one who is frivolous in behavior always ends by hurting himself. Secondly, all conduct will be judged to be right or wrong, and rewards and retributions will surely follow accordingly. Thirdly, by repenting our bad behavior, we will always be given a new chance to live a new life. So, all fictitious stories, idols and deities are the projection and manifestation of human virtue, that is, the divine gift from our Almighty God. They are the manifestations of God Himself. Anyone who is against idols and deities is not only against human virtue but also against God Himself.

V

All fictitious objects can be represented by some sort of abstract spaces, for example — the null space. Every mathematician knows that that null space is a reality. But, what is null space?

Most people think that null space is an empty space. This notion is not wrong but is not useful. Null space comes from a real space whose physical substance has been emptied out. When the substance of a real space is emptied out, the conception of that real space remains. Time is reality and real substance. When we empty out its substance, the conception of time does not possess the real time any more. Space is also reality and real substance. The conception of space does not possess the real space. The conception of a reality is different from its substance. But, both conception and its substance are realities. Substance can be perceived, but conception can only be conceived. The human mind is able to do both.

Not only are the conceptions of time and of space members of null space, but the conception of any object or event is also a member of null space. Furthermore, the conceptual time is different from the conceptual space, although both of them are null elements. The null space is not an empty space but a space with an infinite number of members, which are transcended from both time and space. The perceptual space is a mortal world that is associated with and confined in time and space. The conceptual space is an immortal world that is transcended from both real time and real space. The language of God of this mortal world is the physical science. In this physical world, a decayed body can never arise from death; a human head can never grow on a lion's body. In the conceptual world, all fictitious events are indeed real. Moreover, the conceptual world is not only as real as the physical world, but is much more superior to the physical world because the conceptual world is immortal.

The reality of immortality is often expressed in the form of myths. Myths are not something of superstition but a conveyor of something intangible. A myth is not only an expression of a social ethos but is related to metaphor, in which an object or event is compared to an apparently dissimilar object or event in such a way as to make its otherwise inexplicable essence clear. A myth always conveys higher truths or higher realities, which may not have physical reference. Only mortal realities have physical reference. In short, the reality of the immortal sphere is often expressed in terms of symbolic language. The immortal reality often reveals its vivid existence through the common mythology. Mythology is not a primitive literature of primitive people but a language of immortal sphere. Only with this understanding, can the Revelation of St. John of Divine make sense.

"And I stood upon the sand of the sea, and saw a beast rise up out of the sea, having seven heads and ten horns, and upon his horns ten crowns, and upon his heads the name of blasphemy. And the beast which I saw was like unto a leopard, and his feet were as the feet of a bear, and his mouth as the mouth of a lion; and the dragon gave him his power, and his seat, and great authority. ... And the doeth great wonders, so that he maketh fire come down from heaven on the earth in the sight of men, And deceiveth them that dwell on the earth by the means of those miracles which he had power to do in the sight of the beast; saying to them that dwell on the earth, that they should make an image to the beast, which had the wound by a sword, and did live. And he had power to give life unto the image of the beast, that the image of the beast should both speak, and cause that as many as would not worship the image of the beast should be killed." Revelation 13:1-15.

There are two kinds of symbolic language, the explicit symbolism and the interpreted symbolism. Most of the Hindu mythology have the form of explicit symbolism. For example, Lakini, a goddess of Hinduism, has three heads and four arms. Obviously, this goddess is explicitly meant as a symbol. In one of her hands, she holds a thunderbolt, which symbolizes that the deep uncontrolled passion of a storm is still with her. In another hand she holds the fire of the spirit, which symbolizes her passion and compassion. She also has three eyes on each head. Two mundane eyes can see only mortal things or beings. The third eye sees immortal spirits. In short, Lakini symbolizes the existence of both mortal and immortal realities, of both uncontrolled desire and controlled passion and of both ignorance and spiritual enlightenment.

On the other hand, many symbols in the Bible are not in the form of explicit symbolism. Very often, we cannot be sure if they mean to be symbols or to be facts. Their meaning or lack of meaning is completely dependent upon the interpretation of the beholder. The best example is the virgin birth story. In the Gospel of St. Matthew, it was written in the form as a symbol, but in the Gospel of St. Luke it was stated as a fact.

"But while he thought on these things, behold, the angel of the Lord appeared unto him in a dream, saying, Joseph, thou son of David, fear not to take unto thee Mary thy wife: for that which is conceived in her is of the Holy Ghost. And she shall bring forth a son, and thou shalt call his name JESUS: for he shall save his people from their sins. ... Then Joseph being raised from sleep did as the angel of the Lord had bidden him, and took unto him his wife." Matthew 1:20-24.

"And the angel came in unto her, and said, Hail, thou that art highly favoured, the Lord is with thee: blessed art thou among women. And when she saw him, she was troubled at his saying, and cast in her mind what manner of salutation this should be. And the angel said unto her, Fear not, Mary: for thou hast found favour with God. And, behold, thou shalt conceive in thy womb, and bring forth a son, and shalt call his name Jesus. ... Then said Mary unto the angel, How shall this be, seeing I know not a man? And the angel answered and said unto her, The Holy Ghost shall come upon thee, and the power of the Highest shall over-shadow thee: therefore also that holy thing which shall be born of thee shall be called the Son of God. ... For with God nothing shall be impossible." Luke 1:28-37.

The interpreted symbolism is always ambidextrous as it is ambiguous. It is always written with both hands and each tells a different story. Regardless of what kind of symbolism they are, they all reveal the realities which are as real as any touchable physical object, although they themselves may not have physical reference. All fictitious objects or events are vivid realities existing in the conceptual universe which is a subset of the immortal sphere. Thus, myth is a vehicle that takes men into this immortal sphere. However, we must read any myth as a myth. To read any myth as a fact is nothing but lying to ourselves.

VI

Since nothing can be outside of God, all human languages are subsets of God's language. Not surprisingly, there are two types of human language, which indeed are evolved from these two distinguishable aspects of God's language. The one is perceptual language, the other conceptual language.

English is a good example of a perceptual language. In English, there are many grammatical rules: such as tense, subject-predicate structure, parts of speech, numbers, etc. The purpose of tense is to record and to express the real time. The subject-predicate structure is for relating the relationship between time and space of events or things and to distinguish the knower from the known or the doer from the act. The parts of speech are trying to clarify the real time sequences and the relationship of real space or the relationships of their derivatives. In other words, English is a real time language, a perceptual language.

On the contrary, Chinese is a conceptual language. There is no tense in Chinese. All events can be discussed in the conceptual level. The time sequence can be marked by time marks. Therefore, there is no reason to change the word form for identifying the time sequence. Thus, there is no subject-predicate structure in Chinese, because there are no real verbs. All actions can be expressed in noun form when they are transcended from time and space. There is no need to have parts of speech in Chinese. In short, there is no grammar in Chinese. The following are a few examples to show the difference between a perceptual and a conceptual language.

Perceptual: I went to school yesterday.

Conceptual: I go school yesterday.

Perceptual: I am trying to find three pegs now.

Conceptual: I try find three peg now.

Indeed, Chinese language can express a truth or a picture with only a few words, without any grammar, especially the subject-predicate structure.

For example: "Dead vine, old tree, evening bird; small bridge, running water, flat desert; broken heart traveller at far away place."

No doubt, the above utterance paints a very vivid picture. A heart broken traveller at a far away desert looks at a dead vine, an old tree, an evening bird and a small bridge over a small stream. But, this clear written sentence loses much meaning of the original piece, which emphasizes not only the desertion of the place but the desolateness and the homesickness of a heart broken traveller.

The modern Chinese writing is now somewhat westernized by artificially inserting subject and predicate structures into a sentence, but the writing style of the above example is not only for poems but is in fact for all "genuine" old Chinese writing. I always write to friends in Chinese with the following beginning, "Long no news, much thought, hope more come letter." It means, " I have not heard from you for a long time and have thought about you very much. Please write often, and I am looking forward to your letters." This English translation contains three times more words but no additional meaning.

In other words, the notion that all truths have to be expressed in some form of structure, especially in a subject-predicate arrangement, is no doubt absolutely wrong. Those who believe that the subject-predicate relation is the "only" basis for an emerging consciousness of the distinction between categories related to the "self" (personhood) and those related to entities classifiable as "nonself" is definitely mistaken not only because of their ignorance of Chinese language but also because of the lack of understanding what consciousness is and means. Language is not necessary for the emergence of high order consciousness, although it helps for its later elaborations. Grammar is not needed for language.

The Absolute Totality is the oneness and can be expressed best with the conceptual notion without a symmetry broken structure of subject and predicate. Subject and predicate structure becomes useful only in a symmetry broken realm, such as the mortal universe. Not surprisingly, most computer languages are conceptual languages.

VII

Seemingly, God needs two types of language to express His paradoxical nature, being both mortal and immortal. On the other hand, these two types of languages must be unified into a harmonic oneness because God is the Absolute Totality. Indeed, it does.

Science and mythology can indeed be unified into a harmonic oneness in God Space. The God Space can be expressed in terms of mathematical abstract space, and it also can be represented with a new mathematical concept — the ontological possibility.

Physicists have long used the concept of possibility to represent the virtual entities, the quanta. These quantum possibilities all directly associate with energy, although not always with matter. They are well-understood, by now.

With a quantum leap from the concept of quantum possibility (mortal possibility), we obtain the concept of ontological possibility, which is not directly associated with both energy or phenomena.

There is a significant difference between quantum and ontological possibility. There is no way to derive the concept of God from the conception of quantum possibility, but the concept of ontological possibility can do it. Only under the framework of ontological possibility, the true "nothingness" (not virtue nothingness) can become a possibility, and this possibility can actualize, such as the the first creation, without the help of anything which is already actual. Furthermore, in "nothingness," there are an infinite number of possibilities. Regardless of how small a probability of any possibility is, the "nothingness" is not only a possibility but a certainty — a certainty of a process, the creation process, from nothing to something. Any possibility, however small, is infinitely larger than the nothingness itself. Any possibility, however small, is no doubt a certainty compared with the nothingness itself. God's free will is indeed the highest, but even God Himself is confined to His own essence. God does not have the freedom of not creating. The only way to maintain the perfect symmetry (God's spirit) is by breaking it, beginning with the absoluteness that creates relativity by a symmetry breaking process, and then the relativity regenerates the absoluteness by reconciling all paradoxes, by entering into eternity.

The quantum possibility exists in a universe that is confined in a traditional conservation law, the energy-mass conservation law. Thus, no lump of matter can come out of blue in this quantum universe. On the other hand, the ontological possibility exists in a universe that is confined to a new set of conservation laws, which has a much larger framework. A lump of matter can indeed come out of blue by borrowing energy from the ghost partner (see my book — Truth, Faith, and Life).

The mortal universe — being associated with energy, matter, time and space — must obey physics laws, especially the limitation of light speed. Quantum possibilities cannot be actualized arbitrarily but are confined by eleven dimensions. On the other hand, ontological possibility exists in the realm that is not governed by any physics law. It is not associated with neither energy, nor matter, nor space, nor time. All myths can be represented by ontological possibilities. Every myth is an ontological possibility. The probability (IP — Immortal Probability) of any ontological possibility is always equal to 1, meaning the certainty of its vivid reality, until it makes an association with mortal attributes — energy, matter, space and time. When an ontological possibility becomes a quantum possibility, its probability (MP — Mortal Probability) will then be often less than 1. So, the conceptual reality is much more real than any physical object. Nonetheless, not every ontological possibility is able to transform itself into a quantum possibility. The domain of ontological possibility, God Space, is infinitely larger than the domain of quantum possibility, the mortal universe. Science describes the mortal universe, but mythology describes the complement of the mortal world, the immortal sphere. They exist in two disjoined subsets of God Space. God Space is the union of them.

VIII

Now, we are able to define what truth or falsity is. "All" ideas, either real or fictitious, are ontological possibilities. The probability (IP) of every ontological possibility is always equal to 1 (one). Every ontological possibility is always an ontological truth. By definition, there is no a such thing as ontological falsity. Not only can't we humans create any ontological falsity because God is the Absolute Totality, but even God Himself is unable to do it. God cannot create anything which is not of Himself.

When any ontological possibility associates with the mortal attributes — time, space and energy — it becomes a quantum possibility (a mortal possibility), and the probability (MP) of this mortal possibility has three possibilities.

One, MP equals 1 (one), meaning actuality and mortal truth. This ontological possibility has a physical reference.

Two, MP is less than 1 (one) but larger than 0 (zero), meaning potentiality or mortal possibility. This ontological possibility has a possibility to become an actuality.

Three, MP equals 0 (zero), meaning non-reality and mortal falsity. This ontological possibility has no physical reference and has no mortal possibility to become an actuality.

Even when MP (mortal probability) equals 0 (zero), being a mortal falsity, its corresponding IP (immortal probability of its corresponding ontological possibility) remains to be 1 (one), being an ontological truth still. All mortal falsities are still immortal truths.

In fact, the immortal sphere does not exist apart from the mortal universe but overlaps with it although they are disjoined in terms of Set Theory. The immortal world resides not only in a transcendent heaven but is also here on earth. It is before life, during life and after life. The mystery of existence, of nonexistence, of goodness, of evil and of God can be expressed in terms of mythical or symbolic language. For ancient people, in their search for explanations and solutions, they invent anthropomorphic images (deities). The history of the past is, in essence, the history of the deities, their life and their death and the history of the life and death of the cultures they successively inspired.

This mythical language and symbolic expression is irrational and illogical. With this irrational tool, man became conscious of the immutable ethical law that rules his life long before the age of enlightenment. With this illogical tool, man became aware of the eternal truth without grasping the underlying meaning and without any explanation long before the age of science. These mysteries of mystery can be concretized into mythical images. Although all mythical images do not express a tangible reality, they all really and truly live. They live in man under the form of animating intention. They live in man as the struggle between right and wrong motivations, a conflict which is nothing else than inner human deliberation. Furthermore, symbolic language can express the mystery of mystery because it can create an unlimited number of combinations.

Both the mortal universe and the immortal sphere reside in God. God expresses Himself with two types of language, the perceptual and the conceptual. We are indeed images of God, possessing both properties of mortality and of immortality. In other words, God is embodied in each of us. Our bodies are confined in the mortal universe, but our consciousness exists in the immortal sphere. God's body is the manifestation of the material universe; His essence is the unification of nothingness, infinity and the utmost chaos.

The immortal world is expressed in terms of conceptual vocabularies, often in the form of fictitious stories or myths. The physical science can only describe the mortal and perceptual world. Furthermore, this mortal universe is only a "degenerated" subset of the immortal sphere. "All" scientific models are expressed in terms of fictitious concepts. The ideal gas in the ideal gas model is a fictitious substance or concept. All real gases, including the inert gases, are not ideal gas. The rigid body model in physics is another example. All substance in the world, including the most rigid steel, does not posses the rigidness as described in the rigid body model. Those fictitious concepts of science come from a scientific approach — to simplify the real world; they are on the surface seemingly different from the approach of mythology. Nonetheless, these two approaches are only different in degree, not in kind.

In the West, the fictitious world and the perceivable realities are two irreconcilable opposites. On the other hand, Chinese think of them as a harmonic oneness. The Chinese character for "thinking" is written with a field above a heart. The fictitious world is not something unreal but a field that has been cultivated by consciousness. Thus, both science and mythology can be expressed with a notion of ontological possibility, which can be described completely in terms of mathematics. Indeed, on the one hand, mathematics seemingly has no physical reference and is only a pure form of logic and relation; on the other hand, it always acts as language to represent all physical realities. Mathematics is God's unified language, unifying both science and mythology with the concept of ontological possibility.

Chapter VI
The Moral Truths

Is there moral truth? Is the moral philosophy a genuine knowledge or only a mere opinion? What is the issue? Why shall these questions even be asked in first place?

Since antiquity to present time, most philosophers believe that moral issue is a matter of value, not a matter of fact. Therefore, moral philosophy is subjective and relative, not objective and absolute. Hobbes stated that good and evil are relative to the person who uses these words; and when people are joined together in a commonwealth, then good and evil are subject to the determinations of the commonwealth.

On the other hand, all theologians strongly insist that moral standards are divinely set, and therefore they are absolute. But, all of them believe in their position only with blind faith and cannot provide an intelligent argument or an understandable proof. They prove the absoluteness of moral truths by first postulating the existence of God; then, because of the absoluteness of moral laws, the existence of God is affirmed. In other words, their arguments are no more than a vicious circle, using the conclusion to prove its premises, or vice versa. In general, they provide three types of vicious circles.

First, since moral laws are "commands," a "commander" must exist. Furthermore, the commander cannot be a human moral agent, for what today he commands us to do, he can tomorrow command us not to do. Thus, we can have absolute moral obligations only if God exists to command them; then, because we do have absolute moral obligations, it follows that God must exist.

Second, if we recognize moral authority, we must first recognize that existence of God as alone able to confer that authority. Because the moral law retains its authoritativeness whether particular human wills are at any time actually accepting its rules or not, God must be the source of this authority.

Third, the notion of moral law itself is said to be incomplete without reference to God, for law implies lawgiver, a divine legislator. On the other hand, our very acknowledgment of a moral law presupposes the existence of God.

Do these arguments make any sense? God and moral truth are as the chicken and the egg. Which one came first? Kant presented another view with his presupposition of the highest good. He believed that moral truths are absolute but unattainable by humans. He wrote, "The idea of the highest good ... cannot be realized by man himself ...; yet he discovers within himself the duty to work for this end. Hence he finds himself impelled to believe in the cooperation or management of a moral Ruler of the world, by means of which alone this goal can be reached." As for Kantians, the moral perfection is unattainable; therefore, we can have no obligation to attain it but, at best, only an obligation to strive toward it.

In summary, the chicken and egg argument does not prove anything. Even the postulation of God, either by Kant or by all theologians, can by no means insure that the ultimate moral goals will, in fact, be reached or be understood, although it was precisely to insure their attainment that the postulates were made. This is because they simply do not know what God is. A postulation itself, without the understanding of what the postulation is, can neither insure a true conclusion, nor attain a true understanding. The moral truth can be understood only if three issues are clearly understood: 1) The essence of God — the infinite recursion of absoluteness and relativity, 2) The manifestation of free will and equal rights, 3) The definition of goodness and evil.

II

Up to now, most philosophers, scientists and theologians accept a notion that the matter of value is different from the matter of fact, that ought to be is different from that that is. So, the descriptive statement is different from the prescriptive statement, and the relative is different from the absolute. David Hume even proved that the prescriptive statement can never be proved by using descriptive truths. Later, G.E. Moore came up an idea of 'naturalistic fallacy,' that is, the ethical concepts could not be defined in terms of those of natural science or metaphysics, such as: that 'good' is defined by means of common sense psychological characteristics, or in terms of the notions of some scientific theory. In short, the 'ought' statement cannot be deduced from an 'is' sentence.

For many moral philosophers, there are many meanings for 'ought,' such as: the moral 'ought' as he ought to do good deeds, a technical 'ought' as he ought to use a pencil instead of a pen and an epistemic 'ought' as it ought to rain tomorrow. The moral 'ought' is relative to a desire to obey certain moral rules or a moral principle or more directly for the end or ends specified in such a principle. The moral utterances are calculated not only to express our feelings but to arouse feeling in others. In deciding whether a moral principle, such as abortion, is right or wrong we are not finding out fact, but deciding what to do about the facts or what to encourage others to do about them. 'This is good' said by John does not contradict 'This is not good' said by Smith at the same time and in the same context. In short, the disagreement in moral is not about the truth or falsity of a proposition, but is a disagreement in attitude, in belief and in desire.

Amazingly, most philosophers accept these arguments and their proofs. Einstein even rejected the existence of the absoluteness because he found that everything in nature is relative. Amazingly again, not only all scientists and all philosophers accept this gross mistake of Einstein, but even all theologians lack the courage to challenge it.

No doubt, not only are both Hume and Einstein but also these moral philosophers wrong, partially wrong at least. All 'ought' statements make sense if and only if there are options. We can never say that we ought to be born or we ought to live forever because we do not have option for these matters. Often, an 'is' sentence states a fact, something absolute. An 'ought' statement always only expresses the existence of relativity and options. But, the relativity is only a derivative of absoluteness and can never come to be if there is no absoluteness. This statement can be proved easily.

If there is only one person existing in this universe, then whatever moral value that he happens to have is no doubt absolute. When there are two persons in this world, then their moral values may differ. If there is a common ground between their values, this common ground is then absolute. In mathematics, this common ground can be expressed as a set that is the intersection of the two original sets. If there is no common ground between these two persons, then their common ground is an empty set. But, this empty set is a genuine set in set theory. It is as genuine as any other non-empty set. It is as real as any other non-empty set. Therefore, there is always a common ground, either empty or non-empty. Both of them are realities.

The more people in the world, the higher relativity will be. The higher relativity is, the smaller non-empty common ground can be. With an infinite high relativity, the common ground will surely become an empty set that is the synonym of nothingness. Again, we always come back to the nothingness. The nothingness, our Almighty God, is everywhere.

If you cannot see that the nothingness is the absolute absoluteness, you ought to see that an one person world is much more absolute than a two person world. From this example, the absoluteness has to preexist the relativity. In the real world, the relativity (the difference) always forces compromises and creates non-empty common ground. The difference in value judgement among people is a force both to narrow and to widen the difference. In other words, the relativity itself creates both absoluteness and relativeness. The civil laws are created with this process. The modern name of this process is "democracy". Amazingly, the difference and the relativity are the source of the sameness and the absoluteness. The difference and the relativity are the result of breaking down of absoluteness. But, the difference and the relativity turn around to become a force that recreates the absoluteness. The relativity and the absoluteness are not only closely related but indeed inseparable. Lo-Chen Gong, my father and a professor of Chinese Philosophy, wrote, "This universe is forever changing, and this phenomenon of forever changing is the only absoluteness in the entire universe." In fact, the moral truth is the reflection of God, the process from absoluteness to relativity, then back to absoluteness. Both Hobbes and Kant are, therefore, only partially correct.

Thus, the difference between the prescriptive truths and the descriptive truths are very superficial, not fundamental. The divine law is the law of all laws, of either descriptive or prescriptive laws.

Incest is not only morally wrong but is also punished by physical law. The genetic law will significantly weaken the ability of any group or culture, that accepts the incest practice, to survive the evolution challenge. Incest practice is always punished and thus prohibited by the genetic and evolution laws in a longer time scale. No society that is practicing incest survives to present time. This moral value against incest is indeed supported by descriptive laws; furthermore, it is often implanted in genes with God's own hands. Many species, house mice as one example, can choose between potential mates that differ at a single genetic site in the Major Histocompatibility Complex (H-2), which specifies the antigens responsible for distinguishing between self and nonself. For example, male mice prefer to mate with females whose H-2 type is different from their own.

Adultery is not only morally wrong but is also punishable by physical laws. Every sexual act outside of the marital boundary increases the chance of contracting some kind of social disease. Some of them are deadly. The laws of statistics and probability will ensure the punishment of those adulterer and adulteress. Furthermore, the economical laws are also descriptive laws. Adultery will often cause the breaking up of a family, and the adulterer will surely be punished with economical loss. Again, this moral value is supported by descriptive laws.

The supporting physical laws for any moral truth are often deeply hidden, and the punishment for the violators is seemingly slow. An engine built by violating thermodynamics will surely break down instantaneously during the trial run. A moral truth violator will be punished by the underlying physical laws slowly but surely. No doubt, David Hume's theory and his proof is wrong. The difference between descriptive and prescriptive laws is very superficial. In short, the naturalistic fallacy itself is a fallacy.

III

The moral laws are often supported by many physical laws, but by no means are they inferior to physical laws. The moral truths are not the derivatives of physical laws. They are legitimate in their own right. They are the result of a supreme divine gift, the free will.

Most people believe that there is no free choice in the arena of descriptive truths. No one is able to design a car or an air conditioner by not following the thermodynamic laws. No one is able to design a computer by violating the electronic laws. No one is able to fly space ships by ignoring the gravitational law. But, we are able to design many different cars and engines, in different sizes and different styles. We are able to design many different computers with different capabilities and with different features. In other words, we do have some freedom of choice even in the physical world. In fact, we do have a lot of freedom of choice in the physical world. The notion of free choice is indeed a very important issue for both the physical and moral world.

What is freedom? Some define freedom as the right to do what they want to do, when they want to do it, to whom they want to do it and under circumstances of their own choosing. This kind of freedom is fatally flawed because it teaches that we are entitled to complete freedom or liberty for ourselves without thinking about others. Thus, most people believe that personal freedom is not an escape from but an escape into responsibility toward others. Lincoln said, "Those who deny freedom to others deserve it not for themselves." Is then freedom only an induced notion? Or, does it have a real substance and a life of its own? Can freedom exist independent of something else, such as responsibility? In short, does free will and freedom of choice really exist?

Many philosophers and almost all theologians insist that free will and freedom of choice indeed exist all by itself, without depending upon anything else. They argued that free will is divinely given. They said, "No one, not even the slave in chains or the prisoner in solitary confinement, is totally devoid of freedom to will what he wishes to do." For theologians, free will is the foundation of many religious doctrines, such as goodness and evil, heaven and hell. For philosophers, free will is also the foundation of many philosophical issues, such as political liberty and moral choice. No doubt, there is a need to have free will and free choice for supporting many current dogmas and doctrines. It is also nice if they are indeed real. But, can a need be justified as a proof?

Many determinists, who strongly denounce the existence of free will and free choice, concede that causal laws are not perfect. There are indeed many practical needs for accepting the notions of free will and free choice. How can we hold anyone responsible for an act that he could not avoid having chosen to perform? How can we punish a criminal if he was not morally responsible for what he did because it was not a free choice on his part?

After the invention of statistical and probabilistic laws and the discovery of Quantum Mechanics, those determinists admit that there is indeed some indeterminacy in the realm of natural phenomena. But, the exponents of free choice still argue that this causal indeterminacy of physical world bears no resemblance to the indeterminacy involved in freedom of choice. They insist that the freedom of choice does not act in accordance with the physical laws because it is immaterial.

There is a third opinion, that is, whether the universe is deterministic or indeterministic we do not have free will. If determinism is true, then our actions are determined by some physical laws; so we do not have free will. If indeterminism is true, then our actions may happen by pure chance. If an action happened by pure chance, might we not find ourselves doing something we did not want to do? Would not such indeterminism take away our freedom?

IV

Time and again, I cannot agree with the arguments of all three sides. God's law is the law of all laws. Physical laws and moral laws are cousins. Sure, there shall be some difference between them, but the difference can only be superficial, not fundamental. The free choice and free will are indeed real existences, but they do not exist only in a moral world. They are a vital part of our mortal world. They can be clearly defined and understood. Amazingly, the key to its understanding again lays in physics.

In physics, a free particle is defined as a particle that is not influenced by any external force; thus, it will not lose any of its own energy or essence. With this definition, does any free particle exist in this world? Most electrons are not free because they will be pushed or pulled by any nearby electrons and protons. Physicists tell us that a free particle can only exist in a potential well with an infinite depth. In other words, it can only exist in solitary confinement.

Surprise! Surprise! The total freedom can only come from the complete solitary confinement — the stronger the confinement, the greater the freedom. A neutron, when it is confined in a nucleus, is closely to be a free particle, and it can survive for a long time, almost forever. When it is expelled from this confined environment and enters into the open world, it will die or decay in a matter of one millionth of a second. Not only the freedom of a neutron but its survival are completely dependent upon the strength of the confining force. The stronger confining force acts on a neutron, the stabler this neutron will be.

This notion of freedom seems ridiculous and absurd, but it can be understood very easily. If there were only one person in this world, he would have the right to do whatever he wants to do, when he wants to do it, to what he wants to do it and under circumstances of his own choosing. He has absolute freedom because he is in a complete solitary confinement and in a state of absolute loneliness. If there are two persons in this world, then one person's freedom is reduced and checked by the freedom of the other person. The confining force of this 2nd person is much less than the force of the solitary confinement; therefore, there is much less freedom between either of them.

Every tyrant rules his subjects with his own hands. When we fight against any tyrant, we only fight against a single man. So, the confining force from any tyrant is very weak and often short-lived. On the other hand, democracy has a much stronger confining power. When we fight against democracy, we are fighting against the majority of population. Because democracy is a much stronger confining force, there is much more freedom in a democratic society.

This notion of freedom can also be demonstrated in mathematics. When we live in a one-dimensional world, that means that we are confined with only one-dimensional force, our maximum freedom can never go behind one degree of freedom. When we are confined by a two-dimensional force, our maximum freedom also has a chance to be two degrees of freedom. The more dimensions a confining force has, the more degrees of freedom we can possibly have.

We are confined by gravity force; so we have earth as our nice home. We are confined by thermodynamics; so we are able to build cars and air conditioners. We are confined by Electrodynamics; so we are able to invent televisions, video machines and computers. But the most important of all, we are permanently confined in God; so we have free will and free choice. God allows us to do whatever we choose and please because there is absolutely no way that we can get out of His hand. Indeed, we absolutely have no choice of not choosing. Jean-Paul Sartre viewed that freedom of choice is a curse to human existence. Even God Himself is confined in His own essence. His essence is infinitely powerful, therefore, He has infinite freedom. Our bodies are only confined in the mortal world, which is only a very small part of God's body; so our bodily freedom is somewhat limited. Our souls are permanently confined in God's spirit, which is a larger part of God's body; so our souls can live beyond this mortal world.

V

Since we genuinely have free will, the moral truths are indeed realities. They are not notions dreamed up by theologians. Thus, there are indeed goodness and evil. But, what is goodness and what is evil? How can we determine what is what?

Not only is there a big confusion of why there is goodness and evil, but there is a bigger confusion of how to define what good is. Aristotle and his followers said that happiness is good. But, what is happiness? "Happiness is pleasures," they said. Then, they distinguished between lower and higher pleasures. The pleasures of the intellect are more desirable than the pleasures of the senses. But, what is more desirable and how to determine it? Those who pursue sensual indulgences to the injury of their health may regard the sensual pleasures as the greater good and are willing to sacrifice their own health to pursue sensual pleasures. How can we provide a rational argument to persuade them that they are wrong? How can we prove to them that health is indeed a greater good than sensual pleasure?

Consequentialist distinguishes 'good as an end' from 'good as a means,' or 'intrinsically good' from 'extrinsically good.' Thus, the sensual pleasures is only extrinsically good but intrinsically bad. But, how can we distinguish and define what are intrinsic and extrinsic? Goodness corresponds to a cluster of properties, none of which are necessary or sufficient for goodness.

Because of the inability of defining what goodness is, the moral philosophy is viewed again by most philosophers as only a mere opinion, not genuine knowledge. They give it a fancy name, noncognitive ethics. A few philosophers did try to overcome the difficulty that is imposed by David Hume, that he said the moral value cannot be induced and proved by any descriptive truths. Some, thus, try to combine a prescriptive and a descriptive premises into a "First Principle" of moral philosophy in order to argue for the truth of a prescriptive conclusion. Some insist that human nature has two aspects. One is divinely given. The other is acquired. The acquired can differ from individual to individual. The divinely given are the same for all mankind. So, this divinely given human nature is the common ground for the base of moral truth. This moral truth is, therefore, absolute. The divinely given human nature is the First Principle of moral philosophy. This argument is indeed elegant and correct. But, their notion of divine intervention is again unproved and undefined but is accepted by mere blind faith. Their major problem is that they simply do not know what divine is. The phrase of "the divinely given human nature" is, therefore, a meaningless and an undefined slogan. It will become meaningful only if the divine nature is clearly understood.

Aristotle and his followers have failed to define what good is in a meaningful way. Augustine came up a different idea. Since he, with his blind faith, believed that God is infinitely perfect, he concluded that there cannot be any evil. He made two arguments. One, everything that is evil in our view is indeed good, especially in God's view. For example, scorpions often kill not only animals but also humans; so they are evil. But, they are good for themselves. The male scorpion is good for a female one, and vice versa. Two, he thought that every evil is the corruption of something good. He introduced a new meaningless word, corruption. What is corruption? How does corruption work? His notion of goodness and evil seems elegant but does not reach their ultimate meanings. Saint Augustine simply did not truly know what and who God is. God is an eternal process, moving from the absoluteness to relativity, than back to absoluteness.

VI

The essence of God is infinitely perfect; therefore, it is indivisible. Being indivisible, when a good is created, the evil will be created right beside the good. This is because of the inseparable property between absoluteness and relativity. When someone is a winner, the others will be losers. The goodness and evil are created by relativity. Not only is the physical world governed by relativity, but the moral world is also governed by relativity. In the physical world, Einstein invented a set of relativity equations. There is no relativity equation in the moral world. The relativity in the moral world is created by democracy, the common sense of the majority.

What is the common sense of the majority of people, then? Common sense of the majority of people can by clearly defined by the principle of Pragnanz — the idea that the visual system converges on the most regular and symmetric perception consistent with sensory information. When a circle covers a corner of a square, common sense tells us that a square corner is underneath the circle. This kind of mind-set was discovered by Gestalt. In fact, the covered part can be anything, a part of a triangle or of a circle. But, anything other than a square corner, which can match the other three visible square corners to make a complete square, will be perceived as abnormal. The common sense pursues two properties: continuity and perfection.

Continuity means without symmetry breaking, without discontinuity. Perfection means perfect symmetry, again without symmetry breaking. Continuity and perfection are two sides of the same coin.

In fact, goodness is defined in terms of continuity and perfection. The simpler a system is, the easier the perfection can be maintained. In "Information Theory," good is defined in terms of amount of information, that little information means good and that many connotes "bad". So, perfection connotes simplicity. On the one hand, the "nothingness" has the most complex structure that contains an infinite number of possibilities; on the other hand, it is the simplest entity, therefore, the highest perfection, meaning the highest goodness.

Continuity means indivisible, but it is defined in terms of discontinuity, with terms such as: proximity, similarity, closure, common region or connectedness. When a part of the whole is grouped with the above processes (closure, connectedness, etc.), both the continuity and the perfection (symmetry) of the whole is broken. Thus, goodness is defined in terms of returning to continuity and perfection (the simplicity). Many moral values are indeed built on traditions, which is the continuity of the past. Moral values, therefore, differ from culture to culture.

Both continuity and perfection are characteristics of God. They are in God and in us. Anything that lacks these two properties will be viewed as less good or even evil. The common sense simply pursues God, wanting to unite with God. The common sense is the embodiment of God. The common sense of the majority of people is a force which defines moral truths. Moral virtues are, therefore, both divinely given and acquired commodities.

VII

Moral truths are defined by the interplay of free will of both the individual and the public. The degrees of freedom of any system are defined as the number of possibilities that may be assigned arbitrarily without violating the conservation laws which govern that system. The degrees of freedom for any individual is always less than the degrees of freedom of the system. How to calculate the degrees of freedom of any given system for any given variable is not difficult but quite lengthy. The rule of thumb is that the more members a system has, the higher degrees of freedom it has. Seemingly, moral truth is only a derivative of physical laws because free will is defined in terms of physics (the permanent confinement) and of statistics (degrees of freedom). Not so! Although moral truths indeed exist in the mortal universe and are initially defined in terms of physical laws, their substances are immortal.

Moral truth is not a "state" nor a dogma but a direct reflection of God Himself, being a Spirit as a dynamic union of absoluteness and relativity. Moral virtues are forces which drive us to unite with God. Moral truths also demonstrate that the immortal sphere does not exist apart from the mortal universe but overlaps with it.

In the mortal world, every system is finite; therefore, the degrees of freedom of every system is also finite. In fact, our bodily freedom is surly finite. On the contrary, the immortal sphere is an infinity; thus, the degrees of freedom of it is also an infinity. Our mind space is a reflection (a subset) of God Space; thus, the degrees of freedom of our consciousness is infinite.

Each of us is a member of God Space. Every member in God Space is the center of God Space, by definition, which means every member has an equal right of all rights. In fact, practically and theoretically, freedom can only be defined in terms of equal right. In turn, equal right can only be defined in terms of permanent confinement, that the right of every individual is confined by the right of the rest of universe. That all men are created equal is guaranteed by the property and the definition of God Space. The equal right of all mankind is the foundation of all moral truths.

It is now very clear that God Space has all three properties — as infinite degrees of freedom, as permanent confining force and as equal right. In fact, "the permanent confining force" is synonymous with "an infinite degrees of freedom," and "freedom" is synonymous with "equal right". Since there is no way of escaping from God's hand, we are given free will and free choice; therefore, moral values differ from place to place and from time to time. Moral truth is not only a genuine reality but the ultimate truth.

Chapter VII
The Origin and the Rise of Consciousness

I watched a TV program about how beavers repair their damaged dam. First, they gathered together to assess the damage. Then, they went different ways to saw and gather tree trucks. They seemed to know exactly how long of a piece of wood is needed. They worked together in excellent coordination and cooperation. Finally, they repaired the dam, a job well done. Even us humans cannot do much better than beavers on this particular task. The program narrator, then, asked a question whether beavers have intelligence or not. By answering himself, he quickly concluded that beavers do not have intelligence. Can his conclusion possibly contain any intelligence?

The above example demonstrates the fallacy of all studies on the subjects of consciousness and intelligence. They deny the existence of those things that they are trying to study. Then in a great wonder, they admire themselves for trying to tackle an impossible problem. They deny that beavers have intelligence. They deny that a larva has consciousness while it will indeed react to any disturbance. For these reasons, the origin of consciousness is unable to be found by them. They like to play word game, therefore, have blocked the path to truth, which they are trying to find.

II

There are many definitions for consciousness. Some say that consciousness is a property of matter. They state that the succession of subjective states, which we feel in introspection, has a continuity that stretches all the way back through and beyond into a fundamental property of interacting matter. Others say that consciousness is the property of all living things. Still others insist that consciousness began not with matter, nor at the beginning of animal life, but at some specific time after life had evolved. They insist that man's consciousness could not possibly have been developed by means of the same laws which have determined the evolution paths of all other lives. The interiority of consciousness cannot possibly be evolved out of mere assemblages of molecules and cells. There has to be more to human evolution than mere matter. Something must be added from the outside, such as the divine intervention, to account for something so different as consciousness. After all, we humans are the only creatures who build space ships, write songs and poems, and play quartets.

Worst yet, many psychologists insist that consciousness is not even for thinking. They used an H. Watt's experiment, which is a word association test, as the supporting evidence. They concluded that thinking was automatic and not really conscious once a stimulus word had been given. In other words, one does one's thinking before one consciously knows what one is to think about. They again said, "The very reason we need logic at all is because most reasoning is not conscious at all. Our minds work much faster than consciousness can keep up with." From these arguments, they concluded that judging, reasoning and learning, that supposed hallmarks of consciousness, do not exist in consciousness at all.

For these modern psychologists, what is consciousness, then? Do you know? I certainly do not! This is why they cannot see and find the origin of consciousness. They have blocked the path to a true understanding of their own choosing.

There are at least one trillion cells in human body. Our mind consciousness will never be conscious of the event when a single cell of ours is under attack by either bacteria or poison. On the other hand, the cell that is under attack will quickly respond according to the strength of the attack. For example, when a cell's ability to produced protein (a vital substance for cell's survival) was interrupted by a poisonous agent, it will quickly "summon" the enzyme RNA to rush into the nucleus in order to continue the protein production. If the poison is too strong and if the first survival "strategy" has failed to provide enough protein for cell's survival, it will "enact" the second survival strategy by "sacrificing" part of its own body in order to make more protein. When this cell have won the battle, it will immediately proceed to replicate for increasing the chance of future survival. It passes through one or more cycles of growth and division before the daughter cells finally come to rest. In some cases, this cell's survival "struggle" will turn this cell into a cancer cell because it is unable to come to rest. Obviously, our mind consciousness is not only unable to help our own cell's survival at cell's level but also unable to eliminate the possibility that it could turn into a cancer cell which could in turn devour us. Which one has consciousness, cell or mind?

III

As for me, a thing definitely has consciousness if it can do two tasks; one, if it is able to recognize the self and non-self boundary; two, if it is able to recognize the real time and real space. By this definition, a honey bee definitely has consciousness. Honey bees definitely know the boundary of self and non-self. They will sacrifice their own lives to defend their hive. Furthermore, they not only recognize the real time and real space, but also the conceptual time and space. When a scout bee discovered food some distance from the hive, it will first find its way back to the hive because it can travel through the real space. Then, it will inform the other bees about where the food is by dancing. This bee dance converses the information of distance and direction. Since bees measure the distance and direction by judging the position of sun, which moves with time, the information of distance and direction has to be recalculated by using the conceptual time. So, this bee dance is not only conversing the real time and real space, but also the conceptual time and space. Bees not only can perceive time and space, but can also conceive time and space. No doubt, bees have consciousness, although their consciousness is quite different from our own. Maybe, bee's consciousness is coded in genes; it is hard wired. Either hardwired or soft-programmed consciousness is consciousness nonetheless the same as a computer program whether it is coded in hardware or is written on software; it does the same job and reaches the same aim.

With my definition, even the eyeless and mindless electron has consciousness. In Relativity Theory, time will slow down for the observer on a high speed traveling train. The entire Relativity Theory is wrapped around the observers. But surprisingly, an eyeless electron also obeys the Relativity Theory. It can indeed observe the slowing down time when it itself is traveling at high speed.

This electron consciousness is also supported by Heisenberg's uncertainty principle. It says that the observer will in fact change the course of an event by his observing act, which he is merely observing. By only observing the Vietnam war on TV, the observers finally stopped this aimless bloody war. Although this uncertainty principle is true in both mirco-world and marco-world, it was intended only for describing the phenomena in mirco-world originally. When an electron looks at another electron, it will in fact change either the position or the direction of the other electron.

This kind of lifeless consciousness shocked both Einstein and Heisenberg; therefore, they were forced to draw a terrible conclusion, which is the worst mistake in the human history, that this lifeless material consciousness is the only supreme reality and that there is no such a thing as the absolute absoluteness. Although their conclusion and interpretation is wrong, the lifeless material consciousness is indeed a reality.

Electrons not only can sense time but also recognize the self and non-self boundary. This electron self awareness is described with Pauli's exclusion principle: "In a multi-electron atom there can never be more than one electron in the same quantum state." It means that no two electrons can sit at the same spot. It means that no two electrons can have the same identification number. It means that every electron is able to distinguish itself from others. It means that every electron has self-awareness. In other words, electrons have consciousness.

IV

I do not imply that the life consciousness is only a derivative of the lifeless material consciousness, but rather they came from the same source, the God Space, the Almighty God. In fact, I cannot easily derive the life consciousness from the lifeless material consciousness, but I can derive both of them from God Space.

At supper time, Andrew sits at my right hand side, two feet away from me; Henry is five feet away from me. You, the reader, are many miles away from me. Furthermore, both Andrew and Henry are my sons; I love them much more than I love you, a stranger. So, my sons are much closer to me than you can ever be. This seems to be an obvious fact, doesn't it? But, if we look deeper, the distance from my sons to me can never be any closer than from you to me. As soon as they were born, I can never become anyone of them exactly the same as I can never become you.

You, my sons and all humans are selves. We form a self space. Every member of this self space can never be replaced by another member regardless of how close the relationship is. In other words, the distance from any member to the rest of members in this self space is all the same. The self space is God Space by definition. Every member in God Space is the center of the rest of members. This is Einstein's Relativity Theory that every frame is equivalent to all other frames, isn't it? This is also Pauli's exclusion principle that no two particles can have the identical set of quantum numbers, isn't it? This is the immanent nature of God, that God is present throughout all and God's spirit does not exist apart from human spirits.

I called God Space impossible space in Chapter IV because it seems very difficult to be understood. In fact, God Space is not impossible and exists everywhere. The number line is an excellent example. No doubt, 101 minus 1 is 100 times larger than 2 minus 1. But, if you ask any mathematician, he will tell you that the amount of numbers between 1 and 2 is exactly the same as the amount of numbers between 1 and 101. In fact, the number line has the property of God Space, that the amount of numbers between any number to the rest of numbers is the same, whether between 0 to 1 or 0 to infinity.

Both life consciousness and lifeless material consciousness are coming from God's consciousness, which is described with God space. Every self, whether life or lifeless, is a member of self space, which is indeed a subset of God Space. Thus, every self is able to distinguish self and non-self.

V

Both lifeless material consciousness and life consciousness originate from God. Then, consciousness will indeed evolve into a higher level of consciousness. There are four levels of consciousness. The first is the consciousness that can only recognize self and the real time, such as lifeless material and all lives.

The second is the consciousness that can recognize the consciousness itself, which is the consciousness of consciousness. At this level, the consciousness is not only an "I" who is seeing, but is also a "me" whom is seen by the "I".

The third is the consciousness that sees the unobservable. This is the transcendental consciousness. Only this transcendental consciousness can do the imagination, recognize the existence of a fictitious world, see the unobservable Almighty God and the immaterial souls.

The fourth is the consciousness that can see the past, the present and the future simultaneously. This is the consciousness of God.

But, how is this hierarchy evolved and governed? What is its underlying law? Again, this can be understood very easily if we can get rid of a terrible notion in physics, that all physicists today still believe that time is continuous. In fact, time seems to be continuous in marco-world. We divide time into three sections, the past, the present and the future. We even believe that the past has passed and does not exist any more; the future has not yet come and also does not exist. Only the present is a reality. But, what is the present and how big is the present? Einstein did not believe that there is such a thing as "the present". He used a thought-experiment to prove his point.

Two observers sat beside a railroad track, 1000 feet between them. A train, running with near light speed, flashes a light when it passed the exact center between these two observers. This light signal reached one observer, who saw the train that was coming toward him, 10 seconds earlier than it reached the another observer who saw the train that was going away from him. So, this single event, a light flash, was seen at two different times. Which time is the true time when the light flashed? Or, are there indeed two flashes?

These are very important questions. Einstein's thought was indeed deep, but again he made a terrible mistake for trying to reconcile these differences. He announced that the word "simultaneous" has no meaning whatsoever unless the watches in each frame are synchronized. There is nothing wrong with synchronizing the watches, but for what? By doing what he had done, he found a small coin — the Relativity Theory, but missed the big pot of gold — the God's consciousness.

In fact, Einstein's thought-experiment is the greatest example that tells us that time is not continuous but a quanta. The single fresh light does not have an instantaneous life, but has a lengthy life time. "The present" is not a single point on a continuous time stream. "The present" is an interval, a time packet, the same as a quanta.

Einstein's interpretation not only prohibited him to grasp the truth, but the whole physics community is still trapped by his mistake. This is as if he is standing at a fork in the road: one, the superhighway to the ultimate truth; the other, a dirt path. Instead of following the superhighway, he blocks the superhighway and followed the dirt path. Instead of finding the ultimate truth, he found a relative truth, the Relativity.

The size of "the present" depends upon the eyes of the observer. A super nova explored a quarter million years ago but was observed on my 37th birth day, February 24th, in 1987. The flash of light of that super nova lasted only a few days for the dying star itself. It only lasted a few days in our eyes a quarter million years later. Millions of years from now, someone else might be still able to see it, also for a few days only.

Are we only seeing the past? Or, is the past still part of the present? In the eyes of the universe, "the present" of this single event has endured for millions of years. Furthermore, it is inconceivable that space in a micro-world is quantized but time remains to be continuous. This can be true only if the velocity of travelling through this quantized space is infinitely fast, and we all know it is not so for all mortal items. Even the uncertainty principle tells us that time cannot be pinpointed as a continuous point in the mirco-world. The fact is that the uncertainty principle is a bad name for its context. It shall be named "Time Quanta Principle". It in fact points out that time is a quanta. This time quanta itself is the observing eye of an eyeless electron. The time quanta itself is the lifeless consciousness of a mindless electron.

VI

We can look at this time quanta issue from another angle. Let us draw a straight line on a piece of blank paper and mark two points on the line about 5 inches apart. Then, label the point on left t1 (as time 1), t2 on the right. Then, place a pencil at the top of t1. Now, ask ourselves a question of how this pencil can be moved from t1 to t2. There are two ways to do this. The first way is by holding the pencil still and then pulling paper to left until t2 is covered by the pencil. The second way is by lifting the pencil and placing it on t2. Both ways require some efforts and energy.

Moving through "time" needs a lot of energy. It will cost me a fortune to bring up my four children. How much energy is needed to push the entire universe from the past to the future? And, where does this energy come from?

No doubt, there are two answers ready for these questions, and both of them are correct. First, God is infinity and has infinite energy. So, it is not very hard to move the entire universe from past to future by God. Second, God is immortal and eternal. So, there is no past, nor future in the eyes of God. As for God, all is "the present". God sees all things, either in the past or in the future, with a single glance. In God's view, there is no difference between t1 and t2. Thus, no energy is needed to move the universe from t1 to t2. "The present" is infinitely long in the eyes of God.

Most of us, with blind faith, believe that God is immortal, which means timelessness. But, what is timelessness? We often accept this kind of undefined word without any question, again because of blind faith. Now, timelessness can be defined in two ways. First, it is timelessness if and only if time has no direction, while nothingness and infinity cannot be distinguished. Second, timelessness can be defined in terms of time — past, present and future. When past and future merge into "the present," time is no longer a flow and time becomes timelessness. So, timelessness has no past, nor future. Timelessness is all "Present". In the immortal sphere, "the present" is not a single point on a continuous time coordinate but an infinity.

In fact, the transformation from immortal sphere to mortal sphere is accomplished by changing the size of "the present". In the immortal sphere, "the present" is infinite in length and in size. In the mortal sphere, "the present" has a finite length and size. At an early stage of the universe, "the present" is much longer in length; therefore, the gravitational constant is much stronger then. So, those old images of galaxies seem not to have enough mass today to be held together by using today's gravitational factor; thus many cosmologists invented a "cold dark matter theory" for trying to explain this phenomena. They say that there are many cold dark matter, which is invisible, that binds the galaxies together. No doubt, this cold dark matter theory will fail because those old galaxies was bonded with a much stronger gravitational factor, which is the result of larger time quanta (the present) at those early stages.

We can look again at this issue from a different view. By induction, we can find truth in the unknown territory by observing some known facts. we now know that all flows produce force. The flowing water can generate electricity. The flowing electrons can power a computer. The flowing bosons bind the protons together. But, what force does the "flowing time" create? Or, is the time indeed flowing? These are very simple but fundamental questions. No physicist today asks these questions.

No doubt, time does flow in the mortal world, and the "flowing time" creates a force, the unified force. The time force can be defined easily with the following equation.

Force (time) = (A coupling constant times Planck constant) divided by (Time square times light speed)

All four fundamental forces evolve from this time force (Please read my book — Truth, Faith, and Life — for details). In the immortal sphere, time is not a flow, meaning timelessness. Thus, there is no such a thing as force in the immortal sphere. There is no confining physics in the immortal sphere.

VII

The consciousness of life can be further divided into two levels, the mortal consciousness (2nd level) and the immortal consciousness (3rd level). The mortal consciousness is the consciousness of consciousness. The immortal consciousness is the transcendental consciousness which is conscious of the timelessness.

So, consciousness is not substance, but a process. This process not only exists in both mortal and immortal spheres, but also is a link between them. It is difficult sometimes to imagine that something immaterial is indeed a reality. All processes are immaterial but are all real. The evolution process is the manifestation of God Himself. Anyone who is against the truth of evolution is in fact against God. The evolution process is the soul of God; not only all lives evolve but the universe also evolves.

I have discussed the first and fourth level of consciousness in detail. Every cell has the first level of consciousness. As I stated before, every cell is able to mobilize its resources and to rapid replication of genetic material and cell division when its survival is threatened. But, how does the 2nd level of consciousness evolve? The 2nd level of consciousness not only has the first level of consciousness as a seeing and acting "I" but has additional consciousness as a be seen "me". This 2nd level of consciousness is the result of a self and non-self conflict. When a single cell multiplies into many cells, it creates many non-selves. Even with an identical division, two new cells are no longer one self. They are not only seeing the other cell but also the mirror image of itself. This situation gets even more complicated when the division is not identical. For an embryo, some new cells become head, others toes. We now have two problems. First, how does non-identical division proceed? Second, How do those cells reconcile the self and non-self problem?

Starting as a single fertilized egg with a homogeneous appearance, this single cell turns into a complex structure (consisting of distinctly different parts — such as: head, trunk, arms and legs) through the division of cells. At the stage of midblastula (having about 4,000 cells), the embryo has the shape of a "hallow sphere," which is the same as the cosmology model for the universe. With our transcendental faith, it is not hard to see that every life is replaying the divine creation act.

Around the equator of midblastula, there is a layer of cells called mesoderm which eventually moves into the interior of the embryo. This movement transforms the hallow sphere into a donut-shaped object and divides the embryo into three parts — the mesoderm, the endoderm and the ectoderm. The mesoderm gives rise to most of the body, including the muscles, the bones and the body wall. The endoderm produces a digestive tract as well as various other organs. The ectoderm develops into a nervous system.

From the above facts, three very important truths have been revealed. First, every life is a replay of the creation act. Second, every life performs a ball-donut transformation (see my book — Truth, Faith, and Life — for the meaning of ball-donut transformation). Third, life begins with a non-identical division.

But, how? How can a cell divide into two non-identical cells? This non-identical division is accomplished by a starvation division process. When a cell divides under a starving condition, that is, there is no additional genetic material available, it cannot always divide everything evenly. Thus, the two new cells will be slightly different. Finally, one becomes brain cell, the other something else.

So, during the starvation division process, many non-selves are created. Now the task is to unite them as a new self. This unification effort results in the 2nd level of consciousness. This 2nd level of consciousness is a force that unifies many non-selves; it is the bond of those many non-selves.

There are more than one trillion entities, that have the 1st level of consciousness, in the human body. Thus, those entities can sometimes attack one another, and all autoimmune diseases are the result of this. Reiter's syndrome is because the T-cells attack tissues in eyes, joints and the genital tract. Insulin-dependent diabetes is because the T-cells attack insulin-making cells in the pancreas. On the other hand, the majority of people are able to unify all these trillions of entities into a harmonic oneness.

In Immunology, this unifying force is described in terms of biochemistry. First, every cell carries a passport — a Histocompatibility complex (MHC) proteins — to identify its relation to other cells. Second, there is a censor bureau in the body (by using three mechanisms — deletion, anergy and suppression) to weed out dangerous T-cells.

Regardless of what kind of mechanism is at work, this mechanism has the 2nd level of consciousness. It bonds trillions of non-selves together into a harmonic new self. Furthermore, it controls the territory that cannot be controlled by mind consciousness.

VIII

The 1st level of consciousness arises from physics laws. Relativity and the time quanta principle (uncertainty principle) make all things conscious of real time and real space. Pauli's exclusion principle gives rise the awareness of self. The 2nd level of consciousness is expressed in terms of molecular biology, such as: genes, histocompatibility complex protein (MHC), antigens, etc.. At this level, self and nonself are recognized. A detailed mechanism is highly developed to unite trillions of nonselves into a harmonic new self. On one hand, this new self needs a powerful immune system to destroy all foreign entities; on the other hand, this powerful army not only must be able to distinguish self and nonself but must have "self-tolerance," that is, this powerful army must be pacified during the peace time.

Today, many attempts are made to develop a model for consciousness that is based on neurosciences and the structure and function of brain. But, psychologists and philosophers have discussed consciousness in detail for centuries without reference to the detailed organization of the brain. No doubt, we can never fully understand the functions of the brain unless the meaning of consciousness is understood completely, but on the other hand, by understanding the structure and functions of the brain alone, it will not guarantee the understanding of consciousness.

Any brain based model for consciousness can only address the 2nd level of consciousness. The brain is only a hardware. With an analogy, the brain is as the hardware of a TV station. This TV station can send out millions of different programs — soap operas, news, movies, etc.. Although the hardware is no doubt a finitude, the number of different programs that could be sent is infinite. So, the brain is like the hardware of a TV station, and consciousness is as the union of all different programs that were and will be broadcasted by the hardware. In short, the brain is finite, but the 3rd level of consciousness is infinite. Nonetheless, the 2nd level of consciousness — which is expressed in terms of biochemistry, the structure and function of the brain — is the foundation of the 3rd level of consciousness. In this case, we are using the transcendental faith (principle of example-in-kinds) to obtain truths.

Being an infinity, the 3rd level of consciousness cannot easily be defined as what and where it is. First, the location of this 3rd level of consciousness cannot be pinpointed. For example, if you close your eyes, you are able to see yourself swim, something that you have never observed at all. Your consciousness seems to be outside of your body in this experience.

Second, many psychologists and philosophers are still debating today what consciousness is. As for many philosophers, unconscious means that we are unaware of whatever is happening in the world around us or even in our own bodies or that we are living through an unexperienced interval of time; so, when we are sleeping and not dreaming, we are unconscious. As for psychologists, the issue becomes more complicated. On one hand, consciousness is viewed as the foundation of concepts, of learning and reasoning and of thought and judgment. On the other hand, they say that consciousness is not for thinking because one does one's thinking before one knows what one is to think about, nor for reasoning because the very reason we need logic at all is because most reasoning is not conscious at all, nor for concepts because concepts can never be seen or perceived by the senses, nor for learning whether it be the learning of signals, skills or solutions.

In fact, the 3rd level of consciousness consists of two parts. The first is the consciousness of senses, and it is expressed in terms of perceiving, sensing, feeling, thinking, reasoning and remembering. I will call it 3rd level p- (perception) consciousness.

The second is the consciousness of conception, and it can be further subdivided into three sub-levels. The first sub-level is expressed in terms of conceptualizing by emptying out the substance to form concepts, by freeing from the bondage of present time and confining space. With the freedom from immediate time constraints and with its increased richness of social communication, eventually it led to capabilities allowing the anticipation of future states and planned behaviors. As I stated before, not only can most animals construct concepts but even honey bees are recognizing conceptual time. I call this sub-level 3rd level CE- (by emptying out substance) consciousness. The second sub-level is expressed in terms of imagination by creating something with concepts without any physical reference, such as the beast in the book of Revelation. This level is conscious of the reality of a fictitious world, and it is the force of creation, which is the genuine creation instead of only being a replay as an embryo does the replaying act of the divine creation during its growth. This creating ability creates language. So far, it seems to be that only humans have this level of consciousness. I call this level 3rd level CI- (by imagining) consciousness. The third sub-level is expressed in terms of worshipping for being conscious of God's consciousness. Being conscious of God's consciousness is quite different from having God's consciousness. We are conscious of the existence of other galaxies but not only are not them but also are unable to get there. I call this level 3rd level CW- (by worshipping) consciousness.

CE-consciousness is possessed by most animals. CI- and CW-consciousness seemingly are possessed only by humans; thus they can be called transcendental consciousness. The acuteness of this transcendental consciousness is different from individual to individual. Some of the differences come with birth, but the major differences come after birth because transcendental consciousness is an acquired virtue.

Both the 1st and the 2nd levels of consciousness and the perceptual consciousness are confined to the mortal universe, in turn controlled by all physics laws. They are the stepping stones for and the source of the rise of transcendental consciousness. The transcendental consciousness not only is conscious of the existence of immortal sphere but exists in the immortal sphere, and it is not confined to or controlled by physics laws.

Only by understanding the utmost truth, are we then able to begin the pursuit of moral virtues. Only by pursuing the moral virtues, we are then able to perfect our transcendental consciousness. Only by perfecting our transcendental consciousness, are we then able to unite with God's consciousness.

UNIVERSITY OF TORONTO

CENTRE FOR COMPARATIVE LITERATURE

ROBARTS LIBRARY
14th Floor – Room 14045
Toronto, Ontario M5S 1A5

8 Elgar Avenue
Scarborough, Ontario
Canada M1J 1M4
January 24, 1992

Dr. Jeh-Tween Gong
P.O. Box 1753
Bristol, VA 24203
U.S.A.

Dear Dr. Gong:

I read your book with great interest and admired the diversity of perspectives greatly. In many respects your book draws conclusions which all modernists and post-modernists will necessarily be compelled to recognize sooner or later. Of course, it is a common place to say that our age cannot contemplate its own shifting image outside of the frame of reference for Taoism and Enlightenment calculus. However, Truth, Faith and Life extends this reference for our flickering existence beyond the common place.

I was particularly interested in your discussion of the infinity problem with reference to (Pi)I and (1/3)I. It is all together conceivable that your colour theory is correct. The whole of the theory seems to be soundly argued and most persuasive. I feel that it is in this area where I most profited from your book.

As I indicated in Toronto, my concern with the constants of time is the subject of ongoing research related to our evolution as intelligent being in relationship to perceptible curvatures.

I thank you for your consideration in this matter and look forward to hearing from you.

Yours sincerely,

P.S. di Virgilio Ph.D.
University of Toronto.

Chapter VIII
The Sutra of all sutras,
The Buddha Lands

Around fifth century B.C., while all other religions were led by those who were able to communicate with God through hallucinations (results of the illness Schizophrenia), two religions had matured. These two religions went beyond trying to communicate with God but in earnest to search for the essence of God. Indeed, they both reached some marvelous understanding of what God is. One of the two is Buddhism.

I grew up in a city which has more Buddhist's temples than Christian churches. But most of the occasions that I went to temples were going there for picnics because almost all of them are located around scenic areas. I not only despised Buddhism, while I had not the slightest idea what Buddhism was all about, but I also had a strong hatred for it because I firmly believed that it had dragged China into a second grade nation. I often saw many old ladies who worshipped the wooden image of Buddha or one of their favor Bodhisattva. After a long prayer, they decided their future actions with sortilege. I also often saw many monks chanting Sutras for forty-nine days for trying to liberate the soul of the dead from the rebirth. I simply could not stand their ignorance. How can a wooden idol intervene in human affairs? How can the sortilege, which is the same as throwing a dice and gambling, reveal the future? How can those monks forgive the sins of the dead and deliver its soul to Heaven? I was grew up in a Christian family. Only a 'Personal' living God made sense to me in those days, although I also had not the slightest idea of what this personal living God was or why this God was better than a wooden image. I was taught that it was and believed the teaching without any doubt.

I did not know anything about Buddhism until seven years after the completion of my physics theory, the Super Unified Theory — the Theory of Everything. After I had finally studied it, I was greatly surprised that Buddhism was indeed groping at the gate of the utmost truth twenty-five centuries ago. I finally came to appreciate the compassion and the wisdom of Buddhism. The old ladies, the wooden image of Buddha or Bodhisattva, the sortilege and the ritual for the dead are indeed part of Buddhism, and suddenly they all make sense now. There is great wisdom in Buddhism.

Buddhism is shrouded in many superstitions, myths, legends and rituals. Furthermore, all sutras are summaries of a small subject. Firstly, they cannot be understood easily unless you already know the text which were taught verbally in ancient time. Secondly, there is no sutra of all sutras. Ideas are scattered in many sutras. Thirdly, too many important ideas are omitted in those sutras because of the writing style of sutra, as a summary. Fourthly, the awkward terminologies in Sanskrit language, which is not a common language today, do not help the situation one bit. In other words, the Buddhist's text is a big hodgepodge. Being a big hodgepodge, many people disdain it as superstition without trying to study it. Being a big hodgepodge, many believers worship it as something incomprehensible without trying to understand it. In fact, Buddhism is amazingly simple.

II

Gautama Sakyamuni is generally recognized as the founder of Buddhism, but he himself refers in his discourses to Buddhas who had preached the same doctrine before him.

"Then said Mahamati: Blessed one, you speak of the sameness of all the Buddhas, but in other places you have spoken of Dharmata-Buddha, Nishyanda-Buddha and Nirmana-Buddha as though they were different from each other; how can they be the same and yet different?" (The Lankavatara Scripture)

In fact, five fundamental religious beliefs of Buddhism are inherited from the "Three Vedas". Firstly, it is the conception of God. Buddha said, "There is an Unborn, Unoriginated, Uncreated, Unformed. If there were not this Unborn, this Unoriginated, this Uncreated, this Unformed, escape from the world of the born, the originated, the created, the formed, would not be possible."

Many Westerners think Buddhism is a religion without God, but even the Dalai Lama Tenzin Gyatso made the same mistake; he said, "In Buddhism, the emphasis is on self-creation; there is no Creator, so strictly speaking, it is not a religion; it is closer to science." No doubt, this ignorance about Buddhism is caused by worshipping the western science. In Buddha's own words, "There is an Unborn," and this Unborn is the Buddha's God.

Secondly, all souls are trapped in the eternal suffering cycle of death and rebirth. Buddha said, "Subhuti, I recall that during my five hundred previous lives, I had used life after life to practice patience and to look upon my life humbly as though it was some saintly being called upon to suffer humility. Even then my mind was free from any such arbitrary conceptions of phenomena as my own self, other selves, living beings, and a universal self." (The Diamond Sutra)

Today, many Buddhists do not believe in the conception of immortal soul. This is again a great misunderstanding. In the final stage, Buddha indeed has to transcend and to detach the immortal soul in order to reach Nirvana, but Buddha must accept the existence of immortal soul at the beginning. In fact, the immortal soul is "the thing" that Buddha tries to detach and to transcend; without "it," there will be no Buddhism. Furthermore, Buddha must detach from not only the immortal soul but also the Divine Atman or the Sovereign God for two reasons. First, he must denounce the old Vedic conception of the godhead in order to establish his new teaching. Second, the notion of godhead is still "something" and must be detached in order to reach the true enlightenment. Buddha said, "The doctrine of the Tathagata-womb [Buddha's God] is disclosed in order to awaken philosophers from their clinging to the notion of a Divine Atman as transcendental personality, so that their minds that have become attached to the imaginary notion of soul as being something self-existent, may be quickly awakened to a state of perfect enlightenment. All such notions as causation, succession, atoms, primary elements, that make up personality, personal soul, Supreme Spirit, Sovereign God, Creator, are all figments of the imagination and manifestations of mind. No, Mahamati, the Tathagata's doctrine of the Womb of Tathagatahood [Buddha's God] is not the same as the philosopher's Atman." (The Lankavatara Scripture)

Thirdly, every soul has its own karma. Karma is the accumulative record of this soul's activities, deeds, sins and wisdom from all its many rebirths. Only when karma is matured, is the soul then able to be free from rebirth. "In the outward activities of the discriminating mind, karma is the record of its habit-energy urging it on to further differentiation, but in the inconceivable integrating activities of Intuitional Purity, karma is the record of it unifying attractions reducing multiplicities to unities and resulting in all manner of transcendental syntheses and mysterious wonder. ... This karma going on accumulating from beginningless time develops a strong and stronger tendency to action that enslaves the thinker until he more and more loses his freedom." (Awakening of Faith)

"Subhuti, should there be among the faithful disciples some who have not yet matured their karma and who much first suffer the natural retribution of sins committed in some previous life by being degraded to a lower domain of existence and should they earnestly and faithfully observe and study this Scripture and because of it be despised and persecuted by the people, their karma will immediately be matured and they will at once attain Samadhi [self-realization of Noble Wisdom]." (The Diamond Sutra)

Fourthly, it is possible to escape from the rebirth. Buddha said, "But since there is an Unborn, Unoriginated, Unformed, therefore is escape possible from the world of the born, the originated, the created, the formed."

Fifthly, the goal of life is to escape from rebirth and to unite with the Unborn God. "Vasettha replied: Various Brahmans, Gotama, teach various paths to union with Brahma: is one true and another false, or are all saving paths? Are they all paths which will lead one who acts according to them into a state of Union with Brahma?" (Tevigga Sutta)

III

The similarity between Buddhism and Veda dogma vanishes beyond these five shared religious beliefs. Their views of the essence and the nature of God are quite different.

"Now, Vasettha, when you have been among Brahmans, listening as they talked among themselves, learners and teachers and those aged and well stricken in years, what have you learned from them and of them? Is Brahma in possession of wives and wealth, or is he not?

He is not, Gotama.

Is his mind full of anger or is it free from anger?

Free from anger, Gotama.

Is his mind full of malice or free from malice?

Free from malice, Gotama.

Is his mind depraved, or pure?

It is pure, Gotama.

Has he self-mastery, or has he not?

He has, Gotama.

Now what think you, Vasettha? Are the Brahmans versed in the Three Vedas, are they in possession of wives and wealth or are they not?

They are, Gotama.

Have they anger in their hearts?

They have, Gotama.

Do they bear malice, or do they not?

They do, Gotama.

Are they pure in heart or are they not?

They are not, Gotama.

Then you say, Vasettha, that the Brahmans are in possession of wives and wealth, and that Brahma is not. Can there be agreement and likeness between the Brahmans with their wives and property and Brahma who has none of these things?" (Tevigga Sutta)

From this point onward, Buddhism departed from Brahmanism, and Sakyamuni invented his famous Four Noble Truths and Noble Eightfold Path. The first Noble truth is the truth of suffering.

Buddha said, "And that which is transient is subject of suffering; and of that which is transient and subject to suffering and change, one cannot rightly say: — This belongs to me; this am I; this is my Ego.

"All formations are transient; all formations are subject to suffering; all things are without an Ego-entity. Form is transient, feeling is transient, perception is transient, mental formations are transient, consciousness is transient.

"Birth is suffering; Decay is suffering; Death is suffering; Sorrow, Lamentation, Pain, Grief and Despair are suffering; not to get what one desires is suffering; in short: the Five Aggregates of Existence are suffering.

"Whose delights in bodily form, or feeling, or perception or mental formations, or consciousness, he delights in suffering; and whose delights in suffering will not be freed from suffering."

The second Noble Truth is the origin of suffering. Buddha said, "It is that craving which gives rise to fresh rebirth, and bound up with pleasure and lust, now here, now there finds ever fresh delight. There is the Sensual Craving, the Craving for Eternal Existence, the Craving for Temporal Happiness.

"Thus, whatever kind of Feeling one experiences, — Pleasant, unpleasant or indifferent — one approves of and cherishes the feeling and clings to it; and while doing so, lust springs up; but lust for feelings means clinging to existence; and on clinging to existence depends the Process of Becoming; on the process of becoming depends Birth; and dependent on birth are Decay and Death, sorrow, lamentation, pain, grief and despair. Thus arises this whole mass of suffering."

The third Noble Truth is the extinction of suffering. Buddha said, "And released from Sensual Craving, released from the craving for Existence, he does not return, does not enter again into existence. ... For, through the total fading away and extinction of Craving Clinging to Existence is extinguished; through the extinction of clinging to existence the Process of Becoming is extinguished; through the extinction of the process of becoming Rebirth is extinguished; and through the extinction of rebirth Decay and Death, sorrow, lamentation, suffering, grief and despair are extinguished. Thus comes about the extinction of this whole mass of suffering.

"This I call neither arising nor passing away, neither standing still, nor being born, nor dying. There is neither foothold, nor development, nor any basis. This is the end of suffering."

The fourth Noble Truth is the path that leads to the extinction of suffering. Buddha said, "It is the Noble Eightfold Path, the way that leads to the extinction of suffering, namely:

1. Right understanding.
2. Right mindedness.
3. Right speech.
4. Right action.
5. Right living.
6. Right effort.
7. Right attentiveness.
8. Right concentration."

IV

The entire Buddhism is indeed built upon these four Noble Truths. The first three truths are philosophical cornerstones of Buddhism. They were evolved and supported with the following philosophical views.

Firstly, all objects in the world are transient, and therefore they are not realities. Buddha said, "Suppose, a man, who can see, were to behold the many bubbles on the Ganges as they are driving along. And he should watch them and carefully examine them. After carefully examining them, they will appear to him as empty, unreal, and insubstantial. In exactly the same way does the monk behold all the bodily forms, feelings, perceptions, mental formations and states of consciousness — whether they be of the past, or the present, or the future, far or near. And he watches them and examines them carefully, and, after carefully examining them, they appear to him as empty, void and without an Ego."

Secondly, all objects in the world not only are non-realities but rise from the mind itself. Buddha said, "They do not recognize that the objective world rises from the mind itself; they do not understand that the whole mind-system also rises from the mind itself; but depending upon these manifestation of the mind as being real they go on discriminating them." (The Lankavatara Scripture)

Because of the discriminating mind, the ignorant cling to words, the transient and relative existence. Buddha said, "It is because the ignorant cling to names, signs and ideas; as their minds move along these channels they feed on multiplicities of objects and fall into the notion of an ego-soul and what belongs to it; they make discriminations of good and bad among appearances and cling to the agreeable. As they thus cling there is a reversion to ignorance, and karma born of greed, anger and folly, is accumulated. As the accumulation of karma goes on they become imprisoned in a cocoon of discrimination and are thenceforth unable to free themselves from the round of birth and death." (The Lankavatara Scripture)

These philosophical views are the same as the view of Immanuel Kant who lived 2200 years after Buddha, and he was the founding father of the modern philosophy. Both Buddha and Kant believe that the external world is only the manifestation of the mind. Furthermore, they both believed that the words, the logic and reasoning are unable to reach the utmost truth. Buddha said, "Words and sentences are produced by the law of causation and are mutually conditioning, — they cannot express highest Reality. Moreover, in highest Reality there are no differentiations to be discriminated and there is nothing to be predicated in regard to it. Highest Reality is an exalted state of bliss, it is not a state of word-discrimination and it cannot be entered into by mere statements concerning it. The Tathagatas [the Unborn God or those who have united with the Unborn God] have a better way of teaching, namely, through self-realization of Noble Wisdom [Samadhi through Dhyana]." (The Lankavatara Scripture)

But, their agreement ended at these points. Kant believed that this imperfect tool of reasoning and discriminating is valuable and useful for analyzing the external world. Thus, science got a boost from Kant's philosophy. On the other hand, Buddha believed that all words and reasoning were the causes of suffering and must be eliminated in order to reach the highest Reality. Buddha said, "While the Tathagata, in his teaching, constantly makes use of conceptions and ideas about them, disciples should keep in mind the unreality of all such conceptions and ideas. They should recall that the Tathagata, in making use of them in explaining the Dharma [Buddha's teaching] always uses them in the resemblance of a raft that is of use only to cross a river. As the raft is of no further use after the river is crossed, it should be discarded.

"Moreover, what has just been referred to as 'a system of teaching' has no meaning, as Truth cannot be cut up into pieces and arranged into a system. The words can only be used as a figure of speech." (The Diamond Sutra)

From this point onward, Buddha affirmed that the Highest Reality is the Emptiness, and it cannot be understood by or be described with words or logic but can only be realized through Dhyana. But, what are dhyana and emptiness? This question becomes a major subject of study in Buddhism for twenty-five hundred years after Buddha. Buddha said, "What is emptiness, indeed! It is a term whose very self-nature is false-imagination, but because of one's attachment to false-imagination we are obliged to talk of emptiness, no-birth, and no-self-nature. There are seven kinds of emptiness: emptiness of mutuality which is nonexistence; emptiness of individual marks; emptiness of self-nature; emptiness of no-work; emptiness of work; emptiness of all things in the sense that they are unpredictable; and emptiness in its highest sense of Ultimate Reality. ... By emptiness in its highest sense of the emptiness of Ultimate Reality is meant that in the attainment of inner self-realization of Noble Wisdom there is no trace of habit-energy generated by erroneous conceptions; thus one speaks of the highest emptiness of Ultimate Reality." (The Lankavatara Scripture)

V

Very clearly, Buddha did not believe that any logic is able to probe the domain of either the creation process or the essence of God which is the emptiness in Buddhism. The emptiness cannot be described or understood but can be recognized and be united with by becoming it. In Buddhism, death itself cannot reach the emptiness but will only cause a rebirth. The only way to become emptiness and to unite with the Unborn God is through detachment, detaching from the external world and from the internal mind itself.

The way to detach from the external world is to live a homeless life, to give up all relations with his family and to give up the relations with the social life of the world. Buddha said, "In order to discard more easily discriminations and erroneous reasonings, the Bodhisattva should retire by himself to a quiet, secluded place where he may reflect within himself without relying on anyone else, and there let him exert himself to make successive advances along the stages; this solitude is the characteristic feature of the inner attainment of self-realization of Noble Wisdom." (The Lankavatara Scripture)

The way to detach from the internal mind is by practicing dhyana. What is dhyana? Buddha said, "There are four kinds of concentrative meditation (dhyana): The dhyana practised by the ignorant; the dhyana devoted to the examination of meaning; the dhyana with 'suchness' for its object; and the dhyana of the Tathagatas.

"The dhyana practised by the ignorant is the one resorted to by those who are following the example of the disciples and masters but who do not understand its purpose and, therefore, it becomes 'still-sitting' with vacant minds. This dhyana is practised, also, by those who, despising the body, see it as a shadow and a skeleton full of suffering and impurity, and yet who cling to the notion of an ego, seek to attain emancipation by the mere cessation of thought.

"The dhyana devoted to the examination of meaning, is the one practised by those who, perceiving the untenability of such ideas as self, other and both, which are held by the philosophers, and who have passed beyond the twofold-egolessness, devote dhyana to an examination of the significance of egolessness and the differentiations of the Bodhisattva stages.

"The dhyana with Tathata, or 'Suchness,' or Oneness, or the Divine Name, for its object is practised by those earnest disciples and masters who, while fully recognizing the two fold egolessness and the imagelessness of Tathata, yet cling to the notion of an ultimate Tathata.

"The dhyana of the Tathagatas is the dhyana of those who are entering upon the stage of Tathagatahood and who, abiding in the triple bliss which characterizes the self-realization of Noble Wisdom, are devoting themselves for the sake of all beings to the accomplishment of incomprehensible works for their emancipation. This is the pure dhyana of the Tathagatas. When all lesser things and ideas are transcended and forgotten, and there remains only a perfect state of imagelessness where Tathagata and Tathata [suchness] are merged into perfect Oneness, then the Buddhas will come together from all their Buddha-lands and with shining hands resting on his forehead will welcome a new Tathagata." (The Lankavatara Scripture)

What is Suchness? Buddha said, "When appearances and names are put away and all discrimination ceases, that which remains is the true and essential nature of things and, as nothing can be predicated as to the nature of essence, it is called the 'Suchness' of Reality." (The Lankavatara Scripture)

"One should think: there is walking, there is doing, ...; Not, I am walking, I am doing." (Awakening of Faith)

What is Oneness? Buddha said, "All dualistic views of existence and nonexistence are transcended and by self-realization of Noble Wisdom the true imagelessness of Oneness is made manifest.

"Those attached to the notion of relativity are attached to the notion of the multitudinousness of things which arises from false-imagination.

"Oneness gives birth to the highest Samadhi [self-realization of Noble Wisdom]: which is gained by entering into the realm of Noble Wisdom that is realizable only within one's inmost consciousness." (The Lankavatara Scripture)

By practicing dhyana, one can attain Samadhi, enter Nirvana [a state of union with the spirit of God]. He will go through an inconceivable transformation-death and then receive a new transformation body which possesses the transcendental transformation power. Furthermore, the love and compassion for all sentient beings will arise in him. Then, a Buddha-land will be given to him. Buddha said, "Free from the domination of words you will be able to establish yourselves where there will be a 'turning about' in the deepest seat of consciousness by means of which you will attain Samadhi. There you will be stamped with the stamp of powers, self-command, the psychic faculties, and will be endowed with the wisdom, and will become radiant with the variegated rays of the Transformation Bodies. Therewith you will shine without effort like the moon, the sun, the magic wishing-jewel, and at very stage will view things as being of perfect oneness with yourself, uncontaminated by any self-consciousness. Seeing that all things are like a dream, you will be able to enter into the stage of the Tathagatas and be able to deliver discourses on the Dharma to the world of beings in accordance with their needs and be able to free them from all dualistic notions and false discrimination."

With the 'turning about' at the deepest seat of consciousness, the Bodhisattva will become conscious that he received the second kind of Transcendental body. This transition from mortal body to Transcendental body has nothing to do with mortal death, for the old body continues to function and the old mind serves the needs of the old body, but now it is free from the control of the mortal universe. There has been an inconceivable transformation death by which the false imagination of his particularized individual personality has been transcended by a realization of his oneness with the universalized mind of Tathagatahood. In short, he has entered Nirvana.

Nonetheless, the Bodhisattva who has entered Nirvana not only should not be attracted to stay in Nirvana but should not even be aware of the fact that he has indeed entered Nirvana. If he knows that he has entered Nirvana, then he certainly does not. If he is trying to stay in Nirvana after he has entered, then he will certainly be expelled from it.

There are two reasons for this paradox. First, it is because of his original vow. Second, it is because of the nature of Nirvana. Buddha said, "Owing to their original vows they are transported by emotions of love and compassion as they become aware of the part they are to perform in the carrying out of their vows for the emancipation of all beings. Thus they do not enter into Nirvana, but in truth, they too are already in Nirvana." (The Lankavatara Scripture)

What then is Nirvana? Nirvana is the final aim of Buddhism; thus it is a state of the supreme Bliss; it is a "state" of union with the Unborn God. In fact, it can be defined in two ways, negatively or positively. In the negative sense, Nirvana is the total annihilation of everything — desire, consciousness, external universe, immortal soul or even the Unborn God. In the positive sense, Nirvana is the Perfect Love and the Utmost Wisdom. Buddha said, "Perfect Love is that Tathagatahood expresses itself in Noble Wisdom for the enlightenment of all — there, indeed, is Nirvana." (The Lankavatara Scripture)

Because of its positive attribute, no one can stay in Nirvana after he has indeed entered it because he will be overwhelmed by the Perfect Love and the Infinite Compassion. Buddha said, "Tathagatas and Buddhas look upon sentient beings as being their own sameness not cherishing any conceptions of separation and individuation." (Awakening of Faith)

Although Nirvana itself is a "state" of total annihilation, this "state" itself is still something and must be detached in order to reach the true Nirvana. Thus, the only way to stay in Nirvana is by detaching it.

In either case, there is no Nirvana for Buddhas. Buddha repeated this statement many, many times throughout many sutras. Paradoxically, by detaching from Nirvana, the Bodhisattva will gain a Buddha-land. Buddha said, "Having attained this exalted and blissful state of realization as far as it can be attained by disciples, the Bodhisattva must not give himself up to the enjoyment of its bliss, but should think compassionately of other beings.

"He passes through the bliss of the Samadhi to assume the transformation body of a Tathagata that through him all beings may be emancipated.

"Thus passing beyond the last stage of Bodhisattvahood, he becomes a Tathagata, ..., he will find himself seated upon a lotus-like throne in a splendid jewel-adorned palace and surrounded by Bodhisattvas of equal rank. Buddhas from all the Buddha-lands will gather about him and with their pure and fragrant hands resting on his forehead will give him ordination and recognition as one of themselves. Then they will assign him a Buddha-land that he may posses and perfect as his own." (The Lankavatara Scripture)

VI

Buddha firmly believed that there is one and only one God who is the Oneness, the imagelessness and the emptiness. But he also firmly believed the immanent nature of God, that everyone possesses the spirit of God. Buddha said, "Sentient beings are like a man with a magic gem hidden in his garment of which he is ignorant. He becomes poor and ragged and hungry and wanders about to far countries. Although he is actually suffering from poverty, he still possesses the magic gem. One day a very wise man tells the poor man of his magic gem and forthwith the poor man becomes a millionaire. It is the same with your own nature of Intuitive Mind. You should forthwith realize that this magic gem of Enlightening Essence of Mind, is not to be acquired from some difficult source, but is already within your possession." (The Surangama Sutra)

In Buddhism, all sentient beings are enslaved by the karma and are ignorant of their own Buddha Nature. They have to be liberated by Buddha or Bodhisattva. They must have faith in Buddha and in Dharma (Buddha's teaching). "Even if they have a Buddha Nature but do not chance to meet a Buddha, or a good learned Master, or a Bodhisattva, they could not of themselves attain Nirvana.

"But by reason of Buddha's compassion, they sooner or later meet causes and affinities that enable them to awaken a pure faith and attain emancipation from their bondage to Ignorance.

"If by chance they should come in contact with a Buddha, give offering to him, worship him or his image, they would develop their germ of faith and after ten thousand kalpas [cosmic cycle, one kalpa is 4,320,000 human years] would have so far matured their faith that all Buddhas and Bodhisattvas would teach them how to start their devotion." (Awakening of Faith)

Furthermore, the transcendental transformation power can never be comprehended with logic and words. It can only be realized by a lifetime practicing of dhyana. Therefore, the novice disciple must accept it with faith in the beginning. In Buddhism, faith is not a dogma but a vehicle for reaching the ultimate truth. There are four levels of faith in Buddhism. The first level is the faith in the Unborn God, the perfect Oneness. The second level is the faith in Buddha, who has united with the Unborn God. The third is the faith in Buddha's teaching, the Dharma. The fourth is the faith in Brotherhood. "There are four kinds of faith: First, the novice disciple must have faith in the fundamental, ultimate Principle of things, that it is perfect Wisdom and perfect Compassion, and perfect Oneness. He should think joyfully of his own identity with its pure Mind-Essence. Second, the disciple should have abounding faith in Buddhahood. This means that he should cherish a sincere faith in the merits and virtues of the Buddhas, that he should constantly remember them to feel his fellowship with them, to make offerings to them of adoration and gifts, to seek instruction and guidance from them. Third, the disciple should have an unshakable faith in the wisdom, the compassion, the power of the Dharma. This means that he should look to it and rely upon it as an infallible guide in his practice of its Paramita (spiritual ideal) ideals. Fourth, the disciple should have an unfeigned, affectionate and abounding faith in the Brotherhood of Homeless Bhikshus (monks), caring for them, supplying their few needs, looking to them for instruction and sympathy in their own practice, that they may perfect their faith and move toward Buddhahood together." (Awakening of Faith)

Furthermore, although the bad karma can only be purified gradually, the self-realization of Noble Wisdom can be attained instantaneously. Buddha said, "The evil out-flowings that take place from recognizing an external world, which in truth is only a manifestation of mind, and from becoming attached to it, are gradually purified and not instantaneously. ... But the good non-outflowings that come with self-realization of Noble

Wisdom, is a purification that comes instantaneously by the grace of the Tathagatas." (The Lankavatara Scripture)

Therefore, there is a chance to liberate a person from the suffering of rebirth at the time he is ready to depart from his body, to detach from his loved ones and to detach from the objective world. This time and space is called Yin-Yang domain, a term borrowed from Taoism. Yang is the lively earth world. Yin is the netherworld. Yin-Yang domain is the space between the lively world and the netherworld. This Yin-Yang domain is called "Bardo" in Tibetan language. The book of Bardo, commonly known as 'The Tibetan Book of the Dead,' describes the Buddhist way of salvation while the soul enters the bardo. The ritual for the dead, therefore, makes sense. The following is one lesson that monks sing to the dead.

"O son of noble family, you have a mental body of unconscious tendencies, so even if you are killed and cut into pieces you cannot die. You are really the natural form of emptiness, so there is no need to fear. The Lords of Death too arise out of your own radiant mind, they have no solid substance. Emptiness cannot be harmed by emptiness. Be certain that the external peaceful and wrathful deities, the blood-drinking herukas, the animal-headed deities, the rainbow light, the terrifying forms of the Lords of Death and so on have no substantiality, they only arise out of the spontaneous play of your mind. If you understand this, all fear is naturally liberated, and merging inseparably you will become a Buddha."

VII

Buddhism firmly believes in one and only one Unborn God whose essence is the emptiness and the imagelessness. This Unborn God has the immanent nature, and His spirit and essence is manifested as the Mind-Essence that is carried by every human. This pure Mind-essence is contaminated and buried by the karma since the beginningless time. This karma creates the discriminating mind which in turn causes the manifestation of the external world. The desires arise from this discriminating mind, and the soul is then trapped in the eternal suffering cycle of rebirth and death because of the desire of Becoming. The Transcendental Intelligence (the spirit of the Unborn God) is covered up by the Ignorance that is created by karma. The only way to unite with the spirit of God is by performing three transcendental steps. The first step is to transcend from all objects which we perceive with our discriminating mind. Therefore, all seekers should live a homeless life, for detaching from the external world. The second step is to transcend from the discriminating mind itself. This can only be reached by practicing dhyana, by seeing the reality of Suchness, Oneness and the highest Reality of Emptiness. The third step is to transcend from the Highest Reality (Nirvana) itself. Therefore, all seekers will attain the bliss but without being intoxicated by it. Thus, the love and compassion for others arises. This love and compassion is the Highest Wisdom. This highest wisdom is the transcendental transformation power. With this transformation power, Buddhas and Bodhisattvas who have united with the Unborn God cannot be trapped by the real space and the real time any more. With this power, Buddhas can liberate all other sentient beings. Therefore, worshipping the image of Buddha becomes the first step in the long journey of seeking the union with the imageless Unborn God.

No doubt, Buddhism not only has a superb philosophical system, it is also a genuine religion. It indeed points a path to the Utmost Truth, but it has not yet entered the gate of this utmost truth.

Firstly, the emptiness in Buddhism is a "state" reached by a lifetime or many lifetimes of religious practice. Although Buddha recognized that the Unborn God is the Creator, he does not emphasize the phase of creation. The whole Buddhism starts from recognizing the existence of the transient world, then places the aim as to transcend and to detach from this transient world. Therefore, the religious act of Buddhism is of transcending and of detaching. The emptiness in Buddhism is the "end result" by emptying out the transient world. This emptied "state" (the Emptiness) is quite different from the "Nothingness" in my doctrine. The Nothingness in my doctrine is the source of creation; it has creating power. It is the Creator. The emptiness in Buddhism is the "End"; on the other hand, the Nothingness is the beginning. In other words, the Nothingness is unbounded, but the emptiness is bounded to the nutshell of its preempty state. Today, many scholars wrongly conceive that the Nothingness is the same as the Emptiness. Buddha said, "There are some Brahman scholars who, assuming something out of nothing, assert that there is a substance bound up with causation which abides in time, and that the elements that make up personality and its environment have their genesis and continuation in causation and after thus existing, pass away.

"Again, if it is true that something comes out of nothing and there is the rise of the mind-system by reason of the combination of the three effect-producing causes, ... they must do it on the principle of cause and effect, that is, that something comes out of something and not out of nothing. As long as a world of relativity is asserted, there is an ever recurring chain of causation which cannot be denied under any circumstance, therefore we cannot talk of anything coming to an end or of cessation." (The Lankavatara Scripture)

Secondly, the concept of infinity is not well-developed in Buddhism. The meaning of the unification of Nothingness and Infinity was not known by Buddha. Nonetheless, he did have a fuzzy understanding about infinity. First, the essence of infinity can be grasped by the human mind. Second, infinity has the same meaning as Oneness. Buddha said, "If an infinity of universes arises because of infinite space, and if because of an infinity of universes there are an infinity of sentient beings, and if because of infinite beings there are an infinitude of mentalities and predispositions and conditions and circumstances and differentiated activities, how can even a Bodhisattva-Mahasattva attain perfect understanding, or command of adequate skillful means, or highest perfect Wisdom? The explanation is, that all these infinity of infinities are fully embraced in the perfect self-awareness of the Bliss-body of Buddhahood which is the ineffable Dharmakaya [the essence of the universe, also the teaching of Buddha], which is free of all differentiation or premonition of differentiation." (Awakening of Faith)

Buddha said, "In Tathagata's Womb Oneness has the same meaning as Infinity, and Infinity has the same meaning as Oneness, the minimum is embraced in the maximum and the maximum in the minimum. The tranquillity and peacefulness of my concentration of mind in Samadhi prevails all over the ten quarters of the universes, my body embraces the vast spaces of the ten quarters, and even within a single pore of my skin there is a Buddha-land with a Buddha sitting on a seat no larger than a particle of dust, absorbed in Samadhi, but endlessly radiating there from all the forces of Life - giving Truth and ceaselessly drawing inward into its perfect unity all of its multitudinous manifestations. Since I have ignored and forgotten all worldly objects, I have fully realized this mysterious, enlightening nature of the Pure Essence of Mind." (The Surangama Sutra)

Thirdly, Buddhism divides the Absolute Totality into three parts — the Unborn God, the wheel of life (Samsara) and a river which divides the formers. At this level, the Buddha's God (the Unborn God) is not the Absolute Totality; the Buddha's "final" aim (Nirvana) of liberating all sentient beings from the bondage of the wheel of Samsara and of uniting them with the Unborn God is still not the "final" aim. In other words, Buddha has to transcend the final aim in order to reach the final aim. The only way to stop this infinite recursive paradox is by using an absolute Negation — denying the entire Buddha's doctrine, that there is no Nirvana, no Dharma (Buddha's teaching) and no God. Buddha said, "Subhuti, that is why I say that the Dharma of all things can never be embraced within any arbitrary conception of phenomena however universal that conception may be. That is why it is called the Dharma and why there is no such thing as the Dharma." (The Diamond Sutra)

By doing so, Buddha finally touched the Absolute Totality but has lost the chance forever to understand the essence of the Absolute Totality. The Absolute Totality can indeed be understood in terms of words and reason. The Absolute Totality has an infinite rich structure — as the unification of Nothingness and Infinity, as the perfect symmetry, as the utmost chaos, as the infinite powerful force, and as .... With Buddha's methodology, detachment and negation, only a small part of God's essence was understood by Buddha. Buddha had no idea of that the utmost chaos is also the essence of God.

No doubt, the understanding of the essence of the Unborn God in Buddhism is indeed remarkable in the philosophical sense, but Buddha or all Tathagatas nonetheless did not discover Thermodynamics, Quantum Mechanics and Elementary Particle Physics in either their Samadhis or their Nirvana. Buddhism did not enter the gate of the utmost truth. For over two thousand years, all intellectual men in China were groping outside the gate of the utmost truth but unable to enter it by following Buddhism. Buddhism did prohibit the development of science in China and therefore did drag China to become a second class nation, but not because it is superstition and wrong. On the contrary, it is because of its wisdom. For two thousand years in China, there was no reason to search for any other options and possibilities; there was no chance for China to develop western style science.

September 23, 1991

Dr. Jeh-Tween Gong
P.O. Box 1753
Bristol, VA 24203
U.S.A.

Dear Dr. Gong:

It was a very pleasant experience for me to gain your personal acquaintance in Scarborough, Toronto, Canada. I really admire your excellent idea about the unification of everything. I have learned much from your hand-out at your session in Scarborough, as well as your book.

I was very glad to learn that you liked my paper "Teaching the Constructive Phase of Philosophical Theories". It is my present pleasure and effort to apply the fundamentals of "Constructics" to the inquiries into some unique theories, like your super unified theory, which have been developed and presented by living thinkers like you, as well as those developed and presented by classical thinkers such as Plato, Descartes, Kant, William James, or Russell. For the constructics inquiry I have a checklist called "The Checklist of Constructics Approach to Theories," which consists of 110 questions in the constructive phase of theories. If you will take much interest in giving me your response to the checklist, so that we might publish it in Japanese and use it as one of our teaching materials in our philosophy courses here in Japan under the title of, say, "The Super Unified Theory by Jeh-Tween Gong" in a category of theories developed and presented by living thinkers.

Enclosed is a picture of you at your excellent session. I hope you will like it. Hoping this letter will find you well and happy.

Sincerely Yours,

Shokichi Uto

Shokichi Uto Ph.D.
Professor of Philosophy
Nihon University, Japan

Chapter IX
Tao of Life and of God,
the first TOE (Theory of Everything)

Buddhism pursues the absoluteness by denying and denouncing relativity. Buddha said, "Likewise based upon the notion of relativity false-imagination perceives a variety of appearances which the discriminating mind proceeds to objectify and name and become attached to, and memory and habit-energy perpetuate."

Taoism pursues the absoluteness by embracing relativity and by reconciling all paradoxes. Laotse wrote, "To yield is to be preserved whole. To be bent is to become straight. To be hollow is to be filled.

"We put thirty spokes together and call it a wheel, but it is on the space where there is nothing that the usefulness of the wheel depends. We turn clay to make a vessel, but it is on the space where there is nothing that the usefulness of the vessel depends. We pierce doors and windows to make a house, but it is on the space where there is nothing that the usefulness of the house depends.

"Being and nonbeing interdepend in growth. Difficult and easy interdepend in completion. Long and short interdepend in contrast. High and low interdepend in position. Tones and voice interdepend in harmony. Front and behind interdepend in company."

II

My father, Lo-Cheen Gong, is the greatest scholar in Chinese philosophy. He earnestly advocates that the Laotse doctrine is the greatest philosophy in the entire human culture while also earnestly denouncing the neo-Taosim which has become pure superstitious nonsense. Therefore, I despised neo-Taoism since I was only a child, when I had not the slightest idea of what neo-Taoism really is. I despised it because it is non-Christian. I despised it because of its superstitious rituals. I saw the Taoism rituals a few times in movies. A priest set up an altar. A few talisman flags were hung around the altar. First, the priest performed a sword dance, then sacrificed a chicken and sprinkled the blood around the altar. Finally, he burnt the talismans and fed the ashes to the sinners or patients. By performing this ritual, the evil spirit or the ailment will surely be driven out from the patients. I was simply unable to swallow this kind of stupidity when I was younger than ten.

Twenty years later, at age twenty-nine, I finally understood exactly what God is and where God is. Ten years after that, I began looking back and looking around the traditional religions. To my the greatest surprise, I found that Taoism is the only religion that has entered the gate of the utmost truth, although it has not yet reached the innermost secret of the utmost truth. Unfortunately, most of the people are unable to understand this fact fully, simply because Taoism matured too early. I despised Taoism when I was young, simply because I did not know the slightest bit of what Taoism was.

III

All lives and the entire universe were and are created by God. So, mankind originated from a single beginning. But soon, this single beginning evolved into two distinguishable cultures, the Chinese culture and the Indo-European culture. There is a lot of evidence that Indo-European culture was indeed united once, such as the languages, the conception of the soul of Plato which is quite similar with the teaching of Vedas. No doubt, Judaism is also a small breach of this Indo-European culture. The evidence of this is the Serpent. In Hinduism, the serpent represents a good life-force, and they try to harness this serpent power with kundalini yoga. In Judaism, the serpent represents evil. The Judeo-Christian God has fought with this serpent eternally without any sign of victory. In Christianity, God even lost the first round of battle with the serpent; so He drove the man and woman out of the garden of Eden. Then, this Judeo-Christian God sent His only son to earth trying to rein in this serpent but failed again and promised a second coming. Regardless of what the serpent represents — goodness or evil, it is the center point of both cultures, Hinduism and Judaism. On the other hand, the sexual force is not symbolized with a serpent in China. There were a few stiff-necked historians who insisted that Chinese culture was only a subculture of Indo-European culture. They tried to derive the Chinese system of writing from cuneiform and even from the Hebrew alphabet. But their ignorance was quickly ignored by the world after the discovery of the Yang-Shao culture in 1921, at a village in western Honan, south of the Yellow River. Not only is Chinese writing quite different from the languages of the rest of world, but China also has a very unique theology.

This unique theology was developed by a few sage kings. Suijen discovered the use of fire. Fuhsi domesticated animals, invented eight Kwa (Trigram), conception of Tai Ch'i and the Yin-Yang theory. Shennung taught agriculture and medicine. Huangti (the Yellow Emperor) invented Chinese writing, compass, vehicles, ways to harness silk and sexual yoga. The Emperor Yao established law and order, the conception of Li. The Emperor Shun taught the virtues of God, the conception of Jen. The Emperor Yu seduced the Flood and established the Hsia Dynasty. Five hundred and some years later, the Shang Dynasty was established. Another five hundred and some years, King Wen and King Wu established the Chou Dynasty. Duke Chou, a brother of King Wu, used Li to rule the entire Empire. Another five hundred and some years, Confucius aroused to teach and to edit all that ancient knowledge into six classics.

Those dates and years were recorded in the book of Mencius, written around 300 B.C.. So, the Hsia Dynasty began around 2000 B.C. According to Chinese legends, the Yellow Emperor ruled China around 3000 B.C.. There is no way to know how many years lapsed between Shennung and the Yellow Emperor, between Fuhsi and Shennung. According to Chinese legends, each era lasted more than 1000 years. So, Fuhsi lived around 6000 B.C. or earlier.

Again, I do not know whether it is true that Fuhsi is the father of Chinese theology or not. Chinese legend says yes, and I have no reason to disbelieve it and have no way to disprove it.

IV

Chinese theology and science is based entirely on two cornerstones — Fuhsi's conception of God and Five Walk (Wu-Hsing) theory. All western books translate Five Walk as five elements while in Chinese the term literally means Five Walk. Anyone who translates it as five elements is no doubt having absolute zero knowledge of Chinese philosophy and theology. Absolutely not, Five Walk is not five elements.

Buddha talked about Four Great Elements — earth, water, fire and air. The ancient Greek also talked about a similar idea the same as Buddha's. Those elements were supposed to be the building blocks of the universe in the eyes of Buddha and the Greeks. This conception of elements is quite primitive and has no valid meaning any more after the advancement of modern knowledge. On the contrary, the Five Walk — metal, water, wood, fire and earth — are five forces. They are not building blocks laying upon each other to build up the universe but are five forces acting upon one another.

No one in the world knows who invented this Five Walk theory because no Chinese legend talks about it. Confucius did refer to Five Walk in some of his sayings; so it had to exist long before him. I do know who invented another cornerstone of Chinese theology — Tai Ch'i and Yin-Yang theory, because Chinese legend told me that Fuhsi did it 8000 years ago.

As for Fuhsi, Tai Ch'i is the creator God. Tai literally means the greatest. Ch'i means pole, the monopole. Tai Ch'i gives birth to Yin and Yang. Yin and Yang are two forces. Yang is aggressive and is always moving forward. Yin is passive and yielding. In time of conflict, they are opposite forces. In constancy, they not only complement each other but are imbedded in each other. After reaching their full strength, they transform into the opposite, that is, Yang becomes Yin and Yin to Yang. Thus, Yin can conquer Yang by yielding and allowing Yang to reach its full strength. On the other hand, Yang can only conquer Yin temporarily. Being conquered, Yin transforms into Yang and leads the ultimate conversion of Yang to Yin at end. Yin is represented with " | " and Yang with "1". Then, Fuhsi stacked Yin and Yang into Kwa (the Trigram).

I do not know why Fuhsi stacked Yin-Yang into trigrams instead of four's and five's. A numerology recorded in Tao Teh Ching, the book of Laotse, gives us a clue. Laotse wrote, "Out of Tao (Tai Ch'i), One is born. Out of One, Two. Out of Two, Three. Out of Three, the created universe. The created universe carries the Yin at its back and the Yang in front." Although all Chinese, from ancient to today, believe that all lives are the result of an interaction of Five Walk and ultimately of the two principle of Yin and Yang, that these principles govern both natural phenomena and human society, I don't believe that anyone in the world before me, including all Chinese and Fuhsi himself, realized what Fuhsi had discovered. He found the most basic building blocks of the universe, six quarks and two leptons. For the reason of convenience of typing, I rotated the kwa form 90 degrees in the following comparison table.

Kwa name	Kwa form	Quark form	Quark name
Khien	lll	(A, A, A)	Electron
Tui	|ll	(V, A, A)	Red Up-quark
Li	l|l	(A, V, A)	Yellow Up-quark
Chen	| |l	(V, V, A)	Blue anti-Down-quark

Sun	ll		(A, A, V)	Blue Up-quark
Khan	|1|	(V, A, V)	Yellow anti-Down-quark
Ken	1| |	(A, V, V)	Red anti-Down-quark
Khwun	| | |	(V, V, V)	Neutrino

According to the modern elementary particle physics, the entire material universe is constructed with these six quarks and two leptons. Proton is (u, u, d) — two up-quarks and one down-quark. Neutron is (u, d, d) — two down-quarks and one up-quark. Every up-quark or down-quark has three varieties. They are distinguished with three color labels. So, we say that quarks are colored or are having a color dimension. On the other hand, protons and neutrons have no color dimension, meaning colorless. Those colors obey a color complementary rule. Red plus yellow produces blue. Red plus yellow and blue becomes colorless. So, protons and all other hadrons can only be produced by obeying some special color combinations. As for protons, one such an example is by using one red up-quark, one yellow up-quark and one blue down-quark. In this arrangement, both the electric charge and color dimension are in balance for a proton. In fact, this proton can be written with Kwas, that proton is (Tui, Li, (-)Chen). Eight Kwas are indeed the foundation of the universe, and they were discovered 8000 years ago by Fuhsi, in China.

The surprise does not stop here. Today, the elementary particle physics finds out that there are three sets of quarks and leptons, although only one set (the eight listed above) is needed for the present universe. The other two generations of quarks and leptons are for the evolution process of the universe. In China, the whole cosmos, from the beginning to the present, is described with Yin-Yang and Five Walk. To my greatest surprise, I discovered, ten years after the completion of my Super Unified Theory, that the Five Walk theory is "identical" to the modern elementary particle physics.

Superficially, there are only two sets of rules to control the interactions of the Five Walk.

Rule one is the Generation rule which is also called the Mother and Child rule. Earth generates (gives birth to) metal. Metal generates water. Water generates wood. Wood generates fire. Fire generates earth. Thus completes a cycle of generation and birth.

Rule two is the rule of Conquest or destruction which is also called the Man and Woman rule. Metal conquers wood. Wood conquers earth. Earth conquers water. Water conquers fire. Fire conquers metal.

These rules were not drawn up arbitrarily. They are the summation of nature phenomena. No doubt, actual "wood" can indeed produce fire, and Fire produces Earth (ashes). Earth produces metal because metal comes out of mines. Metal produces water (as molten liquid), and Water produces wood (viz. vegetation).

Again, there is no doubt that Earth can stop Water, and Water vanquishes Fire. Fire melts Metal, and Metal chops Wood. Wood sets roots deep into Earth.

These rules seem to be very primitive and non-scientific. Not only I was outraged by its apparent stupidity, but all educated modern Chinese and Westerners think of it as nothing but a big joke. Only by discovering and understanding the modern elementary particle physics and the Super Unified Theory, can these seemingly primitive assignments of Five Walk begin making sense.

According to the modern elementary particle physics, this universe is controlled by seven color dimensions — three quark colors, three generations and one colorless dimension. Their interactions can be described with a diagram of four connected triangles. Please get a piece of paper and a pencil, then follow the following instructions to draw up this diagram which represents the operations of the universe.

First, draw a triangle and mark 1, 2 and 3 on each vertex to represent the three generations. The interior area of the triangle is colorless for generations (genecolors).

Second, from each vertex, extending outward, draw a smaller triangle and mark the three vertexes on the small triangle with R, Y, B (Red, Yellow and Blue — the quark colors). The interior area of each small triangle is colorless for quark colors.

With these four connected triangles, this universe is described as having three generations (1, 2, 3), and each generation is constructed with three quark colors and one colorless dimension. But, this four-triangle diagram can be reduced to a pentagon overlaid on a pentagram without losing any information. In other words, with a pentagon and a pentagram, all relationships of quark generations and quark colors can be described in detail.

Surprise! Surprise! The rule of Generation of Five Walk forms a pentagon. The rule of Conquest forms a pentagram. Again, the surprise does not stop at here. The Five Walk theory clearly describes that this universe is constructed with three generations. There is a hidden rule that is called the rule of Revenge. That is, the Child, on behalf of the Mother, takes revenge on the latter's conqueror. Now, this Five Walk becomes a cycle of three generations — Man, Mother and Son. Not only do the Westerners not understand what the Five Walk really is, but no Chinese before me truly understood the meaning of these three generations.

I do not know how the ancient Chinese developed this Five Walk theory. No doubt, they did not know quantum physics, modern elementary particle physics, or modern Super Unified Theory. They invented it with some very primitive observations, with a non-scientific generalization and with seemingly arbitrary logic. They not only invented it somehow and believed in it, but they used it to develop a first TOE, Theory of Everything. This TOE is the foundation of Chinese medicine, geomancy, Kung-Fu, philosophy and religion. It describes the precise laws of "life" and "universe".

This unification between life and lifeless is not only demonstrated with the success of both quantum physics and Chinese medicine but with the Golden Section. As I have said, the rule of Generation of the Five Walk forms a pentagon, and the rule of Conquest forms a pentagram. The Golden Section, the Divine Proportion, is the ratio between the side of the pentagon and the side of the pentagram. Directly related to the Golden Section is the Fibonacci Series; 1, 1, 2, 3, 5, 8,...,34, 55,.... This series is constructed by adding up the last two numbers in a sequence to give the next number; such as the next number after 55 is 89 (=34+55). As the numbers rise, their ratios correspondingly creep closer and closer to the Golden section, which is 1.618014, and $5/3=1.66$, $8/5=1.6$, $55/34=1.617$, $89/55=1.6181$,.... Surprisingly, the Fibonacci Series is not only a mathematical concept invented by Leonardo Fibonacci, but it is a basic principle in nature. The Fibonacci Series is found in many life and natural formations: the leaves on trees, the formation of stars, the skins of onions, the arrangement of pads on cats' feet, the shells of microscopic protozoa, the crystalline forms of minerals, the shape of rams' horns and of nautilus shells. Each section of the spiral, such as the rams' horns, relates to the next section in the sequence in the same progression as the Fibonacci Series. Five Walk theory contains the principles of both the Golden Section and the Fibonacci Series.

Chinese science and theology is completely derived from these two cornerstones — Yin-Yang and Five Walk theories. This combined theory is not only identical with the modern elementary particle physics, but has much more meaning. The modern elementary particle physics has not yet become the law of medicine or religion, but all Chinese science, philosophy, medicine, religion and even superstitions are based on Fuhsi's theory. No doubt, Fuhsi did not have the slightest notion of what elementary particle physics is. He just simply found the ultimate truth, by pure luck perhaps, and all Chinese people believe him since the day he found it. All Chinese people did not wait for me to tell them that Fuhsi was right. For eight thousand years, no one in China can find any error in Fuhsi's theory in any discipline, medicine, geomancy (Feng Shui), Kung-Fu, philosophy, etc. Therefore, the western style of science was not and could not be invented in China. There was no reason to look into or search for any other options and possibilities.

V

Chinese medicine is the biggest proof that Fuhsi is right. According to Fuhsi, everything, being or nonbeing, is a spirit, the manifestation of the interaction of Yin-Yang and Five Walk. This manifestation, therefore, has a life-force, Chee. Tian-chee is the weather. Di-chee is the life-force of the earth. In other words, the lifeless material world is indeed alive.

As for humans, chee flows along 14 Meridians. There are a few Vital Points along each Meridian. Every vital point is not only a check station along the meridian, but a window or an opening connecting the internal organs with the external environment. By applying pressure with fingers or stimulant with acupuncture needles or the heat of Moxacautery on those windows, the ailment of the internal organs will be cured, and the immune system will be strengthened to ward off any contagious disease. In other words, all the function of the intestinal organs can be adjusted through those windows, the acupuncture vital points.

Those chee paths (meridians) do not overlap with the blood circulatory system, although chee does control the circulatory system and the autonomic nerve system. These chee paths cannot be found by cutting up the body (the anatomical procedure), and the mind-consciousness is unaware of their existence. Therefore, almost all modern doctors deny the existence of the chee and chee paths because of their ignorance, not because they are able to disprove it. Ignorance is in no way science.

My right shoulder became very stiff and painful after a few days of typing this book. Two days later, this pain moved to my hip joint; the moving path was followed exactly the chee meridian. Too many modern doctors ignore this kind of personal experience and discredit it as non-scientific. I am now going to teach those stiff-necked doctors a lesson about science. In science, when any event happened or was observed even only once, its existence is confirmed, although the probability of its occurrence cannot be determined by only one observation, although that event cannot be explained scientifically, and although it cannot be understood by many scientists. Every experience is the foundation not only of philosophy but of science. Science can never go beyond the totality of human experience. Science has no right to deny any single experience. Furthermore, since all scientific observations are theory-dependent, thus the western science is incapable of epistemically observing the Chinese truths. When I was a kid, I despised Taoism and Buddhism. Thirty years later, I despise many scientists. On the summit of science, I see no science but God who is both transcendent and immanent.

Although our will is unable to manipulate both the chee paths and the autonomic nerve system, our moods and emotions indeed have a strong influence on those systems. The ancient Chinese not only realized this fact but developed a system (Chee-Kung) to control the moods and emotions, in turn to control the chee and chee paths. The Chinese discovered the chee meridians and vital points by meditation and Chee-Kung. Acupuncture was not discovered accidentally but is a result of a comprehensive medical system based on Fuhsi theory.

Fuhsi and all Chinese regard the human body as the Microcosm, and the rules which govern the universe also govern the human body, to the exact same degree. The table below shows the relationship between the external universe and the human body.

Yin organs	Liver	Heart	Spleen	Lungs	Kidneys
Yang organs	G. bladder	S. intestine	Stomach	L. intestine	Bladder
Five Walk	Wood	Fire	Earth	Metal	Water
Five seasons	Spring	Summer	Midsummer	Autumn	Winter
Five directions	East	South	Center	West	North
Five Planets	Jupiter	Mars	Saturn	Venus	Mercury

Five colors	Blue	Red	Yellow	White	Black
Five smells	Rancid	Scorched	Fragrant	Fleshy	Rotten
Five tastes	Tart	Bitter	Sweet	Hot	Salty
Five evils	Wind	Heat	Wetness	Dryness	Cold
Five emotions	Anger	Laughter	Worry	Sorrow	Fear
Five Fluids	Tears	Sweat	Saliva	Mucus	Spittle
Five senses	eye	tongue	mouth	nose	ear
Five windows	nail	body hair	breast	breath	head hair
Five cereals	wheat	millet	rye	rice	beans
Five meats	chicken	mutton	beef	horse	pork
Five notes	chio	chih	kung	shang	yu

In this table, the entire external world is classified with Five Walk, and they influence each internal organ according to those seemingly arbitrary assignments. The wind is evil for the liver and gall bladder but not for other organs. Seemingly, this table provides a unified scheme between the universe and the human body. It is the TOE (Theory of Everything) of China. Furthermore, it shows the first time how the Yin-Yang and Five Walk theories are unified; the ten vital organs are divided into five pairs, each consisting of one 'solid' Yin organ and one 'hollow' Yang organ. The pairing is not arbitrary. The solid organ is the master, the hollow the slave. The Yin, the female power, is the master, the Yang the slave. Yin-Yang is in fact imbedded in Five Walk. Yin and Yang manifest themselves in every conceivable contrast, large scale or small. In the human body, Yin controls internal surfaces, lower regions and back part, both on the body as a whole and on each individual organ, while Yang governs external surfaces, upper regions and front parts. Yin is always stronger and more abundant than Yang, but Yang is more obvious and active.

Chinese medicine is very complicated, but this table summarizes it all. Chinese doctors take those seemingly arbitrary assigned attributes very seriously in two ways, the diagnosis and the treatment. The four steps of diagnosis in Chinese medicine are looking at the colors, smelling, taking pulses and questioning. The best doctor shall know what the patient's problem is immediately after he sees the patient. The second grade doctors need the aid of smelling. The mediocre ones need the aid of taking pulses. If any doctor needs to ask questions for diagnosis, he shall be ashamed of himself. Questioning is only for confirmation and comforting. For example, if the nose color lacks whiteness, then no doubt the lungs and large intestine system is out of balance. This way of diagnosis seems very non-scientific or even down right absurd. Worst yet, they treat this ailment with herbs which have a hot taste, fleshy smell and whitish color, according to the above table. I was sick of this kind of stupidity when I was a kid while I did not know the Chinese philosophy the slightest bit.

At age 18, I got a very bad eye infection. A western eye doctor treated me with shots, eye drops and pills for two months, and my eye infection was cleared. But soon, I found out that I could not do any reading longer than five minutes without feeling a serious pain in my eyes. They teared involuntarily for every five minutes of study. No western eye doctor could help me because there was no more infection in my eyes. They tried all kinds of eye glasses on me, but it failed to do me any good. Finally, I went to see a Chinese medicine doctor. He put my wrist on a small pillow and used three of his fingers to take my pulse. He closed his eyes, concentrating or falling asleep, for almost one hour. Then he waked up by opening his eyes and wrote me a prescription with fifty some herbs with a different proportion of quantity for each. I took this prescription to a Chinese herb drug store. The next day, I went to pick up a big bag of pills. After only taking the first dose, my eyes were able to read nonstop for five hours that day. No one, including myself, believed that can be true. In six months, I had a pair of excellent seeing eyes I did not have before, even before my eye infection. I had a few more similar situations that the western doctors sent me home with pills and bills but was unable to cure my discomforts which were finally all cured by Chinese medicine doctors. At that time, if anyone doubted the effectiveness of Chinese medicine, I would surely slap his face to wake him up from his stupidity. Today, I will still feel sorry for his ignorance. Chinese medicine is based on a unified view that unites the Macrocosm and the Microcosm. On the other hand, western medicine is only an encyclopedia of many trivia facts, a big hodgepodge. The western doctors are no more than body mechanics; they can no doubt cure a body's ailment while not knowing exactly what life really is.

VI

The ancient Chinese probably did not know the connection between Five Walk, Golden Section and the Fibonacci Series, but no doubt they did formulate a very accurate and elegant unified theory, which is able to describe both the human body and the universe. The other Chinese masterpiece is Feng Shui, the Chinese Geomancy. Feng Shui is quite different from the western geomancy. The western geomancy is a self-centered belief, by creating a self-declared Omphalos stone, by defining a self-defined boundaries, by imaging a self-created labyrinth, by aligning the church buildings with the sun path, by sacrificing a life to be a guardian of an entrance, by applying the sacred geometry in the architecture. On the other hand, Feng Shui seeks harmony between the Macrocosm and the Microcosm. Feng Shui consists of two cornerstones, a unified world view and a religious belief.

All Chinese people regard birth and death as a transition from one realm of existence to another rather than as absolute beginnings or endings. Chuangtse, the greatest disciple of Laotse, wrote, "How do I know that in clinging to this life I am not merely clinging to a dream and delaying my entry into the real world? How do I know that love of life is not a delusion after all? How then do I know but that the dead may repent of having previously clung to life?" Confucius wrote, "When a relative died, they went up on the roof and cried aloud to the spirit, saying to him, 'Ahooooooooo! So-and-So, will you please return to your body?' If the spirit failed to return, then they used un-cooked rice and baked meats for sacrifice, and they turned their heads towards the Heaven to looking for the spirit and buried the body in the earth. The material spirit then descended to earth, while the conscious spirit went up to Heaven. Therefore the dead were buried with their heads toward the north, while the living had their houses facing the south. These were the ancient customs."

It is very clear from Confucius' writing that Feng Shui existed long before him, and he identified two main functions of Feng Shui: one pertaining to premises occupied by the living, known as Yang dwelling — facing the south, and the other concerned with the abodes of the dead, known as Yin dwellings.

Since the dead are not really dead, then the correct positioning of the burial sites of the dead will surely afford good fortune either to the spirit of the deceased or his descendants. Now the task is how to determine what burial site is good. Again, Feng Shui is entirely based on Yin-Yang and Five Walk theories with two additional tools, the magic square and the compass (the Lo P'an, invented by Yellow Emperor).

According to Chinese legend, the magic square was discovered in the markings of the shell of a tortoise emerging from the River Lo.

This magic square has a special symmetrical property. The sum of any three numbers — either vertical, horizontal or diagonal — is 15. Now, most of the people, either Westerner or Chinese, consider the magic square little more than a mathematical oddity which produces a pleasing pattern, or it is only relegated to the realms of mythology and fairy tales. Obviously, those people do not understand the meaning of the magic square. God is the perfect symmetry; therefore, no direction can be defined or distinguished. God creates this mortal world with the process of symmetry breaking, and the directions are created after this symmetry breaking. The magic square is created by reversing the symmetry breaking process, and symmetry is regenerated.

God created directions with the process of symmetry breaking, and the ancient Chinese defined directions with a reversed process, the magic square. By doing this, the directions are no longer arbitrarily defined but are linked to the law of universe. In general, there are four arbitrarily defined directions — east, west, south and north. In India, there are six directions, four plus up and down. In China, there are eight directions, which are defined with the magic square; 1 is north, 9 south, etc. All cardinal points are all associated with odd, or Yang number, and the corner points with even, or Yin numbers. Then, these eight directions are tied to eight Kwa, Five Walk, twenty-four seasons, twenty-eight celestial mansions, ten Heavenly Stems (denary cycle), twelve Earthly Branches (duodenary cycle), and twenty-four stellar positions. By doing so, the earth, the heaven and the laws of the universe (Yin-Yang and Five Walk) are unified into a harmonic whole. All those associations are placed in many concentric rings on Lo P'an, the Chinese Feng Shui compass. In general, there are 33 rings on Lo P'an. All those associations are not arbitrary but are observable facts. Not only was the movement of the magnetic north around the true north discovered by Chiu Yen-Han, a Feng Shui master, around 700 A.D. — at least 1000 years ahead of western science, but the amount of movement was also measured with precise accuracy. Feng Shui was a highly refined science. All Chinese sciences — astronomy, meteorology, geology, philosophy, numerology, theology and metaphysics — are summarized on

Lo P'an. Feng Shui is a unified knowledge and belief of both Chinese science and religion. In ancient time, only a very small percentage of the population were educated. The majority of Chinese people did not read five classics or Tao Teh Ching. But, all of them had some knowledge about Feng Shui and believed in it. Without Feng Shui, there would be no Chinese culture.

The reputation of Feng Shui was badly damaged because many people tried to benefit from the dead by burying the deceased in a beneficial spot; in turn, it often deprived many of the dead of a decent and timely burial. Therefore, many Confucian scholars came out to denounce Feng Shui. Today, most of the Chinese people despise Feng Shui because of worshipping western science and because of not knowing what Feng Shui really is.

VII

The combined theory of Yin-Yang and Five Walk is indeed a Theory of Everything. It is not only the foundation of Chinese medicine, Feng Shui, religious belief, dietary laws and of martial arts (the Kung-Fu and Chee-Kung), but it is also the foundation of the laws of social order, of the laws of moral and even of the rules of a chess game —the "Go" game. Every discipline is not only solid and valid on its foundation but improves human life and society immensely.

For two thousand years, Yin-Yang, Five Walk and Feng Shui were classified as Taoism theories. Chinese historians often refer to Taoism as Huang-Lao-Tao, the teaching of Yellow Emperor and Laotse. But, this is a big mistake. The linage of Taoism is from Fuhsi, Huangti, Yao and Shun to Confucius. It was Confucius who summarized the five classics of the ancient. The Yin-Yang and Five Walk theories were passed on to today by Confucius. He wrote, "Therefore man is the product of the forces of heaven and earth, of the union of the Yin and the Yang principles, the incarnation of spirits and the essence of the Five Walk."

On the other hand, the term of Yin-Yang was only used once in the entire book of Laotse, and he did not mention Five Walk at all, not even once. No doubt, Laotse was a revolutionist. He wanted to break away from the Fuhsi-Huangti doctrine. He wanted to invent a new teaching. In the interview with Confucius, he laughed at Confucius because Confucius knew only the ancient knowledge, which were invented by those who died long ago. Laotse even invented a new theology, that the nothingness created something, the something then became the universe. This Laotse theology is quite different from the Fuhsi doctrine, that Tai Ch'i created Yin and Yang, then eight Kwa, then the universe. Although Laotse was a revolutionist, the majority of his teaching is still the teachings of the ancients, perhaps the non-mainstream teaching. Chuangtse wrote, "Some of the teachings of the ancients lay in this: the root of all things is subtle, while material things are gross appearances of reality; all measurable quantities fall short of the truth of reality; live calmly and dispassionately alone with the spirits. Laotse heard of such teachings and loved them. Their fundamental thesis is that nonbeing is the constant phase of life, and all things can be traced to God. They teach gentleness and humility in appearance, and a passive attitude and the belief that one should not destroy the things of the universe by interference as the substance of their faith."

Although Laotse did not belong to the mainstream Taoism, he did give a great contribution to Taoism by emphasizing three virtues of Tao. First, Tao is inaction, yielding, soft and having the quality of water. He wrote, "There is nothing weaker than water. But none is superior to it in overcoming the hard. That the yielding conquers the strong, and the soft conquers the hard. ... A large kingdom must be like the low ground toward which all streams flow. It must play the role of female in its dealings with all things under Heaven. The female by quiescence conquers the male, by quiescence she gets underneath."

This of course was the cornerstone of China's foreign policy for thousands of years. Conquered several times by Tartar, Mongol and Manchu invaders, China simply lay down and got underneath them, seducing these vigorous barbarian aggressors with the irresistible charms of Chinese culture. Instead of fighting fire with fire, China fought fire with water and won, reducing her rock-hard conquerors to be a part of China. In the long run, China survived and thrived while her various conquerors passed forever from the stage of history. China is not only the world's oldest living civilization, in terms of a continuity of culture, but is also one of the great international powers of today. No doubt, Laotse shall get some credit for this.

Second, Tao is relativity. Laotse wrote, "He who is to be made to dwindle, must first be caused to expand. He who is to be weakened, must first be made strong. He who is to be taken away from, must first be given."

Third, Tao is the oneness, the absoluteness and Tao is everywhere. Laotse wrote, "In embracing the One with you soul, can you never forsake the Tao? ... Tao is absolute and has no name. ... The Great Tao flows everywhere. The myriad things derive their life from it."

No doubt, Laotse did have a fair understanding of what God is and where God is. God the oneness and the absoluteness will break down into parts and creates relativity, then unifies the parts into oneness again.

Although Laotse was not in the mainstream of Taoism, his emphasis and the new interpretations of the virtues of Tao had enriched Taoism immeasurably. Today, Taoism consists of three cornerstones, Yin-Yang, Five Walk and Laotse's conception of God. Yin-Yang, eight Kwa and Five Walk are the laws of the mortal universe. Laotse's conception of Tao describes the essences of God, from oneness to relativity, then to oneness again. Finally, Laotse's Taoism became one of the three cornerstones of mainstream Taoism. For many people today, Laotse is Taoism and Taoism is Laotse.

On the other hand, Confucius was expelled from the mainstream Taoism. Perhaps, it is more accurate to say that the neo-Confucianism abandoned Taoism. After Confucius, mainstream Taoism broke into two groups, the Yin-Yang school and the neo-Confucianism. The neo-Confucianism cared about nothing but Li (the social order and religious rituals) and Jen (the human virtue and the true manhood); in turn, it drove itself out of the mainstream Taoism. The Yin-Yang school, which is despised by both neo-Confucianism and Laotse Taoism, survives among the lower class Chinese people. Mainstream Taoism lives among the common folk.

VIII

All modern historians believe that history began in the Near East for two reasons, many artifacts which are preserved by the desert and the legends of the Bible. Therefore, history might begin in the Near East, but the civilization no doubt started somewhere else. Today, both the gene map and the fossil map conclude that modern humans originated in Africa about 200,000 years ago. Then, there were two major waves of migration from Africa to Asia and to Europe. The first migration took place about 60,000 to 100,000 years ago; the second was about 35,000 years ago. According to a Chinese legend, both Fuhsi and Yellow Emperor came from the west.

By studying ancient theology, the Mesopotamia culture cannot be anything but a subculture of a bigger system. The religious beliefs of the Mesopotamia culture is too primitive compared with the three Vedas.

Regardless of when the written form of the three Vedas appeared, its complex theory cannot reach its maturity around 3000 B.C. without the works of a matured civilization at least a few thousand years before it. Furthermore, the teaching of Vedas is not only a theology but a structure of social order, which cannot come to existence and reach its maturity without the support of a fairly matured civilization for at least many thousands of years. The Mesopotamia culture did have some intercourse with the Egyptian, the Jewish and the Greek cultures, but those were only branches of the Indo-European system. Today, many historians conclude that many myths in the Bible were borrowed not only from pagan stories but also from Hindu sources. Abram, the original name of Abraham, is but the Hindu Brama with the "a" as prefix instead of suffix, and Brama was the original name of the Hindu Creator Brahma (See Chapter XIII — The Grand Detour). In other words, a branch of the branches can never be the root of the roots. There is no doubt that God is the beginning and the root; then there are two cultures — Chinese and Indo-European. The Near East cultures were only a few leaves on one of the branches, and its history incidentally was preserved by the desert. From theologies, it is not very difficult to distinguish which is the root and which is the branch. So, the Indo-European culture must have existed many thousands of years before the Near East cultures, although historians today cannot find any 'history' of that culture beyond 3000 B.C.

On the other hand, Chinese civilization is an entirely separated system. The Chinese theology, the Fuhsi doctrine, matured around 6000 to 10000 B.C.. This very complicated Yin-Yang and Five Walk system cannot be invented in a short time span; a fairly matured Chinese civilization must have existed a few thousand years before Fuhsi. Since the theologies between China and Indo-European are so different, the Chinese civilization, regardless of how early it began, cannot be the forefather of the Indo-European culture, and vice versa.

The early maturity of this Chinese civilization, especially on the area of theology, is not a blessing for China. By and large, China has been standing still since the time of Confucius and Laotse. No doubt, both of them are culprits on this China's misfortune. Confucius insisted that everything from ancient time is good. The ancestral worship is not only a religious notion for Confucius but a conviction that the ancient knowledge is perfect and complete. Confucius said, "I taught the truth originally handed down by the ancient Emperors Yao and Shun, and I adopted and perfected the system of social and religious laws established by the Emperors Wen and Wu. ... This Li is the principle by which the ancient kings embodied the laws of Heaven and regulated the expressions of human nature." Therefore, there is no reason to pursue any new knowledge after his completion of the six classics, and Chinese scholars in the two thousand years after him simply did just that. Furthermore, his teaching of filial piety encourages the parental dictatorship, and all creative abilities of the young are murdered.

On the other hand, Laotse and Chuangtse believed that knowledge corrupts the human nature; therefore, they both were strongly against any kind of knowledge. Laotse wrote, "The ancients who knew how to follow the Tao, aimed not to enlighten the people, but to keep them ignorant. The reason it is difficult for the people to live in peace, is because of too much knowledge."

From this point of view, both Confucius and Laotse were deeply indebted to China. But, the real reason that China has been standing still for two thousand years is not because all Chinese people obey Confucius' and Laotse's teaching of worshipping the ancient and of denouncing knowledge, but because Taoism has indeed entered the gate of the ultimate truth; no one was able to find any error in it for two thousand years. No error can be found in it even today. Therefore, there was no reason to search for any other options and possibilities. Therefore, there was no chance for China to develop western style science.

Chapter X
The Triune Universe

God is the union of nothingness and infinity. God is the infinite recursion, from absoluteness to mortal universe then back to absoluteness. But, how? How can infinity be transformed into finite? How can order come out of chaos? How can something be born from nothingness? How does life arise from lifeless material? What are the basic building blocks of the universe? What is the basis of the universe? These questions are discussed in detail in my book — Truth, Faith, and Life. In this Chapter, I will only briefly outline a framework of these issues. Readers are encouraged to read that book in its entirety.

II

The Big Bang is thought of being a state of infinity either in temperature, density or energy by most modern physicists, but this state of infinity cannot be expressed in terms of physics equations. All physics equations have to be normalized, meaning that it cannot diverge into infinity. Thus, the question of how an infinity is transformed into finite cannot be answered by physics under its current restraint. A new physics is needed. Fortunately, two infinities, countable and uncountable, are formally recognized by mathematicians today. Both of these infinities are clearly defined in terms of Set Theory and Number Theory; thus, we can deal with these infinities with logic and understanding.

The countable infinity can be understood by counting, 1, 2, 3,..., at least theoretically; this is why it is called countable infinity. Nonetheless, this simple procedure, counting, does not really transform infinity into finite and vice versa. In order to create, either from nothing to something or from infinity to finite, God must accomplish this task by using only a few basic building blocks. The counting procedure involves an infinite number of different kinds of building blocks; thus, it is not a suitable candidate.

The Standard Model of elementary particle physics is a great achievement in the 20th century. It affirms that our mortal universe is composed of only two kinds of quark, up- and down- quark. On the other hand, it is surprised by two unexpected phenomena. First, although only two quarks are needed to construct the entire "present" universe, three families of quark (2 in each family) were discovered in laboratories. Why?

Why are there "three" families instead of one? Are there two more universes somewhere in addition to ours?

Second, Standard Model very accurately predicted the mass of many new particles, such as W- and Z-boson, but in its framework many parameters do not have any theoretical foundations but were forced into equations by the demands of experimental data. This fact gave rise to two questions. Why shall there be a logic gap? Why should those parameters have the values they have and no other possible alternative?

In the equations of Standard Model, there are two very important angles, the Cabibbo angle (13.5 degrees) and the Weinberg angle (28.8 degrees). Not only does the validity of the Standard Model depend upon these specific values, but the universe is indeed constructed with these precise angles. But, why? Today, no physicist besides me understands the reason why.

These two angles are the results of infinite to finite transformation. As I have stated above, the countable infinity contains an infinite amount of numbers, so it cannot be transformed into finite in terms of numbers. On the other hand, the countable infinity can be transformed into finite with a procedure of trisecting an angle. It takes a countable infinite number of steps to trisect any given angle by using only a compass and a straight edge, which are the only tools available for God. Please see my book — Super Unified Theory — for exactly how this trisecting procedure works. I will give only a brief outline of this issue at the end of this chapter.

Nonetheless, a philosophical explanation of why this mortal world is a triune universe can be given here. The word "process" needs to be clearly defined. Many people murmur the word "process" or the phrase of "process theology" without knowing what the word "process" is and means. For many people, "process" always means the association with "time," but this is a very bad definition. "Process" can be defined in terms of a new causal law. That a cause causes an effect is a process. The effect of a cause is often not a single outcome but many possibilities. In the universe, the number of these possibilities is often finite, but it is infinite in the immortal sphere. Moreover, a cause and an effect can appear at exactly the same time. When two rigid bodies collide, the force (cause) and the acceleration (effect) will appear at exactly the same time. Furthermore, the divine creation "process" transforms timelessness into a timed world; time is created by this process. Thus, process can be independent of "time" although many processes are associated with time.

Furthermore, every process must consist of at least three subjects or entities, of a trine. The process of measuring time needs three subjects — event (1), event (2) and a watch. The process of measuring a distance needs point (a), point (b) and a yard stick. The process of clapping hands needs the will to clap, the action of clapping and the non-escapable consequence — the effect of clapping. Any process from A to B must travel on and bridge over the difference (the C) between the two.

Every process can be sustained if and only if it is a trine. Most species have a male, female then a new generation. The virgin birth process (partenogenesis) seemingly violates this rule, but it does not. In the case of partenogenesis, the mother is in fact two entities, being a daughter first then mother; thus this process is sustained by [(daughter) Mother] begetting daughter. Any process from A to B can never form a sustainable process, but A to B then A is always an eternal process.

In fact, the indivisible Oneness can be preserved to be indivisible Oneness if and only if it is divided into three. Every dividing "process" divides "Oneness" into three parts — the dividing force and two disjointed parts. By definition, this dividing process (force) can be nothing other than the Oneness itself; thus, the Oneness remains to be Oneness after it has been divided into three parts. In other words, God creates the Universe and its ghost partner without losing any of His own essence.

In Taoism, Yin and Yang come out of Tai Ch'i but are unable to dissect Tai Ch'i; thus, Yin-Yang and Tai Ch'i are a trine, as being both the Oneness and three separated entities. Buddhism divides the Oneness into the Unborn God and the wheel of samsara; thus the salvation of Buddha is needed to unite all immortal souls with the Unborn God, thus to return the division to Oneness. The Christian Trinity is a forced consequence of this triune phenomenon. Jesus can never be the witness and the messenger of God unless there is the Oneness, God. God can no longer be the Oneness after there is a witness of God. Jesus' message will also absolutely have no value if there is no audience to hear it; thus the church must be the holy spirit.

In short, this mortal world is a triune universe. Not only are both time and space trisected but every process must be a trine. As I stated in Chapter IV, even God is a trine, being the union of nothingness, infinity and the utmost chaos.

III

Since the infinite to finite transformation is done by a procedure of trisecting, not only both "time" and "space" must be trisected but the trisected thing (angle) must be the basic building block of the universe. Indeed, they are.

In 1979, I proposed a prequark model. The entire universe is constructed with two basic building blocks, Vacutron (vacuum or nothingness) and Angultron (Trisected angle).

Since space is trisected, space is divided into three seats. For each seat, it can be either empty (Vacutron) or occupied (Angultron). Thus, only four different kinds of particles can be formed:

1) A particle with all seats which are occupied by Angultrons carries one unit of electric charge, and it is named electron or lepton.

2) A particle with two seats which are occupied by Angultrons carries 2/3 units of electric charge, and it is named UP quark.

3) A particle with only one seat which is occupied by Angultron carries 1/3 units of electric charge, and it is named DOWN quark.

4) A particle with no seat which is occupied by Angultron carries zero units of electric charge, and it is named neutrino.

Furthermore, for a given quark, there are three ways to arrange the seating, and each way is distinguishable from others. Physicists have chosen three color labels to identify these differences. So, two quarks (Up and DOWN) evolve into six distinguishable quarks. The entire "present" universe is constructed with these eight elementary particles (six quarks and two leptons, and their structure can be represented with the following formulas.

Electron is -(A, A, A1) A is Angultron
Neutrino is (V, V, V1) V is Vacutron

For quarks, there are three varieties for each, and they are identified with three color labels, red, yellow and blue.

	Red	Yellow	Blue
Up quark	(V, A, A1)	(A, V, A1)	(A, A, V1)
DOWN quark	-(A, V, V1)	-(V, A, V1)	-(V, V, A1)

Two notions shall be mentioned here. First, the quark color corresponds to a special seating arrangement. I have chosen the first seat to be red, yellow for the second seat, blue for the third. The quark color is identified by the seat's color which is occupied by a minority prequark. For example, V is the minority prequark in (V, A, A1), and it sits on the red seat; so, (V, A, A1) has a red color. The prequarks (A or V) themselves are colorless. Second, there is a number 1 attached on the third seat. Not only space is trisected, time is also trisected. The life time of the universe is divided into three stages, and they are represented by three generations of quarks. These three generations are identified with three numbers, 1, 2 and 3. They are attached to the third seat. The formulas for a second generation elementary particles are as following:

Muon is -(A, A, A2)

Muon neutrino is (V, V, V2)

There are two quarks, Charm and Strange.

	Red	Yellow	Blue
Charm quark	(V, A, A2)	(A, V, A2)	(A, A, V2)
Strange quark	-(A, V, V2)	-(V, A, V2)	-(V, V, A2)

The formulas for third generation particles are:

Tau is -(A, A, A3)

Tau neutrino is (V, V, V3)

There are also two quarks Top and Bottom.

	Red	Yellow	Blue
Top quark	(V, A, A3)	(A, V, A3)	(A, A, V3)
Bottom quark	-(A, V, V3)	-(V, A, V3)	-(V, V, A3)

These generations are three colors (genecolor), and they obey the color complementary rules, such as 2 is the complement of (1, 3) and 3 the complement of (1, 2). In the 1st order, genecolor 2 can be represented as (1, 3); in the 2nd order genecolor 2 can be represented as (1, (1, 2)). In fact, the Muon decay is caused entirely by this genecolor force. Muon will decay into electron, electron neutrino and muon neutrino, that is, -(A, A, A2) becomes electron -(A, A, A1), electron neutrino (V, V, V1) and muon neutrino (V, V, V2). Obviously, the genecolor 2 of muon transforms into (1, 1, 2) and the total Angultrons are also conserved. Nonetheless, the Vacutrons, being vacuum, are not conserved.

In my Super Unified Theory, the quark colors are properties of space, being expressed in term of "seats". The generations (families) of quarks are properties of time. Thus, a particle has no independent entity but is embedded in both space and time. In short, a particle manifests when prequarks (especially Angultron) fall in or drop out of those seats.

IV

The above prequark model not only is consistent with the Standard Model but goes much beyond it. First, the quark colors arise from the trisected space and the generations of quark from the trisected time. Second, the process of trisecting is a procedure of countable infinity to finite transformation. Today, this trisecting theology is supported by experimental physics and cosmology. The trisected quark colors are demanded by experimental data in elementary particle physics, and it has been universally accepted. On the other hand, although currently only three families (generations) of elementary particles are discovered, the Standard Model does not provide a theoretical framework for this trisecting phenomenon. Fortunately, this trisected quark generations are affirmed by two independent studies. From cosmology, the helium is the most abundant of the nuclei synthesized by Big Bang; thus its quantity can be measured with the greatest accuracy. The observed data suggests there are at most four generations of elementary particles. From elementary particle physics, after we are able to produce W- and Z-bosons in large quantity, their decaying paths can be observed and their decaying rate can be measured with the greatest accuracy. Today, the observed data virtually rules out the possibility of the fourth generation particles. In short, the prequark model is the last consequence of searching for the foundation of this mortal universe.

On the other hand, the concepts of time and space in prequark model are defined in physics mainly in terms of operational definition, meaning by being able to measure these variables without the concern of where and how these variables arise. From a theological view point, both time and space are undefined, meaningless null words. Where and how do time and space arise?

No doubt, God creates time, then space manifests itself as the result of this flowing time. But, how? How does God create time?

As I stated before, there is another infinity, the uncountable infinity which is a much higher infinity than the countable infinity. Can this uncountable infinity be transformed into finite?

God is not a being, nor a "state" but an eternal process, the infinite recursion from absoluteness to relativity (the mortal universe) then back to absoluteness. This means that God must wholeheartedly be transformed into finite so this eternal process can be complete. The uncountable infinity must be transformed into finite somehow. But, how?

Infinities have one very important characteristic, softness. All finite numbers are very rigid. Three is larger than two. Three trillion is larger than three trillion minus one. On the other hand, infinity is very soft. Infinity plus one trillion is still infinity. We can even compress an infinite amount of a thing into infinity but will not increase its size. Thus, this characteristic of softness must manifest in some ways in the mortal universe.

Softness, as defined above, really means absoluteness; no amount of external force can either increase or decrease its size. Surprisingly, relativity also means softness according to the Relativity Theory; both space and time can be compressed or stretched. From this point of view, not only are absoluteness and relativity indeed identical but time and space must be the result of this uncountable infinity to finite transformation. But, how? And, what is uncountable infinity?

Uncountable infinity is clearly defined in mathematics; it can be represented with the tail of the number Pi (3.14159...). There is an uncountable infinite number of digits in the tail of Pi. Thus, to transform uncountable infinity to finite is the same as to square or triangle a circle. The order of symmetry of a circle is infinite, but it is finite for a square (four) or a triangle (three).

This squaring a circle problem is now at least three thousand years old, and we now know that it cannot be accomplished by using only a compass and a straight edge. The compass and straight edge are "rigid" tools and can never probe the region of softness. Nonetheless, a circle can be transformed into a triangle with a soft (uniformly moving) compass which is Archimedes' spiral (see my book — Super Unified Theory — for details).

Obviously, only a dynamical moving compass (Archimedes' spiral) can transform the character of softness of uncountable infinity into finite, and this Archimedes' spiral is the projection of a time cone. In other words, "time" is the consequence of this "uncountable infinity to finite transformation". Thus, time retains the character of softness, and this softness character of time is described in the Relativity Theory. Space is the direct consequence of flowing time and will be discussed more at the end of this chapter.

V

Now, both time and space are clearly defined in terms of how and where they arise. Time arises from a triune transformation — the uncountable infinity to finite transformation, and space manifests from time; then, the countable infinity to finite transformation trisects time into three generations and trisects space into three quark colors (seats). These seven color dimensions — three generations (genecolor), three quark colors and the colorlessness — give rise to the prequark model. This is exactly how the essence of God, the infinities, has transformed into the mortal universe.

There is only one God (infinite) but many infinity(ies). Any difference in finite (being — associates with time and is mortal) causes a difference in essence, but the difference in "Infinite" will not change the essence of the Infinite (God). Infinite minus infinite is still Infinite. Because the essence of the Infinite is immutable, an infinite number of finites (beings) can be pulled out (creation) of the Infinite without changing the essence of the Infinite (God).

Thus, there are more features of this mortal universe than we have just discussed. Again, these features present themselves in forms of paradoxes. They are not theological paradoxes as described in Chapter IV but are cosmological puzzles. The most intriguing one is the homogeneous and the lumpy paradox.

With all attempts, cosmologists affirm time and again that the current lumpy collection of stars and galaxies were in fact arising from an absolute smooth and uniform soup of matter and energy. Why and how? How can a bowl of absolute uniform soup turns into a pan of lumpy dumplings? This question is the same as how orderliness comes out of chaos.

In 1948, George Gamow put forward the idea of the Big Bang theory. This Big Bang theory predicted the quantity of Helium in the universe, and it was quickly confirmed. In 1964, its prediction on the cosmic radiation background was also confirmed; thus, it became a widely accepted theory. Nonetheless, it still faced three major difficulties — the horizon problem, the flatness problem and the large-scale structure problem.

The universe today includes a vast number of regions that could never have been in causal contact at any stage of their entire history according to the Big Bang theory. In other words, those regions must come from two or more distinguishable origins and cannot be from the single Big Bang event. Simply, the observation contradicts with the theory. This is the "horizon problem".

Then, there is the "flatness problem". According to the Big Bang theory, the universe shall become more curved as time passes. But observation reveals that the spatial geometry on the part of the universe we can observe is extremely flat. Then, the Big Bang theory cannot adequately explain the origin of large-scale structures, such as galaxies.

Because of these difficulties, the Big Bang theory was modified into having two Bangs instead of the original one — the inflationary Bang and the old fashion one. During the inflationary Bang, the universe would have increased in size by an astounding factor of 30th power of 10.

With this inflationary scenario, all three difficulties are resolved, sort of at least. It solves the horizon problem because the observed universe moved out of each other's horizon because of this huge inflation. The flatness problem vanishes because the huge expansion blows the universe up so much that it appears flat. The large structure problem is also solved because the sudden expansion would have locked in quantum fluctuations that could have "seeded" the formation of large-scale structures.

This inflationary scenario solved three problems, but at the same time it gives rise to three new questions. First, the rate of inflation is faster than the light speed; thus a new physics is needed. At present time, no such new physics law is found. Second, why would such a moment of inflation happen? In fact, all known traditional physics laws break down at this point. Third, what happened before inflation? In short, the inflationary scenario does not really solve the homogeneous-lumpy problem but only pushes it further back in time.

In addition to these problems, there is another problem. With all current data, all galaxies have not enough mass to hold themselves together according to the current calculation for gravitational force. Many models have been presented to deal with these two issues. Today, the prevailing theory is the "cold dark matter model". It says that there is much dark matter that accounts for the missing mass. Nonetheless, this dark matter cannot be the regular building blocks — such as: proton, neutrons or any hadron — because they interact too strongly with light. This kind of interaction would definitely have prevented the original uniform soup to transform into the current state of the universe. Thus, all missing mass must be composed with "cold" dark matter. It must be "cold"; so it will not interact with the ordinary matter strongly but only makes a contribution to gravitation. So far, all candidates except one (neutrino) are fictitious particles.

The dream for neutrino to possess mass was broken after the observation of the 1987 super nova. The neutrinos and visible light of that event arrived on earth simultaneously after travelling almost a quarter millions of years; thus the neutrinos must fly at the same speed as light. According to the Relativity Theory, the neutrino thus cannot have any "rest" mass; so, neutrino cannot be accountable for the missing mass in the cold dark matter model.

Many dreamers insist that neutrinos arrived 10 minutes later than light after a quarter million years of flight; thus it can still have a tiny rest mass with the upper limit as 3 electron volts. Since it "could" have a near infinite number of neutrino, neutrinos can still account for the missing mass. Nonetheless, the entire "cold dark matter model" is now officially dead after the recent x- and gamma ray telescopes sky survey from satellites.

According to my Super Unified Theory, this missing mass puzzle can be easily resolved. The time quanta at the present state of the universe is so small, and it seems to be an instantaneous point on a continuous time coordinate. But, in the early stage of the universe, the time quanta could be a million times larger; thus the gravitational constant was many folds larger, and those old galaxies were held together by a much stronger gravitational constant. No missing mass is needed for those old galaxies.

On the other hand, the homogenous and lumpy transformation puzzle remains to be unsolved. The inflationary scenario only provides a mechanism to "seed" the lumps during the inflationary period but does not provide answers for the pre-inflationary era. Not only did the universe start out from a bowl of absolute homogeneous soup, but the 2nd law of thermodynamics also guarantees that the universe will eventually return to that state of absolute homogeneity. In fact, this homogeneous-lumpy duality is not a unique problem only belonging to the creation myth; it is a general phenomenon embedded in the Cosmos. Then, why and how do lumps come out of this absolute homogeneity?

We can answer the question of why quite easily. God is an eternal process from absoluteness to relativity then back to absoluteness, and this process is expressed in terms of the transformation from the absolute homogeneity to lumps then back to the absolute homogeneity. But the question of how remains to be unanswered.

How? How did the absolute homogeneous state of pre-inflationary evolve into the current state of a lumpy collection of stars and galaxies. Up to now, there is no answer for this question in both physics laws or cosmology models. In fact, all known traditional physics laws break down at this point. On the other hand, this transformation is guaranteed by the Ramsey Theorem in mathematics.

Ramsey theorem states, "If the number of objects in a set is sufficiently large and each pair of objects has one of a number of relations, then there is always a subset containing a certain number of objects where each pair has the same relation." The above mathematical jargon might not be easily understood; it can be restated in common words, "Any large structure, regardless of how homogeneous or how chaotic it is, will necessarily contain an 'orderly' substructure." In other words, the absolute homogeneity itself is the "source" of all lumps.

Perhaps, all physicists are not impressed by a mathematical guarantee that the homogeneous Big Bang must evolve into a lumpy collection of galaxies. They want to know the exact mechanism of how.

VI

The answer of how lies in the 2nd law of thermodynamics. All physicists today interpret the 2nd law to mean the following: 1) It guarantees that all "orderly" states will eventually move toward disorderly states, or lumpy states to homogeneous ones. 2) Heat cannot be converted 100% into "work". A large portion of the heat will be lost into entropy.

These interpretations are not only correct but are the driving force of modern technology. On the other hand, every half-emptied bottle is also a half-filled one. The 2nd law not only guarantees the trend from order (lumpy) to disorder (homogeneous) but also guarantees the creation of order (work) from disorder (heat).

Without the 2nd law, we can never build automobiles, refrigerators, and many other things. The creation of order from disorder seemingly does not happen on a universal scale in nature but is expressed only by two exceptions — the life forces and the creating ability of intelligence.

Only lives can reverse the nature trend of going to disorder and create very complicated orderly states — genes and societies. What are lives and intelligence then?

Are lives not part of nature? Are lives able to escape from the laws of nature? No, absolutely not! Then, what is the difference between being and nonbeing?

Life is not a "state" but a process, from birth, growth, aging to death. In fact, it is a ball-donut transformation, beginning from a single cell (ball) to a donut-shaped system (with digestive track). In my book — Truth, Faith, and Life — life is expressed in terms of seven color dimensions, and it is the same as all nonbeing that can also be expressed with seven colors. In short, the lifeless world is indeed alive. There is no difference between the two trends, going to chaos (entropy) from orderly states or creating orders from the homogeneity.

Not only is the above conclusion correct and is unifying being and nonbeing into a harmonic oneness, but it also helps our quest to understand "how" life can reverse the nature trend of going to chaos, at least while it is alive. Time and again, we experienced that the question itself is its own answer. God created the relative world because only relativity can preserve the absoluteness. Softness, the essence of absoluteness, is preserved only by relativity. Again, the Ramsey theorem points out that "disorder" is synonymous with "order". Thus, lives and intelligence must be the manifestations of Chaos. Today, neuroscience discovers that the physiology of perception can only be achieved by the chaotic activities of the brain. Only a chaotic system can amplify the very small external stimulus. Only a chaotic system can produce infinite novel patterns over and over.

Now, we have come full circle. God is the utmost chaos, and lives are the manifestations of chaos; thus lives are the manifestation of God. God is embodied in lives, and intelligence is a force that creates order out of chaos. In fact, "order" can be defined in terms of entropy and intelligence. Bacteria decomposes many things and pushes those things from orderly states into disorderly ones, but at the same time it is the only way that they nurture their lives which are amazingly highly ordered states. The stronger a force can disorder its neighborhood, the higher order it can create for itself. Honey bees have genetically coded intelligence; they create a orderly hive. We humans have unbounded intelligence, thus created a super organism — the human society. Thus, entropy is the result of the force of orderliness although entropy is also the force that destroys the orderly states. It is both the cause and the effect. In life, there is a seed of death. In death, there is a seed of life. Both life and death belong to the world of appearances, but existence lies beyond both.

The above discussion clearly pointed out a new truth, "the self-cause" that the cause is the effect and that the effect is the cause. Furthermore, the question is the answer, and the answer is the question. The 2nd law of thermodynamics forces all orderly states into disorderly states, but at exactly the same time it also creates the orderly states. This 2nd law is a self-cause.

Life is expressed in terms of this 2nd law, entropy. Life lives on or sucks life from its neighborhood by making its neighborhood less lively, thus higher entropy. The higher entropy a life can cause to its neighborhood, the higher orderliness this life has.

Thus, disorder is caused by orderliness, and orderliness is caused by disorder. But, which one, disorder or order, comes out first? And, how?

In fact, the law of order and the law of disorder is the same law. As I stated before, disorder is the trait of symmetry, and orderliness is the result of symmetry breaking. God is not only the perfect symmetry but also a simultaneous broken symmetry. Thus, orderliness and disorder came out at exactly the same time. God is the utmost chaos and the utmost order at the same time. God is the destroyer and the creator of all lives. Thus, the bowl of absolute homogeneous soup is in fact the cause and the result of the pan of lumpy dumplings. The original homogeneous soup at the Big Bang will inevitably evolve into a lumpy collection of galaxies because it is not only a bowl of lifeless uniform energy and matter but is a spirit which can and must create order out of chaos. Indeed, the lifeless world is alive.

Everyone has some fuzzy understanding about the word "spirit," but it is in fact an undefined, meaningless null word up to this point. A spirit is an intelligence. Intelligence can be defined in terms of a symmetry breaking process. Intelligence is a force that creates orderliness.

Every individual proton is a symmetry in terms of quark color. But, when two protons approach each other, its quark color symmetry breaks, and this residual color force binds them into a nucleus. A nucleus has a much higher order than two free protons. With a similar mechanism, the electromagnetic symmetry breaks to bind atoms into molecules. When many molecules form a helix chain, the space symmetry is broken. When a mutation occurs in a gene, the double helix symmetry is broken. This mutation process is the force of evolution. As I stated in my book — Truth,

Faith, and Life — the evolution process is the source of intelligence. On the other hand, intelligence is the source and the force of evolution. Today, human intelligence not only changes the landscape of the earth but is altering the evolution paths of many species by genetic engineering.

Thus, life is a spirit, and spirit is an intelligence. Intelligence is the symmetry breaking process which is the essence of God. Intelligence is a self-cause. Every self-cause is a trine. Intelligence causes both orderliness (being) and entropy (nonbeing).

God is the supreme intelligence, and the Big Bang is a spirit embodied from God. God is the union of both symmetry and symmetry breaking, of both order and chaos, of both being and nonbeing and of both mortal and immortal. God is the reconciling force for all paradoxes. Thus, God must be a Trine, two opposites and one unifying force. Goodness and evil come out of God, and God will then judge them. The goodness will surly receive award, the evil the retribution.

After 30 years of searching, I reached a conclusion that is the same as Jason's notion, when he was only 7 years old, that God is the answer for all puzzles. Maybe, we all are just wasting our time. We should simply go to church every Sunday and not ask any questions. In fact, I did know the answer also at age seven. On the other hand, I feel much better now by knowing why and how that answer is the answer, and why and how there cannot be any other answer.

VII

This section is somewhat technical. You can go ahead to the next chapter if physics or mathematics is not your favored subject. Now, I am briefly outlining how God trisects space or time. This issue has been addressed in my book — Super Unified Theory, so I will only list some facts here. Readers are encouraged to read the original treatise.

Fact 1: Space is the twin brother of "time". They are inseparable. Superficially, there are one time coordinate and three space dimensions, but in fact there are sixty-four space dimensions according to my Super Unified Theory (page 26). These 64 dimensions are eventually reduced to 7 color dimensions because of the interdependent relationship among them.

Fact 2: Only forty-eight of these space dimensions are occupied with matter; the remaining sixteen are vacuum states.

Fact 3: Half of the forty-eight dimensions are occupied by anti-matter. Thus, 24 fundamental particles (18 quarks and 6 leptons) are needed to represent the material world.

Fact 4: the wholeness is represented by a circle (2 Pi).

With these facts, three numbers (Pi, 64 and 24) become the foundation of this trisecting process. Since there are 64 dimensions, the wholeness (2 Pi) must be divided into 64 parts times and again, beginning from the 1st order, then 2nd, ... to infinite. The sum of this geometric series is 1.0516213.... Obviously, the wholeness cannot be divided evenly. Thus, the best way to divide is to start getting rid of the half of the uneven part. Why half? The other half is the insurance of a safety margin. In fact, this "half" becomes the unit for trisecting. I call it A(0), and it is equal to 1.47895 degrees [57.3 * (1.0516213 - 1)/2].

After having a unit, God is now able to trisect space. Since only 24 dimensions are occupied by matter, each of these twenty-four are given one A(0) first; then the rest is divided evenly into 24 parts, and this new angle A(1) is equal to 13.5 degrees which is exactly the same as the Cabibbo angle which was derived from experimental data. A(1) = (2 Pi - 24 * A(0))/24.

The second order (way) to divide the wholeness is by subtracting what was given out the first time (A(0) and A(1)), then divides it by 24. Since it is a second order division, it has to be doubled. A(2) = 2 * (2 Pi - A(1) - A(0))/24 = 28.8 degrees which again is exactly the same as the Weinberg angle.

Both the Cabibbo and Weinberg angles are foundations of the Standard Model. They are free parameters. They are forced into the equations of the Standard Model by the demand of experimental data. Now, I have derived them from a numerology based only on my theology.

Institut für wissenschaftliche Zusammenarbeit

Institute for Scientific Co-operation
Federal Republic of Germany

Instituto de Colaboración Científica
República Federal de Alemania

Dr. Jeh-Tween Gong
P.O. Box 1753
Bristol, VA 24203
U.S.A.

26. Oktober 1991

Dear Dr. Gong,

You were kind enough to send your book "Truth, Faith and Life" to our institute and our journal "Universitas". In this work, you deal with the position of truth in this field. Your book is an important account that deserves to find thorough and numerous readers. The problem of truth has been treated in depth in our country both by theologians and philosophers (e.g. Hegel), and remains a central problem for spiritual development today. As on P.83f. of your book you also deal more closely with other religions from this point of view, I should like to add that the Catholic theologian Hans Kung of the University af Tubingen has described these encounters in his books and a large symposium.

With our thanks to you once again, and good wishes for your further work.

Yours sincerely,

h. hür

(Prof. Dr. H.W, Bahr)

Chapter XI
The Souls

It is very obvious that there is a striking difference between the animal which a moment ago was alive and is now dead. The ancients postulated a notion of soul that is the principle in all living things, and death occurs when the soul departs from the body.

Socrates argued that the knower must be like the known; thus, the soul's reflexive knowledge knows its own existence. There are a few very obvious facts pointing out the existence of soul to soul itself and to others.

First, the living matter possesses distinctive powers and performs functions — self-nutrition, growth and reproduction — which are not present in any degree in the realm of the nonliving.

Second, death is a process which only living matter undergoes. A quenched candle can always be lit again, but a plucked rose must wither.

Third, the living thing can only come from the living substance of another living thing, but death carries the living to cross the gap between the living and the nonliving. Therefore, life or birth is incompatible with death, and death may not be able to annihilate life entirely.

II

All lives have different levels of consciousness. Without the consciousness, the meaning of life and its existence is certainly threatened and in doubt. Therefore, it is ultimately impossible to conceive of the permanent loss of this consciousness. We find the concept of total dissipation of self after death much more difficult to accept than a postulated notion of soul that exists after death.

The notion of soul not only manifests itself from the facts that life and death are quite different but also solves a major religious and metaphysical issue — the immortality. The notion of immortality is required not only by religions but also by metaphysics. There are many things — such as ideas, intellect, belief, compassion and love — which clearly cannot refer to bodies, the only available corporeal objects, must therefore refer to some incorporeal objects. By definition, an incorporeal substance would be naturally incorruptible and therefore immortal. Soul can be not only the life-force of a life but is also the aggregate of these immortal substance.

Furthermore, the notion of soul can solve another major issue — the moral truth. It is very obvious that justice cannot always prevail on earth. Then, is there moral truth and justice? With a notion of immortal soul, any earthly unjust can be corrected in the after life, and the moral truths will be upheld.

It seems that the notion of soul is not only valid but solid and sound. Nonetheless, the smart alecks of modern science reject the notion of soul because of their mechanism doctrine. This doctrine reduces all phenomena to the interaction of moving parts or particles. They claim that no new principle is needed or is found to explain the physical phenomena of life; the laws of physics and chemistry suffice. Biophysics and biochemistry simply deal with the mechanics of more complex material systems. The apparent difference in function between living and nonliving things represents the same functions. They are altered only in appearance by the more complex organization of the matter which is called living. William James even concluded that "the substantial soul ... explains nothing and guarantees nothing," because he finds the concept of soul useless "so far as accounting for the actually verified facts of conscious experience goes." But, those modern scientists ignore the intellectual and spiritual phenomena of life. They deny the very acts they are acting — the thinking, the investigation and the debates. There is no traditional physics or chemistry law that can generate or control those intellectual and spiritual acts. Therefore, no further discussion is warranted to address this smart aleck doctrine any further.

The notion of soul solves many metaphysical and religious issues but at the same time creates many new questions. Does a soul exist before being united to the body? How does it exist when it exists separately or apart from the body? In short, what is a soul? Where is it? And, how does it live and function both in the body and apart from the body?

There are only two traditional doctrines — Chinese tradition and Indo-European doctrine — which are worthy of any discussion. These two doctrines view death quite differently. One sees death as an existential treat. The other accepts it lyrically, neither fantasying it nor fearing of it.

III

The notion of soul in Vedic tradition is clearly defined. Soul is the true self. Sickness and death are real enough, but they occur only on the profane level of samsaric (cyclic) existence; they do not touch the real self, the soul. The body is only a temporary shelter for the immortal soul.

"The Body change, but the soul remains the same. As the embodied soul continually passes, in this body, from boyhood to youth to old age, the soul similarly passes into another body at death. Just as a person puts on new garments, giving up old ones, similarly, the soul accepts new material bodies, giving up the old and useless ones. The soul can never be cut into pieces by any weapon, nor can he be burned by fire, nor moistened by water, nor withered by the wind. It is said that soul is invisible, inconceivable, immutable." (Bhagavad - Gita as it is).

Surprisingly, the notion of immortal soul in the Vedic tradition does not provide any comfort for facing death and is not an answer to the problem of death. This immortal soul is trapped in an eternal cycle of death and rebirth. The soul's transmigration is experienced as bondage, as a tedious burden, as an eternal suffering, from which deliverance is sought.

In the Vedic tradition, both Hinduism and Buddhism affirm the notion of the immortal, karmic soul, meaning that every individual soul exists from the beginningless and remains its existence eternally. They both also divide the "Whole" into three parts. On the one side there is an Unborn God who is utterly transcendent. On the other side, there is an eternal cycle of death and rebirth — the wheel of samsara or the wheel of life. Between the two, there is a giant river. In Buddhism, there are three vehicles — Mahayana, Hinayana and Vajrayana (the Tantric tradition) — to help the individual soul to cross this giant river and to unite it with the Unborn God. The state of this union is Nirvana. In Nirvana, the soul is liberated from all sufferings and from all human predicaments — birth, death, sickness and all sorts of misfortunes. In Nirvana, all desires are extinct; therefore, only bliss remains. In Nirvana, all ignorance and delusion are eliminated; only wisdom remains.

By Buddhist's definition, there is "nothing" in Nirvana. Thus, neither bliss nor wisdom can stay in Nirvana. Even the immortal soul is annihilated in Nirvana, as a drop of water unites with the ocean, and the drop of water vanishes and becomes one with the ocean.

Not surprisingly, Buddhism, demanded by its religious methodology and definition, at this point turns against its initial position of affirming the existence of the immortal soul. The Buddhists, therefore, claim that there is no enduring individual self or soul. At this point, they even deny the existence of the Unborn God.

Thus, Buddhism asserts that all things are compounded, and those are in a constant state of rearrangement of certain primary material and psychic elements of existence. Life is only a constant arrangement and rearrangement of the things, material and events. Everything is in flux. There is no stable, unchanging personal substance or soul beneath the flux.

Buddhism treats all issues with a paradoxical approach, first to affirm a premise then to deny it at the end. So, Buddha on the one hand provides three vehicles to deliver all individual souls from an eternal trap, the wheel of life, to the yonder shore of Nirvana, but on the other hand proclaims that "there is no Nirvana for the Buddhas (The Lankavatara Scripture)."

By denying the ultimate reality of the immortal soul, Buddhism steps back to square one, sort of at least. To overcome the problem of death the second time around, Buddhists meditate on death, experience the proleptical death experience and perform the rite of passage. In other words, the enlightened Buddhists experience the death of the "Immortal Soul" before the death of the body, and Buddha called this the "Inconceivable Transformation Death". After this inconceivable transformation death is achieved, the Bodhisattva will not only be able to escape from the eternal trap, the wheel of samsara, and is able to enter the Nirvana, but will also obtain the transcendental magical power.

IV

Plato represents the other half of Indo-European tradition. His position on soul is quite similar to the Vedic tradition on two accounts, the idea of immortality and of universality. In Phaedo, Plato argues for the existence of soul before it joins a body and for its existence after it leaves the body to dwell apart before entering another body. He also classifies souls in many kinds, vegetative, sensitive (animal) and rational (human). On the other hand, the Vedic teaching further differentiates the human soul with a caste system. In short, Plato's teaching is almost identical to the Vedic doctrine.

The Vedic tradition was challenged by Buddha on a very deep metaphysical level, by accepting it first then denying it at the end. Plato's teaching was outrightly rejected on a very superficial level by his student Aristotle. Aristotle flatly rejected the notion of immortality. He insisted that the soul and body come into existence together when the organism is generated. Therefore, Aristotle said, "The soul cannot be without a body.

Yet it cannot be a body; it is not a body, but something relative to a body. This is why it is in a body and a body of a definite kind. The soul is inseparable from its body." Aristotle's argument is very shallow, based on a very primitive understanding of some very primitive concepts — matter, form and potentiality. Nonetheless, his nearly meaningless argument did provoke two new streams of thought, Descartes theory of immortality and the Judeo-Christian dogma of shade.

Descartes tried to revive the notion of immortality by identifying the soul with rational thinking substance. He wrote, "I saw that I could conceive that I had no body, and that there was no world nor place where I might be; but yet that I could not for all that conceive that I was not." From the fact that in the very act of doubting the existence of everything else, he could not doubt that he was doubting, and hence thinking; he assures himself of his own existence, or, more precisely, of the existence of himself as a thinking being. He wrote, "I knew that I was a substance the whole essence or nature of which is to think, and that for its existence there is no need of any place, nor does it depend on any material thing; so that this 'me,' that is to say, the soul by which what I am, is entirely distinct from body, and is even more easy to know than is the latter; and even if the body were not, the soul would not cease to be what it is." From this logic, he obtained his famous Cogito — "I think; therefore, I am." Then, he further concluded, "Our soul is in its nature entirely independent of the body, and in consequence that it is not liable to die with it. And then, inasmuch as we observe no other causes capable of destroying it, we are naturally inclined to judge that it is immortal. ... Any persons who are not sufficiently persuaded of the existence and the immortality of the soul by the reasons which I have brought forward, I wish them to know that all other things of which they perhaps think themselves more assured (such as possessing a body, and that there are stars and an earth and so on) are less certain."

Descartes did reaffirm the notion of immortal soul after Aristotle had destroyed it, but his notion of soul connotes mind, thinking and intellect. As for Descartes, soul is then not thought necessary to explain the phenomena of life in plants and animals. He took the souls away from all plants and animals. Later, Locke tried to mend this terrible mistake, that the word 'soul' is synonymous with the word 'mind,' by conceiving soul in terms of not only rational thought but also sensation, imagination and memory.

Locke then gave souls back to animals but might still exclude plants to have souls.

By the time of Kant, the Western philosophical thought finally had enough of those meaningless arguments on the subjects of souls and immortality. Thus, Kant firmly denied the possibility of proof of immortality or the existence of God. He surrendered himself to his own ignorance and declared that "Freedom","Immortality", and "God" are three basic postulates of practical reason. They are theoretical propositions which are not as such demonstrable, but which are inseparable corollaries of an a priori unconditionally moral law.

V

Surprisingly, all the arguments on soul and immortality from Plato to kant involve only metaphysical and philosophical issues and require no reference to a deity. This is not the case in Judeo-Christian tradition.

We all know that Christian tradition comes from three sources — the heritage of Judaism, the teaching of Jesus, and the philosophy and the theology of pagan doctrine. In short, the Judeo-Christian is a subculture of the Indo-European system, but it made a new hodgepodge out from these varieties of doctrines.

In Jewish thought, death was viewed as terror and as the greatest enemy. "The last enemy that shall be destroyed is death." 1 Corinthians 15:26. Its idea of afterlife was also very immature. Originally, the notion of a soul was not in the Jewish thought. After death, what remains is a shadowy, highly attenuated existence in Sheol — the abyss or underworld where "the shades writhe in fear." The prospect of existence after death as a shade in Sheol is dreary and despondent. Those who go down to Sheol are alienated from the community and even estranged from the worship of God.

"For in death there is no remembrance of thee; in Sheol who can give thee praise?" Psalm 6:5.

"Whatever task lies to your hand, do it with all your might; because in Sheol, for which you are bound, there is neither doing nor thinking, neither understanding nor wisdom." Ecclesiastes 9:10.

Therefore, that the shade, the remains after death, survives in Sheol is not a source of consolation in the face of death, but rather of despair, and it is not a reassurance in the face of death, but rather a source of dread. The shade is not an indestructible soul.

Because in Jewish thought there was no matured conception of soul to resolve the problem of death and afterlife and because to be fully alive as a Jew means to have a body, the problem of death and afterlife could only be solved with the conception of resurrection of the body.

"And many of them that sleep in the dust of the earth shall awake, some to everlasting life, and some to shame and everlasting contempt." Daniel 12:2.

Thus, everyone will resurrect, some to everlasting life and some to everlasting contempt. The resurrection is then neither a solution for facing death nor consolation for the afterlife. Moreover, the resurrected body cannot be this mundane body but a different one. Therefore, Jesus could not be recognized by either his close friend or his disciples after only three days of his death.

"..., she [Mary Magdalene, a very close friend of Jesus]... saw Jesus standing, and knew not that it was Jesus." John 21:14.

"..., came Jesus and stood in the midst, and saith unto them, ..., be shewed unto them his hands and his side. then were the disciples glad." John 21:19-20.

In short, the resurrected body of Jesus cannot be recognized by anyone, even his close friends; all confirmations came from the marks on him. Thus, for many people, this resurrected body could well belong to the one of two thieves who were crucified with Jesus, and no one knew the difference because no one did know according to the Bible. This is the first difficulty for the resurrection dogma.

The second difficulty of this resurrection dogma is the contradictory concepts among Bible books. There is a sequential order that is built in Christian dogma. Christ shall be the "first" resurrection, then those who belong to Christ at Christ's second coming. "Every man in his own order: Christ the first fruits; afterward they that are Christ's at his coming." 1 Corinthians 15:23. But, this claim is contradicted by the most important book of new Testament — The Revelation, which denies Christ to be the first resurrection. "But the rest of the dead lived not again until the thousand years were finished. This is the first resurrection." Revelation 20:5.

Nonetheless, the greatest difficulty is raised by common sense which cannot be overcome easily even with dogmatic faith. What state are the dead in before the resurrection?

Thus, the notion of a soul had to be borrowed from pagan tradition into the later Judaism. Firstly, man was besouled by God as a living soul. "And the Lord God formed man of the dust of the ground, and breathed into his nostrils the breath of life; and man became a living soul." Genesis 2:7.

Secondly, any human, body or soul, has to be mortal because of the original Sin. Death is the punishment from God; thus even a soul cannot escape from death. "And fear not them which kill the body, but are not able to kill the soul; but rather fear him which is able to destroy both soul and body in hell." Matthew 10:28.

Thirdly, the relation of love between the devotee and God was so intense, that it was inconceivable that this relation could be terminated because of the biological death. Therefore, life with God must continue even after the death of the body. "For thou wilt not leave my soul in hell; neither wilt thou suffer thine Holy One to see corruption. Thou wilt shew me the path of life: in they presence is fullness of joy; at they right hand there are pleasures for evermore." Psalms 16: 10-11.

In short, both conceptions of soul and immortality in Judeo-Christian tradition are two phantoms; now they are, now they are not. Their appearance or disappearance entirely depends upon the situation. If a situation needs them, they appear; if not, they vanish without a trace. This Judeo-Christian phantomism is quite different from the approach of Buddhism by accepting them at the beginning then denying them at the end. This Buddha paradox is the essence of Buddha's teaching. On the other hand, many people think that this Christian phantom is an one-sided triangle, it can never be wrong because it has never been right yet. Therefore, nobody can either prove the Christian Trinity doctrine or deny it; it has to be accepted with dogmatic faith. In fact, this one-sided triangle indeed symbolizes the ultimate truth but with a reason different from the Christian dogma.

In conclusion, without a wholehearted acceptance of the pagan idea of the immortal soul, the Christian theology becomes a big hodgepodge. Today, all Christians utter the term of "Immortal Soul" without knowing Christian doctrine indeed rejects the notion of an Immortal Soul. If any individual has an immortal soul, there is no need for a Savior; a teacher like Buddha or Confucius will suffice. Today, all Christians are in fact believing in pagan beliefs.

VI

Gilbert wrote, "This one eminent property is the same which the ancients held to be a soul in the heavens, in the globes, and in the stars, ... The ancient philosopher ... all seek in the world a certain universal soul, and declare the whole world to be endowed with a soul. ... We deem the whole world animate, and all globes, stars, and this glorious earth, too, we hold to be from the beginning by their own souls governed... Pitiable is the state of the stars, object the lot of earth, if this high dignity of soul is denied them, while it is granted to the worm, the ant, the roach, to plants and morels; for in that case, worms, roaches, moths, were more beauteous objects in nature and more perfect, inasmuch as nothing is excellent, nor precious, nor eminent, that hath not a soul." Gilbert's position is only one man's philosophy in Western culture, but it is everyone's belief in China. All Chinese believe in some sort of animism and henotheism.

The animism and the henotheism are united as one belief in China. There is one and only one creator, the Almighty God, Shangti or Tai Ch'i. Shangti, the Almighty God, is a spirit, a Chee. Everything, being or nonbeing, that is created by Shangti has chee. Man has human chee. Stone has rock chee. Moon has Moon chee. Being and nonbeing are all alive. Their chee can interact among one another. The science of Feng Shui was developed to seek harmony between beings and nonbeings. Confucius said, "The worship of Shangti, the Almighty God, is for the purpose of recognizing the supreme rulership of Shangti. The worship of the spirit of Earth is for the purpose of displaying the productivity of the earth. Worship at the ancestral temple is for the purpose of recognizing the ancestry of man. The worship of mountains and rivers is for the purpose of serving the different spirits."

Chinese not only worship one Almighty God but also respect all spirits. They find that the path to unite with God is through a process called Wul-Whal. Wul means things or nonbeings. Whal means "becoming" or "changing into". The Wul-Whal state is a state that one has reached a state of symmetry that he (being) and things (nonbeings) become indistinguishable. This Wul-Whal state is a state of union with God. It is quite different from the state of Nirvana. Nirvana is a state of emptiness and annihilation. Wul-Whal is a state of highest symmetry; the difference between beings and nonbeings vanish. The first step of how to reach this Wul-Whal state was described in a butterfly story told by Chuangtse.

Chuangtse wrote, "Once upon a time, I, Chuang Chou, dreamt I was a butterfly, fluttering hither and thither, to all intents and purposes a butterfly, I was conscious only of my happiness as a butterfly, unaware that I was Chou. Soon I awaked, and there I was, veritably myself again. Now I do not know whether I was then a man dreaming I was a butterfly, or whether I am now a butterfly, dreaming I am a man. Between a man and a butterfly there is necessarily a distinction. The transition is called Wul-Whal. All things are in constant flux and change, but are different aspects of the one."

This butterfly story is often interpreted and understood as the existential anxiety and as the identity crisis by the Western philosophers, but it is in fact the first step to unite with the Almighty God, by breaking the barrier between a man and a creature (a butterfly).

The second step is to break the barrier between being and nonbeing, meaning Wul-Whal. Because of ignorance, many lives want to hold on to life but only eventually lost it. In fact, in life there is the seed of death, and vice versa. Death is not an accident. The body of every life is confined to both space and time, thus must die. On the other hand, when the soul of life is no longer limited to its body but has become all-encompassing, it is no longer confined to time and space, thus becomes immortal. Nonetheless, this ability of Wul-Whal is only an acquired virtue.

Chuangtse wrote, "Four men: Tsesze, Tseyu, Tseli, and Tselai, were conversing together, saying, 'Whoever can make Nonbeing the head, Life the back bone, and Death the tail, and whoever realizes that death and life and being and nonbeing are of one body, that man shall be admitted to friendship with us.' The four looked at each other and smiled, and completely understanding one another, became friends accordingly.

"What we love is the mystery of life. What we hate is corruption in death. But the corruptible in its turn becomes mysterious life, and this mysterious life once more becomes corruptible. If life and death are companions to each other, why should I concerned? How then do I know but that the dead may repent of having previously clung to life?"

All lives are preoccupied with death, not predominantly with analyzing it, but with facing and fearing it, struggling against or embracing it. Death is not merely a biological incident that ends the life function of the body; it reaches into the entire course of life long before the end is reached. Montaigne said, "To philosophize is to learn to die. To die well requires greater moral stamina than to live well." Cicero said, "To study philosophy is nothing but to prepare one's self to die." To die well forms the main structure of Chinese moral values.

Although the Chinese accept death lyrically, they do not romanticize death. On the contrary, to be able to live a long life is considered one of the greatest blessing on earth for all Chinese. The Chinese view life as valuable as death although death is the gate to the eternal home of life.

The Chinese have long understood that the Almighty God is the perfect and the highest symmetry. In God, there is in fact no difference between being and nonbeing, therefore no difference between the living and the dead.

By breaking the barrier between life and death, Chinese people reach the highest symmetry state (Wul-Whal), unite with the Almighty God and obtain Immortality. Anyone who attains the Wul-Whal state before the death of the body will become immortal, a deity at the time of his death, and he will be able to dwell in both the Yin and Yang worlds. Laotse said, "He who dies yet remains has long life." Nonetheless, everyone will eventually enter the Wul-Whal state at the time of bodily death and remains to be a spirit without the body, of course, dwelling only in the Yin domain.

Thus, we are not immortal to the same degree. There are at least four levels of immortality. Immortality through offspring is the lowest; it can be attained without a major effort for the majority of all lives. The second is the immortality of soul that will return to God as a drop of water returns to the ocean. The third is the immortal spirit of individual who has reached the Wul-Whal state. The highest is the immortal of virtue which becomes the essence of mankind, such as: Confucius, Buddha and Jesus who are thought of as still being present today.

VII

All notions of soul discussed above do not violate physics laws. In fact, there are many reasons which demand soul to be a reality. From the view point of a human, only the notion of soul can explain five very important realities — immortality, moral truths, religious craving, the incompatibility between life and death, and the rise of intelligence.

The immortality is a reality, not just a notion. The immortality is the base for all knowledge — philosophy or sciences. All sciences are supported with proofs which are limited in number, in time and in space. Thus, their lasting validity is only guaranteed by the property of immortality.

Furthermore, many subjects are very obvious to be immortal, such as: concepts, forms, truths, etc. We are not only conscious of these immortal subjects but we indeed possess them. We can from concepts and understand forms. We even understand the meaning of immortality. Thus, there must be an "entity" in us which is able to reach the domain of immortal sphere, and it must have the property of immortality.

Moral truths are also realities as I have proved in Chapter VI, but justice does not always prevail on earth. Not only are evil doers often prosperous while righteous people often suffer, but death often strikes indiscriminately with no regard of goodness or evil, of young or old, of rich or poor, or of just or unjust. Thus, there must be a "subject" in us which is able to receive the final justice if the moral truths are indeed realities.

Religious craving is also definitely a reality. Taoism was developed ten millennia ago. Then, there was the Vedic tradition. There was pagan teaching; then Judaism arose. Even at the time of Jesus, the people had only very primitive knowledge of nature, which is the body of God. But all people, since time immemorial and from all corners of the globe, recognize the spirit of God. How does this knowledge come about? There is no answer other than Socrates' argument that the knower must be like the known. It is that the soul's reflexive knowledge knows the spirit of God.

Life can only come from another life, but death bridges over the difference between being and nonbeing. Thus, on the view point of metaphysics, life is incompatible with death. So, death can never be equal but must be either more or less than life. Since death seemingly is not a creation process, it is very difficult to be more. Thus, death cannot annihilate life entirely, and "something" must be left over after the death of a life.

As I stated in the last Chapter, life does not live on nonbeing but creates it. Life creates death, thus is the master of death. Life is and has intelligence, and intelligence is a self-cause. Every self-cause is a trine which is an eternal process. Although the material body of a life will surly disintegrate sooner or later, the intelligence of a life can never be annihilated. Descartes wrote, "... for its existence there is no need of any place, nor does it depend on any material thing, ..., the soul by which what I am ... could not cease to be what it is."

Among religions, the Chee of Taoism is the only doctrine that really understood the meaning of self-cause, of intelligence and of being and nonbeing. As for Taoism, even nonbeing has Chee. Chee is the force that transformed the homogeneous Big Bang into a collection of lumpy galaxies. The Taoism doctrine developed ten millennia ago has solved the most puzzling puzzle of the modern cosmology.

The concept of immortal soul in Hinduism is valid but lacks the understanding of the true difference between being and nonbeing. As for Hinduism, souls are not all equal but are graded into castes. The difference among souls arises from karmas and gunas (intrinsic characters). Only by freeing from gunas and karmas, can souls then unite with the Unborn God.

The Plato doctrine of soul is a simplified version of Hinduism. Aristotle's idea of soul arose from his ignorance. That ignorance evolved into the doctrine of Limbo that life after death is an undefined shade suffering in Limbo, waiting for an unspecified time for salvation and for an impossible way of resurrection. In fact, the doctrine of Limbo has said absolutely nothing. On the other hand, being an empty truth, it becomes a living truth. After all, nothingness is the essence of God, thus the essence of soul.

Even from the view point of God, He must give life a soul. God is the Absolute Totality. Death can never bring life outside of God but return it to Him. The soul is an invisible dog leash permanently confining life in God. God is the God Space, thus must be embodied everywhere. This embodiment is soul or Chee.

With a soul, the primitive people recognized God without any modern knowledge. The soul's reflexive knowledge knows its creator. With a soul, we all crave and desire to return to God although we are already permanently confined in God. With a soul, the moral truths will always prevail. The soul (or Chee) is the link between the body and God when there is a lively body and is still the link between the spirit and God after the body has died. Soul is an invisible dog leash permanently confining every life in God.

In my book — Truth, Faith, and Life — soul is an infinity and is represented with the seventh color. Every soul is immutable and unchangeable. No other soul can ever replace yours in the past, at the present or in the forever going future. Even the destruction of the entire universe can never destroy your soul. You have a soul because you are permanently confined in God. You are not only a member of God Space but are the center of it.

Being permanently confined, the soul is given free will and free choice. Being free, the soul is given immortality; thus the moral truth will prevail always. Being a moral being, the soul is permanently confined in immortal virtues, even while it has a body. Love, beauty and truth are something immortal. Not only everybody craves them but indeed possesses them. Thus, by cultivating these virtues, a soul is able to reach a higher level of immortality.

Chapter XII
Providence and Divination

The greatest mystery of God is neither the creation nor the triune nature of the godhead but is the impassibility and providence paradox. On the one hand, God must be immutable and unchangeable; thus, nothing can move God. Even while the entire universe collapses into God, He will neither be moved nor be harmed. In short, the nature of God must ever in Himself of necessity enjoy immortality together with supreme repose. Therefore, many people draw a conclusion that God is far removed and withdrawn from our concerns and that He does neither intervene in the order of nature nor concern Himself with human affairs. God is neither gained by favors nor moved by anger.

On the other hand, God can indeed be moved with sincere prayer and can be gained with meditation although God is indeed immutable and unchangeable. These two opposite views form the impassibility and providence paradox. Furthermore, these two opposite views must be both correct in order to form a paradox. Many people thus think of God as one who interacts with the history of the universe and who concerns Himself with human affairs, must be a dipolar God, possessing a temporal pole as well as an immortal pole.

II

In the past and even today, most people do not understand the issue of providence in a theological context. There are three levels of speculation. First, the concept of providence is viewed as incoherent with or contradictory to the modern scientific world-view; thus providence is nothing other than the imagined illusion and hope that arises from human minds and desires.

Second, God is recognized only as the Creator and the law giver, but His action is limited to that great single Act. After the creation, God is ultimately transcendent from the created world. Thus God is the foundation of a reliable world. Being reliable and fair, God will not give any "special" favor or punishment. God governs the world with laws and ignores either prayer or petition. In short, God will not break His own law to perform miracles for anyone whether he is only a common man or is even God Himself.

169

Third, God is thought of having a split personality. On the one hand, God rules the world with reliable and rigid laws; on the other hand, He performs miracles for those in His favor by breaking His own laws.

What is a miracle then? For almost everyone, an event must meet two requirements in order to be classified as a miracle. One, it must violate the laws of nature. Two, it must be a nonrepeatable event; thus any attempt at finding proof against it cannot be obtained. For all religious people, miracles must have two more meanings — being both God's Creatorly will and a "sign," which is endowed with meaning and is free from caprice.

By the above definition, miracle thus cannot be proved. Anything that can be proved or repeated regardless of how miraculous it is is not a miracle. So, all historically claimed miracles cannot be questioned whether they had actually happened or not. In fact, there is even no need to believe those claims with blind faith because by definition they cannot even be challenged.

Time and again, God's glorious nature is portrayed as an absurdity because of our ignorance and stupidity. The true miracles are not anything out of the ordinary, not the things that cannot happen in nature, not the events that are prohibited by the laws of nature. The true miracles are things that happen everyday and are events that follow the laws of nature. Everything around us is a miracle created by God.

In fact, all historically claimed miracles can and are performed almost daily now. Today, many blind persons receive sight. Many people who were perceived to be dead are brought back to life. Leprosy has been wiped out from the face of the earth. Although the claim of dividing the Red Sea still cannot be performed with today's technology, it is nonetheless possible for geological or cosmological force. The true miracles that are still beyond our reach are those ordinary things and events which obey the nature laws. We still cannot create life out of inorganic substances. We still cannot escape from the confinement of any nature laws — gravity, the limit of light speed for material substance, the second law of thermodynamics, etc.. We cannot even truly create any inorganic substance. In fact, everything around us is a miracle created by God. There is no reason for God to rule the world with reliable laws from his right hand then to break the laws, which are ordained precisely by Him Himself, with the left hand. Thus, the traditional definitions of miracle and providence have in fact prevented us to understand God's will, love and providence. A new definition and a new understanding about miracles and providence are needed.

III

I have shown you in the previous chapters that God is both a reliable process and an infinite possibility. Although we now know God's essence — the Trine (the union of nothingness, infinity and the utmost chaos) — we can never understand even a small portion of all possibilities.

A corollary of the impassibility and providence paradox is the omniscience and free will paradox that God knows the future regardless of the random acts performed by human's free will. By understanding this omniscience and free will paradox, we will then be able to understand the impassibility and providence paradox.

In Chapter IV, I showed you a still picture of God's portrait that God's essence, which is the infinite void, resides in the center of the ball while the entire material universe lies on the surface of the ball. In Chapter X, I briefly mentioned that life is a transformation, from a ball to a donut.

God is the utmost life force. Thus, God is an eternal process — creating a material world out of His essence (the infinite nothingness in the center of the ball) then returning them to nothingness at the end. In fact, all lifeless material and lives come out of nothingness and then return to it. This process of "coming out and returning to" paints a dynamic picture of God's portrait. All material and lives are laid on the surface of the ball (the universe). Inside of the surface is the infinite nothingness, which is not an empty space. The empty space is something, not nothingness. When a life returns to nothingness, it is the same as water draining out of a bath tub; it sinks into nothingness. The birth of a life is as a spring springs out of the ground. So, the ball surface is not a sealed surface. It looks like a donut surface. The universe (the ball surface) and the spirit of God (the center of the ball, nothingness) are connected with these springing springs and sinking holes (the birth and death). The same as all lives or lifeless material in the universe, God Himself is constantly transforming from a ball into a donut. In fact, God is a ball consisting of an infinite number of sinking holes and springing springs.

This birth and death process not only connects the universe (the surface of the ball) with God's spirit (the infinite void inside of the ball surface) and not only transforms a ball into a donut, but it also connects the inside of the ball surface (nothingness) with the outside of the ball surface which is also nothingness. In other words, the universe (the something) is sandwiched by the nothingness. This is a dynamic picture of God's portrait. Nonetheless, this picture is still unable to resolve the problem of the omniscience and free will paradox that God knows the future regardless of the random acts performed by human's free will. Thus, the complete picture of God's portrait is much more complicated than this dynamic picture is.

Time is created by God, but it exists only in the mortal universe. The spirit of God is timelessness, therefore eternal. When one universe collapses, a new one will begin. Moreover, the new universe will be always larger than the old one (see my book — Super Unified Theory). When this process goes on, the God's portrait becomes a series of concentric balls. If we draw them on a piece of paper, it becomes a series of concentric circles.

For the sake of discussion, let us draw ten concentric circles on a piece of paper, and let us assign the fifth circle as the universe we are living in. There are four universes before us and five still yet to come. The four before us have vanished, and their energy has become the flesh and bones of our universe. The five universes that have not yet arrived will come one at a time after we have gone. But, this description is only our view that is confined to the conception of "Time". Our view is quite different from God's. For God, there is no Time, and all these ten universes are existing simultaneously although only one of them possesses Time, Space and Material. The vanished universes have not vanished in the eyes of God. The death of a body does not vanish in the eyes of God. Thus, our souls will never die. The vanished universes and the death of bodies lost only "Time" and entered into the timeless Heaven and united with the spirit of God, the nothingness. Although the future universes have not yet manifested because of not yet possessing Time, they already exist in the eyes of God. God is, therefore, omniscient and knows the future regardless of the random acts performed by our free will.

Why shall anyone believe in the above description as God's complete portrait? Is this only a notion dreamed up by me? Or, can it only be accepted with a blind faith? On the contrary, it can be understood from two directions. First, this is the only answer that can reconcile the omniscience and free will paradox. In other words, it is the problem (the omniscience and free will paradox) as the foundation of the answer. Second, there are many similar examples in the real world.

Let us imagine that you and I were watching a roller coaster ride. You were watching with your naked eyes. I did not want to watch with my eyes but rather with a movie camera. You saw only one cart running around the track. You saw it in the real time. I wanted to see it in a different way. I reconstructed the entire track with the pictures I took. In this reconstructed picture, I saw a few, for example 10, carts along the track. No doubt, all 10 carts are the result of only one cart that was moving around the track. In other words, any single process always has multiple images at off-time. God is both a process and an immortal that is timelessness. This process itself is God Himself. God is also able to see the entire process, that is Himself, in an off-time view.

No doubt, this truth can never be proved or disproved with scientific methodology. Nonetheless, it can be understood with transcendental faith (the principle of example-in-kinds).

In fact, immortality is defined in two ways — one, time has no direction (in Chapter IV); two, the present is infinitely long, and there is neither past nor future (in Chapter VII). Thus, God can see the past, present and future with a single glance because all is just He Himself.

IV

Since God is able to know our future regardless of our random acts, God thus can intervene or change our future and can even foretell our desires before we pray. God is both a reliable process and an infinite possibility. In fact, the reliability of God is the greatest miracle. For every gene reproduction, many billions of genetic codes have to be reproduced. With today's technology and quality control standard, a process produces only 200 defective products per million is considered to be a super reliable process. But, if there is only one error per billion during any gene reproduction process, every species will lose its vital genetic traits in 10 generations. No doubt, God is the symbol of absolute reliability. On the other hand, genetic mutation does exist. In general, genetic mutation will not alter the genetic trait of any species over night or over a short period time but allows many species to survive all "possible" environments. Thus, this reliable God is also the symbol of possibility. In fact, the reliable laws of nature are the cause and the source of all possibilities. Because of the laws of thermodynamics, automobiles and many other things become possible. Because of the laws of electrodynamics, television and many other things become possible. Today, the insights of cosmology, evolutionary biology and molecular genetics, all bear witness to the astonishing potentiality and possibility with which matter is endowed. In short, reliability is synonymous with possibility. The reliable God is an infinite possibility. Being an infinite possibility, God can provide us "special" providence inside the framework of his reliable process. In fact, God provides two levels of providence.

The first is the universal providence. God is the Creator and the Sustainer. Besides the single Act at the beginning, God provides a continuous creative process to sustain the existence of His creation. This universal providence is accomplished with reliable nature laws.

The second is the special personal providence. Fatherly care of God must be concerned with the individual and his specific needs. Being immanent, God has the ability to provide personal encounter simultaneously with all that He has created. Thus, why not?

These two levels of divine action are indeed not contradictory. An infinite number of possibilities can manifest from a set of reliable laws the same as the syntactic system that there are only finite sets of words and grammatical rules, but an infinite number of sentences can be constructed.

I-Ching (Book of Change) is a book about divination. It views God as an eternal changing process. Being eternally changing, God is thus the only unchangeable. The impassibility and providence paradox was reconciled in the Chinese saying "Change, not change; move, not move." It means that the only reason that God can be moved by our prayers is because God is immovable and unchangeable.

In I-Ching, the fact that the phenomenal world is forever changing is the only unchangeable essence of God. Only by understanding God's essence, action and will, the interaction with God becomes possible by following God's action and will which are both a reliable process and an infinite possibility. Being a reliable process, God's actions can be represented with 64 hexagrams. Hexagrams are constructed with two forces, Yin and Yang. Yin and Yang are opposite yet complement forces to each other. These two incompatible forces meet and interact, then become compatible after many complicated changes. By the same token, any harmonic state will also eventually corrupt into incompatible conflict again sooner or later.

Being an infinite possibility, God's will can be revealed by tossing coins. Many smart aleck scientists and many stiff-necked churchgoers will quickly view I-Ching as nothing other than a primitive superstition. In fact, they are the ones who do not understand neither the essence of God nor the divination process — tossing coins or sortilege.

Sortilege is not a game of chance. In probability and statistics, after an infinite number times of tossing, head and tail will appear with exactly equal chance, 50% for each to be exact, and this fairness is the divine nature of tossing coins. In reality, any finite number times of tossing will not always reach this divine value, 50%. If the times of tossing is limited to an odd number, it will always create possibilities instead of going to the probability value. For example, if the probability of getting lung cancer is one per cent and one person in a group of 100 people is already found to have lung cancer, it does not mean the remaining 99 people are home free. The probability of every possibility is embodied in each of our souls. Anyone who views sortilege as a game of chance obviously does not know the meaning of possibility, probability and statistics. Sortilege is not a game of chance but is a way of revealing all possibilities and a way of receiving divination if your heart is sincere.

Every divination process always consists of three parts — formation of questions, action of divination (tossing coins) and personal interpretation. Even though the outcomes of tossing a finite number of coins are finite, the question and the interpretation are definitely personal, thus can have almost an infinite number of outcomes.

V

There are many forms of providence and divination, but I-Ching is the only systemized system of divination. First, God's essence is represented with two forces, Yin and Yang. Then, God's will is represented with eight trigrams. In Chapter IX — Tao of Life and of God, I gave new meaning to these eight trigrams as the building blocks (two leptons and six quarks) of the universe. Traditionally, they represent God's divine attributes — the Creative (Heaven), the Receptive (Earth), the Arousing (Thunder), the Abysmal (Water), Keeping still (Mountain), the Gentle (Wind), the Clinging (Fire) and the Joyous (Lake). Finally, God's actions are represented with sixty-four hexagrams. In I-Ching, God is an eternal flow, from one hexagram to another. Hexagrams start with the Creative (Heaven) and the Receptive (Earth) and ends with Settled (63rd hexagram) and Unsettled (64th, the last hexagram). These 64 hexagrams form an infinite recursion. The perfection and the completion, that everything is at its place and that presupposes no further developments, is reached at the 63rd hexagram, but the completion also means the lacking and the dying of the creative power; thus, it becomes the unproductivity which is the last (64th) hexagram. Even perfection and completion not only cannot be eternal but must move on.

We human beings have no choice but to drift along with this eternal flow. If we drift with the direction of the flow, we will receive benefits and providence. If we drift against the direction of divine flow, we then commit sin and will surly receive retribution sooner or later. Thus, finding out the direction of this divine flow is the first step to interact with God and to receive providence from God. Confucius said, "Music expresses the harmony of the universe, while ritual express the order of the universe. Through harmony all things are influenced, and through order all things have a proper place. Music rises from heaven, while rituals are patterned on the earth. In order to have the proper rituals and music, we must first understand the principles of Heaven and Earth."

After you have understood God's will, for receiving divination you must formulate a "personal" question. This question must be beyond your ability to reason and solve because God already gave you the intelligence to reason and solve all solvable problems. Then your heart must be sincere, and you must concentrate your will in order to receive God.

After God has entered your heart, toss three coins on a flat surface to construct a hexagram. Tail has a value of 2 and head a value of 3.

2 tails, 1 head = 7 is Yang (a solid line)
2 heads, 1 tail = 8 is Yin (a broken line)
3 tails = 6 is Yin (a moving Yin line)
3 heads = 9 is Yang (a moving Yang line)

In statistics, 3 tails or 3 heads are much rarer event than other outcomes; thus this rare event seemingly has higher significance, but in I-Ching this means that it has reached its fullness and must be transformed into its opposite. So, it is a moving line.

After casting three coins six time in all, you will obtain a hexagram. Your first toss will be the first line, starting from the bottom of the hexagram.

Now, the final step is to interpret your hexagram. There are five ways to read any hexagram. One, read it in its entirety as a hexagram; that is to read the main text which describes an action of God. Two, read the meanings of each line which describes the possibilities. Three, read it as two trigrams, top and bottom, which describe the movement (interacting force) of God's will. Four, read the two nuclear trigrams, which are obtained by removing the top and bottom line of the hexagram, and these nuclear trigrams describe the potentiality. Five, when your hexagram contains moving lines, you can then receive a new hexagram — one in which each of the moving lines of your original hexagram has changed into its opposite. For your second hexagram, you would consult the main text only, not the lines.

Furthermore, every line, trigram or hexagram has many attributes. It always is a symbol and symbolizes something, such as: heaven, earth or wind. It always represents a kind of force, creative, receptive or arousing, etc. It always possesses a quality, such as: joyous, perfection or unstable. It also always associates with time (month, season, ...), space (north, south, ...), Five Walk (metal, wood,...), movement, action etc. With all these, the paths of interpretation become very large in number, and the meaning of it becomes infinite in number because both question and interpretation are absolutely personal.

In short, the divination process of I-Ching consists of three parts. One, the hexagram is produced by God's hand (the Divine Possibility). Two, the meaning of the hexagram is by observing and understanding God's will and His laws and is recorded in I-Ching. Three, your question and your interpretation are absolutely personal and subjective. In other words, your objective situation and subjective personal needs are resolved with transcendental divine inspiration and providence.

VI

Although the I-Ching divination process also has psychological significance, the other forms of divination mainly depend upon the psychic. The two most common ones are praying and channeling.

In channeling, otherwise ordinary people seem to let themselves be taken over by divine force to use them as mediums or channels for special information and important messages. In general, all channeling takes place in a trance state which is a very extraordinary psychic state. All mediums believe that they have been possessed by a Holy Spirit. They have been chosen by God as His puppet. They have stopped other people's problems and sorrows with hope and joy. They become the ultimate in authorization since the Holy Spirit is one with the highest source of all being. God has chosen to enter the lowly subjects and has articulated his speech with their lowly tongues. They have received divine messages and divine providence.

Channeling can happen to many common people. Oracle is sort of an official channeling. The most famous oracle is Apollo at Delphi. At Delphi, many simple rural girls were trained to put themselves into a psychological state such that they could make decision at once that ruled Greek world. Even Plato called Delphi "the interpreter of religion to all mankind."

The fact is that humans indeed possess the psychic faculty to receive the divine influence. This receptive faculty does not come to be by itself but is given by the Creator. God wants to communicate with us, thus gives us the ability to communicate with Him.

Humans have three levels of activity — physical, psychological and spiritual. When we are physically present with others, we can project our feelings to others without words or actions. Without the physical presence of others, we can still feel their feelings. In short, the psychological communication, without words or actions, is possible with physical presence of others, and the spiritual communion is possible even without the physical presence of others. Many people think that spiritual communion with others is only a subjective imagination or hallucination because the spirits of others often do not sense or feel our spiritual present in them. They also question how this spiritual message is transmitted.

In the case of spiritual communion with God, no transmission is needed because God is immanent. God is in us and us in God. We only need to make our hearts sincere and God will appear to us. Prayer means yearning for the simple presence of God, for a personal understanding of his essence, for knowledge of His will and for the capacity to obey Him.

Our ability to communicate with God comes from God's embodiment in us. The embodiment itself is not providence or divination but a channel for them. Many religious mania strongly oppose the fact of embodiment because if the Holy Spirit is embodied in everyone, then there is no need for a savior, and then there cannot be more than one God, such as: God of Jesus and God of Buddha. They said, "If God and the world are so closely linked by embodiment, then one must gain the mastery over the other. Either divine impassibility must triumph by the assertion of a divine tyranny over the world, or divine vulnerability must triumph through the world's imposing itself upon God. Only by breaking the tie implicit in embodiment can God be let be to be God and his creation be let be to be itself." This ignorant and stupid notion of those religious mania is caused by lacking of the understanding of the nature and the essence of God. God is not confined by causal law, especially not by the principle of excluded middle. God has no need to triumph one over the other. There is enough room in God for all. The divine embodiment is not only a channel of providence and divination but is the will of God. God wants to be with His creation. Only with embodiment, the abstract God is also the God of Abraham. Only with embodiment, the timeless God of philosophers becomes the God of Isaac. Only with embodiment, the God of reliable cosmic process is also the God of special providence. Only with embodiment, the God of Jesus is also the God of Confucius, of Buddha. A transcendent but not embodied God is only an abstract God on a piece of paper or is only as the hot airs gushing out from the mouths of religious mania, in short, a dead God without a living body. Embodiment is the essence of God according to the definition of God Space. Only with embodiment does the spiritual communion with God and the religious mutual in-dwelling in the Christ-Body or in the Buddha-Body become possible.

VII

Providence and divination in no way mean that they are ways of constant negotiation with God. Thus, the prayer of petition or begging is an improper way to communicate with God. As a father myself, I am always longing to communicate with my kids but can never stand their begging and whining.

On the contrary, providence means destiny and fate. Destiny and fate do not mean to be fatalism. Destiny and fate are God's will that becomes the purpose of life. Thus, all prophets and sages, on the one hand, reproach God for having burdened them with too heavy a load, on the other hand accept their destinies and fates to complete the tasks that are given by God. Mencius said, "Before God chooses a prophet and gives him a divine task, God will first torture his mind and will, then wear out his body, and fail everything he is trying to do. He will be persistently stopped and oppressed by conditions that he could neither remedy nor overcome with the obviously necessary actions. Only if he still accepts his destiny after all these, God will then give him the divine task."

Destiny is the purpose of life and it comes from God's will. We can either fulfill or fail to fulfill our destiny but can never escape from it. God knows our future regardless of our random acts. Only with persistent struggle and faithful faith in God can destiny then be fulfilled. Destiny stands still and waits; no one can ever escape it. Goethe wrote, "You should not resist fate, nor need you escape it; if you go to meet it, it will guide you pleasantly."

King Wen lived around 1100 B.C. when China still suffered from the oppression of the last tyrant of the Yin dynasty. Although King Wen knew that God had given him the task to create order, he also knew that he must pass many divine trials for that end. He was imprisoned; so he developed I-Ching to understand God's will. His superhuman patience seemingly accomplished nothing visible at first, but precisely because of his superhuman patience and his passing many divine trials, the Chou dynasty rose like a bright sun on the horizon. Chou culture become the greatest China had ever seen, and the effects of this culture were felt for millennia hence. China became China because of the heritage of those formative eight hundred years.

The Chinese word "Jeh" means divine trial, and "Tween" means existence or surviving. "Jeh-Tween" means to have survived or passed the divine trial. In early 1950, my parents were moving from mainland China to Taiwan. They got on a ship in Canton, but soon the ship was surrounded by many pirate ships. During the fierce gun fight, Mother gave her seat to a sick old man and sat on floor herself. Two minutes later, a bullet shot the old man right between his eyes. Then, in a great panic, the crowd pushed Mother off from the upper deck to the lower one and she were badly injured. After the ship surrendered to those pirate ships, every valuable thing on the ship was taken away. Then, the ship was floating on the sea for two months without any medicine on board. Everyone on the ship was allowed only one bowl of rice soup a day. Under those conditions, Father was greatly worried about my arrival and did not believe that I could survive, but I was born and lived. Thus, Father named me "Jeh-Tween" to celebrate my passing the greatest divine trial.

Since I was about only 5 year old, I already knew my destiny that I will be the one to speak the words of God. But, how? God did not show Himself to me behind the bush fire and did not descend from heaven as a white cloud. He did not even send any angel to talk to me in my dreams or my imagination. In short, God did not make my task any easier. On the contrary, my mind was tortured night after night. Everything I did was either an outright failure or a non-event. In 1979, I developed a prequark model and unified all four physical forces. Heisenburg won the Nobel prize for his discovering the uncertainty principle. My Super Unified Theory

(SUT) derives the uncertainty principle from another direction and gives it much more meaning, but it is ignored by the physics community. Einstein became a world celebrity by failing to complete a simple version of the unified theory. My SUT unified all four physical forces, but again it is ignored by physicists.

There are two reasons for this. First, if physicists accept my SUT, they would have to destroy the old empire they had built. Their prestige will then surly go down the drain as well. Since they are now controlling many institutions, they can ignore my SUT without encountering a big fuss. Furthermore, SUT reaches the domain that is much beyond the reach of scientific methodology; thus, there is no danger of ignoring my theory because no one can either prove or disprove it at this moment anyway. In 1982, the editor of "The Physics Teacher" wrote to me, "Neither readers nor reviewers would be capable of analyzing your article on a unified theory." In 1983, the editor of "The Physical Review" wrote, "We have made no judgment on whether your work is correct or not, only that the subject matter is not suitable for the Physical Review." Also in 1983, the editor of "Science Digest" wrote, "Naturally, the material is much too advanced for our use." These letters were published in my book — Super Unified Theory.

On the other hand, the main reason that my SUT was ignored is because of God's will. If my SUT was accepted in 1979, I probably would not be able to continue the intense searching for the ultimate truth, and I probably would not be able to break through the old scientific barriers and truly reach and enter the domain of God.

I have found God because God placed many obstacles in my path. Every obstacle is a divine sign and a divine guiding light. Every trial is a shower of divine inspiration. Every sentence of this book is inspired from those divine trials. Life is not suffering but a challenge. Life is a mission to find its purpose and meaning, to plant seeds and to gather its fruits. Then, eventually at the end, life meets its destiny with either fulfillment or failure.

Those who are entrusted with a divine mission are in general never able to see the harvest. They may glance only from afar into the promised land; most often others gather the fruit. This is the greatest divine trial. Laotse, Confucius and Jesus all knew their destiny, to teach mankind the words of God. They all also knew their fate, an inevitable failure during their lifetime. Laotse took his fate lyrically, rode a buffalo into the wilderness and let the divine force take its own course. Jesus cried desperately before his death,

"My God, my God, why hast thou forsaken me?" Confucius sighed and said, "I know I will not succeed. But, if I don't do it, Who will?" They all failed in their lifetime. At the end, they all not only indeed enlightened mankind immensely, but their spirits are the spirit of mankind. No doubt, my teaching will follow their footsteps.

Chapter XIII
The Grand Detour

I had some understanding of both Taoism and Buddhism since I was a kid because Father was a professor teaching Chinese philosophy, but their doctrines and methodologies did not play any part in my thinking process. As a Chinese, I found and understood the essence of God by traveling on the path of western knowledge.

On a Chinese New Year's Eve when I was seven years old, Father held me on his lap and told me, "No one in the world knows Chinese knowledge more than I do, but I have not the slightest idea of what western knowledge is all about. I hope you as my son will mend this defect of mine. You must go and study the western knowledge of which I cannot teach you, and I will teach you all Chinese knowledge you want to know myself." I took his words as my mission.

Father did not formally teach me Chinese knowledge, but his immense wisdom and a large library did help me to build a solid foundation on Chinese knowledge. Many years after my enlightenment, on the one hand, I was astonished that I was only 'reinventing the wheel'. On the other hand, this ancient Chinese understanding is quite primitive. Laotse indeed did understand the essence of God that is entangled with nothingness, large (infinity) and chaos. He wrote, "There is something chaotic yet complete which existed before heaven and earth. Oh how still it is and formless, standing alone without changing, reaching everywhere. Its name I know not. I call it Large and rename it Tao." Nonetheless, this primitive understanding did not develop into science. In Chapter IX — Tao of Life and of God, I infused many new interpretations and meanings into this old Taoism. In short, my enlightenment did not come from Chinese knowledge but enriched it. The root of my thought is no doubt rooted in the West.

The western science was the guiding principle for my thoughts before the completion of my Super Unified Theory. After its completion, I had no choice but to touch and see the essence of God. At the same time, I also realized that the scientific methodology has become a burden and a barrier for any further advancement to understand the true essence of God. Thus, my attention turned to western philosophy and theology.

In my school days, all my classmates despise Christianity because of its absurd claims of a virgin birth and bodily resurrection. They cannot criticize it beyond this level. In fact, I often won arguments by denouncing their ignorance about the Bible and by demanding them to shut up until they have learned what I have read.

After the completion of my Super Unified Theory, I held God's hand through the path of science and thus desperately want to know what exactly the claim and the teaching of Christianity is. I believed that the Bible is the root of my thought, that the Church is the trunk and that the sciences are the branches. Thus, I dived into the works of western historians, exegetes and theologians.

II

To my greatest surprise, all books, that I thought advocated the Christian cause, turned out to denounce and despise it. Many of those authors were Christian theologians. Some of them desperately tried to argue for the Christian cause but only revealed its absurdity. In general, there are three kinds of criticism. The extremists claim that the Bible is not the word of God but a steal from pagan sources. The modest claim that the Bible lacks moral sense. The conservative claim that the Christian churches have broken away from Jesus' teaching.

For the extremists, Christianity is now proved to be a stolen religion. Not only are many individual myths in Bible borrowed from pagan sources but its center piece — the Pauline Trilogy (fall, incarnation, and resurrection) — is also stolen.

In the Pelagian myth of creation, the goddess Eurynome created a wind by dancing over the waters. The more she danced, the greater and stronger grew the wind, until it became the serpent Ophion, who, coiling himself about her, coupled with her. Later becoming angry at the serpent, she bruised his head, kicked out his teeth and banished him to the dark caves below the earth. Thus, the Bible wrote, "... and the Spirit of God moved upon the face of the waters. ... it shall bruise they head, and thou shalt bruise his heel." Genesis 1:2 and 4:15.

The Hindu God Siva sent a woman a fig tree and prompted her to tempt her husband with the fruit. This she did, assuring the man it would confer on him immortality. The man ate and Siva cursed him. The Greek Zeus gave Hesperides a tree that bore golden apples and as they could not resist the temptation to eat them, Zeus placed Ladon, a serpent, in the garden to watch the tree. Finally, Hercules slew the serpent and gave the apples to

Hesperides. These are the original sources of the story of the tree of knowledge.

The Greek Zeus, becoming offended with his own creation, decided to drown the whole wicked lot of them, except Deucalion and Pyrrha, who had found grace in his eyes. These he allowed to escape in a ark which finally landed on Mt. Parnassus. This became the story of Noah's ark.

Even the name of Abram was borrowed by transferring "a" as the prefix instead of the suffix from the word Brama which is the original name of the Hindu Creator Brahma.

There are many more of these kinds of accusations that most of the Bible myths are copied from pagan sources. Worse yet, the Christian theological framework — the Pauline Trilogy which is God's cosmic plan for human salvation — is also proved to be copied from a Greek myth, the story of Perseus.

Perseus is fighting with the monster Medusa whose hair is made of serpents. No mortal can look at her face to face. Athena, the Olympian deity, lends her mirror-shield to Perseus, and he captures the image of Medusa in the protective mirror. Thus Perseus is able to decapitate the monster Medusa. The winged horse Pegasus, devoured by Medusa, flies out the decapitated body of Medusa. Bellerophon, victor over the Chimaera, rides on Pegasus's back and flies up to conquer Heaven but is defeated and sent to hell and is tied by serpents to an endlessly spinning incandescent wheel. He is finally rescued by Perseus. At his death, Perseus bequeathes the head of Medusa to Athena who attaches it to her mirror shield.

This Perseus myth originally symbolized the victory over the human existential predicament. Perseus symbolizes mankind. Medusa represents the subconscious vanity of Perseus and is the ruler of the world. Etymologically, Medusa means 'she who reigns.' If Perseus were exempt from vanity, he would have no need to fight Medusa. Nonetheless, he cannot see her without the mirror of truth from Athena. Chimaera represents false promises. Although Bellerophon conquers Chimaera, he turns his victory over chimerical vanity into vanity over victory, thus is sent to hell. The winged horse rode by Bellerophon symbolizes impetuous desires. It yields to vanity and is devoured by Medusa. It takes flight but is of no help to Bellerophon. Thus, the true human salvation is by conquering the vanity and preventing the vanity over victory.

This Greek myth became the Pauline Trilogy. Medusa is Satan, and Bellerophon symbolizes Adam's fall. Jesus (Perseus) with God's (Athena) help defeated Satan (Medusa) and went into hell to rescue mankind (Bellerophon).

There are many other authors who despise the Bible because they claim that the Bible is a book teaching immorality — the practice of incest, of stealing and of killing.

Some complain that Lot lay with his daughters. "Thus were both daughters of Lot with child by their father." Genesis 19:36.

Some complain that king David was a lecher, a thief and a murderer. David's second wife was Abigail, the wife of Nabal. Then he fell in love with Bathsheba by spying on her at her bath. She was married to Uriah. So David put Uriah in battle, and he was killed. David married Bathsheba.

Some complain that Jesus invented communist principle: From each according to his ability, to each according to his need. "And the multitude of them that believed were of one heart and soul: and not one of them said that aught of things that he possessed was his own; but they had all things in 'common'..., and distribution was made unto each, according as any one had need." Acts 4:32-35.

The very earliest and original Christians not only practiced communism but with a totalitarian form of communism. "But a certain man named Ananias, with Sapphira his wife, sold a possession, and kept back part of the price, ..., and brought a certain part, and laid it at the apostles' feet. And Peter said, Ananias, why hath Satan filled thy heart ..., and to keep back part of the price of the land?... Ananias hearing these words fell down and give up the ghost: and great fear came upon all that heard it. ...three hours after, when his wife, not knowing what was done, came in. ... Peter said unto her, ...behold, the feet of them which have buried thy husband are at the door, and they shall carry thee out. And she fell down immediately at his feet, and gave up the ghost. ... And great fear came upon the whole church, and upon all who heard these things." Acts 5:1-11.

Today, many theologians also conclude that both Judaism and Christianity are in fact polytheism. Not only was the Trinity doctrine worked out by Hellenistic group by borrowing pagan methodology, but the monotheism of Judaism is only a self-proclaimed psedo-monotheism. This proclamation of Judaism in fact affirms the reality of polytheism. On the one hand, this proclamation sprung up because of fears and jealousy of other deities. On the other hand, Judaism being a copied religion did not become a true monotheism but only reduced other deities to a lower rank, such as angels and devils. But, it failed to reduce Satan's status, and the Jewish God has lost every battle with Satan. In short, both Judaism and Christianity do not comprehend the meaning of 'Totality' which is the essence of the true God. Thus, both Judaism and Christianity do not understand the true God.

III

No doubt, a major portion of the Bible was written in mystic or symbolic language because it was written at the age of mysticism and mythical symbolism. Nonetheless, the Old Testament does contain some historical incidents, but most historians discredit the Bible of having any historical accuracy. Engberg wrote in his book (The Dawn of Civilization), "Joshua is so closely associated with the fall of Jericho in Hebrew tradition that it is therefore necessary to place his lifetime around 1400 B.C. Moses, on the other hand, appears to be linked to a period about two hundred years later, for the Hebrews slaved in the cities of Rameses. The story, then, of Joshua following Moses seems to be a confused version of two originally different episodes."

In the Columbia History of the World, the author wrote, "At this point a new cycle of legends begins. Its hero is Moses, a prophet of the God YHWH (probably 'Yahweh') — a god unknown to the patriarchs (exodus 6:3). From here on the tradition seems to be mainly Israelite in origin and, in outline, historical. The details, however, are fantastic; not only minor episodes but major ones like the covenant at Sinai may have been invented to provide Israelite origins for Canaanite ceremonies. ...For historical outline, thus, not much is left save that some Israelites escaped from Egypt under Moses, picked up adherents in the wilderness, fought off attacks by other tribes, were driven out of southern Palestine, and eventually conquered the western edge of Transjordan. The historical connection of Moses with Joshua is uncertain, and the legends of the Joshua cycle have suffered badly from later accretion and invention; they contradict both the archaeological evidence and each other."

Even many prominent Christian historians or exegetes — such as: Albrecht Ritschl, Johanees Weiss, Karl Schmidt and Rudolf Baltmann — do believe that gospels are not historical accounts of what happened but are religious fiction. They used three kinds of biblical science — redaction criticism, source criticism and form criticism. First, the date of each writing was determined. The Paul's Epistle was written 20 years (50 C.E.) after Jesus death, and it is the first Christian written document. Twenty more years later (at 70 C.E.), Mark's gospel appeared. At least fifteen more years later (at 85 C.E.), gospels of Matthew and Luke appeared about the same time. The gospel of John was written ten years later (95 C.E.) still.

The contents of these gospels are different because they grew upon one another. The defects of early versions were removed in the later versions. Many newly invented ideas were added in the later gospels. In short, Matthew and Luke were basically based on Mark but added many newly invented fictions in order to ward off the criticism that Mark had encountered. In short, the difference among gospels did not happen accidentally but was created with desperate efforts by those later gospel writers. The resurrection story is just one of the many good examples about those desperate efforts.

In Mark, the resurrection story is quite simple and straight forward. After Jesus bitterly resented his God who has abandoned him, he gave up the ghost. Joseph asked Pilate for Jesus' body and laid him in a sepulchre and rolled a great stone unto the door of the tomb. Then, after sabbath, Mary Magdalene and Mary the mother of James wanted to anoint Jesus, but they had no way to move the great stone and said among themselves, "Who shall roll us away the stone from the door." To their surprise, the great stone was rolled away at their arrival. After entering into the sepulchre, they saw a young man sitting on the right side. He told them that Jesus has risen and asked them to deliver a message to Jesus' disciples, but these two ladies did not believe or trust this stranger and fled and said nothing to any man for they were afraid.

Mark's narrative not only lacks religious meanings about resurrection but also raises many questions. First, the empty tomb does not guarantee the resurrection. There are many possible explanations. The obvious one is the stolen-body theory that Jesus' dead body was stolen by his disciples. In order to ward off this accusation, Matthew heavily emphasized that the chief priests by violating the sabbath law (a major crime according to Jewish law) went to see Pilate on sabbath day and asked for having a watch at the tomb.

Second, the motive of two Mary to anoint Jesus without the ability to move the great stone was quite absurd even for those primitive people in biblical time. Thus, this motive was dropped in Matthew, and it simply said, "... and the other Mary to 'see' the sepulchre."

Third, it was quite embarrassing that both Mary (not one) not only did not believe the young man but also did not have great joy by knowing that their loved one (Jesus) has risen. Thus, in Matthew, the young man was transformed into an angel and both Mary did have great joy.

According to those Christian exegetes, there are many more of this kind of fabrications. The difference between gospels was not originated from different sect of Christian group but was caused by later fabrications which were desperate intend to mend the defects of the early gospels. Although those Christian theologians did not say it out loud, they have indeed concluded that the Bible is only a collection of religious fiction.

Today, moderate theologians purport to say what in fact really happened to Jesus after his death, but without emphasizing the Bible's mythical imagery. They hold that the resurrection is not a historical fact but nonetheless has ontological meaning. In fact, by believing a falsity, believers can transform this falsity into truth. The liberal theologians prefer to drop the ontological transformation but emphasize the 'fact' that Jesus continued to have significance for his disciples after he died, what he meant to the early believers and could mean to Christians today. The focus is on the significance of Jesus for us without regard to the resurrection legend.

IV

I could never win arguments over my classmates if they had read those books. If the Bible is only a collection of fiction and if the Christian Church is only a congregation of religious mania, my search for the root of my doctrine is no doubt in big trouble. I did not invent my doctrine out of blue. It is originally based on science, especially physics and mathematics. Then, I transcended scientific methodology and entered the domain of metaphysics and religion. Superficially, the history of the West is very simple and clear. Science did spring out from Dark Age during and after the renaissance. The Dark Age was under the absolute control of the Christian Church. Christianity was spun off from Judaism and coexisted with a Hellenistic culture for about three centuries.

Everything is simple and clear. The Bible is the root; Christianity is the trunk, and sciences are the branches. But, why does the true essence of God is quite different from Christian's dogma? In other words, the leaf is seemingly a different species from the root. This situation is simply unacceptable for me. I must find out why they are different and how they come to be as they are.

Many preachers told me that no one can ever comprehend Jesus completely. Thus, we must believe in Him with faith. Their confidence of their statement came from three sources. First, Jesus died two thousand years ago and carried many secrets with him into his grave. Second, Jesus is now God, and no one is able to comprehend God outside of faith. God is a mystery. The more absurdness, the greater the mystery. Thus, God can be embraced only with the madness of blind faith, and thus the Bible can never be understood but must be believed with dogmatic faith.

Furthermore, all preachers have the ability to write a big novel out of a simple Bible verse. One example is the story of Joseph. "And a certain man found him, and, behold, he was wandering in the field: and the man asked him, saying, what seekest thou? And he said, I seek my brethren: tell me, I pray thee, where they feed their flocks. And the man said, They are departed hence; for I heard them say, Let us go to Dothan. And Joseph went after his brethren, and found them in Dothan." We all have the experience of looking for someone and asking information from one or many strangers on the way. But all preachers can transform this common Bible story into a great mystery. They said that this stranger must be an angel. Some do say the man is the angel Gabriel, others that whoever he is he is meant to show the difficulties Joseph had to overcome before reaching his brothers. Thus, the Bible is a book of mystery and can only be understood with dogmatic interpretation. In fact, a blank book contains much higher mystery and must be the highest Sacred book because it contains an infinite number of possibilities.

Third, if you don't agree with their interpretation, they can still win the argument by condemning their opponents. Saint Paul was the greatest expert on this technique. He wrote in his first Epistle, "Someone may ask, 'How are dead people raised, and what sort of body do they have when they come back?' These are stupid question." I Corinthions 15:35-36.

Today, the essence of God is clearly understood. We can embrace God with understanding instead of the madness of blind faith. While the mystery of God can be understood, no mystery of Jesus can be hidden although we indeed can never know how many times Jesus picked his nose. We have no interest in that issue anyway.

Jesus lived in this world. There were people before him, around him and after him. He learned from the people before him and talked to the people around him; so his teaching can be revealed quite easily by simply studying the doctrines before and after his time. The gospels desperately tried to distort the true Jesus, but these desperate acts themselves become the guiding light and the signposts for the task of finding the true Jesus.

V

The Jewish people did not come out of blue, but all prominent modern historians conclude that the Jews did not have an honorable history but have worked out many legends. "But the Yahweh-alone party held to the Deuteronomic code, and the code reshaped the party. Like the laws of Sparta, it was to be learned by heart, ... More over, the Deuteronomist inspired a school of followers, recognizable by their imitation of his style, who augmented his code with a 'historical' framework eventually extended to include earlier collections of legends and court records. These they 'reworked' to make one great 'history,' teaching that only when Israel worshiped Yahweh alone did it prosper, and whenever it worshiped other gods it was punished. Thus, the 'historical' half of the Old Testament began to take shape." (The Columbia History of the World).

Many people also despise the book of Genesis because of its stupidity compared with the truth that we now know. This is indeed an unfair treatment on this ancient book; after all it was only copied from pagan sources. It was just as smart as its counterpart — the pagan mythology. Although the Old Testament does neither contain any godly truth nor historical fact, it does tell us what those ancient Jews did think about, and this is exactly what is needed to begin our journey to find the true Jesus.

There are many names for this Jewish God. The most commonly known name is Yahweh, and this is the name I am going to use. Today, all Christians assume that Yahweh is the Creator God as described in the book of Genesis. This is not the case for those ancient Jews because the book of Genesis appeared one thousand years after their time. For them, Yahweh is only the guardian angel of their tribe. He fed them. He fought wars for them. He brought them out of slavery. He also punished them. In short, Yahweh who lived in a box (the Tabernacle) was the head of the Jewish household.

After the Jewish population grew into the size of a nation, Yahweh became a lawgiver. He anointed kings and high priests. He directed Jewish people's history. He was the God of Law and of History. For many centuries, Israel was a kingless theocracy governed by a timeless Law. Around 400 B.C., the five books of the Pentateuch, called the Torah, or Law, were edited to their final form and became the religious and legal constitution of the Jews. Besides the famous ten commandments, there were six hundred and thirteen more commandments, three hundred and sixty-five prohibitions, corresponding to the number of days in the solar year, and two hundred and forty-eight positive precepts corresponding to the number of the member of man's body.

The perception and conception of Yahweh soon changed after His captivity in Babylon. Regardless of the sincere calls and prayers, Yahweh seemed to have fled to the higher heavens. He was either unable or unwilling to intervene in the Israel's political history for the Jewish people.

Zoroaster of Persia (550 B.C.) had taught that the world was the scene of a dramatic cosmic struggle between the forces of Good and Evil, led by the gods Ormazd and Ahriman. But this conflict was not to continue forever because, according to Zoroastrianism, history was not endless but finite and in fact dualistic, divided between the present age of darkness and the coming age of light. Time was evolving through four progressively worsening periods toward an eschatological cataclysm when Good would finally annihilate Evil and the just would receive their otherworldly reward in an age of eternal bliss. Zoroastrianism's profound pessimism about present history was thus answered by its eschatological optimism about a future eternity.

Under the desperate condition of being exiled and by the influence of Zoroastrianism which was encountered by the Israelites during the Babylonian Exile, many prophets (especial Daniel) dreamt up a radically new idea of eschatology, the doctrine of the end of the world. The apocalyptic eschatology spelled the end of the prophets' hope for a future revival of the past and replaced it with mythical hopes for a cosmic cataclysm followed by the eternal new age. In this new hope, the long fled Yahweh was imagined as an apocalyptic destroyer. At this point, Judaism shifted the focus of its religious hopes from the arena of law and of the historical to that of the eschatological and cosmic, from political salvation in some future time to preternatural survival in an afterlife. This radical change can be seen in late Judaism's adoption of notions like the fall of Adam from grace at the beginning of time, the workings of Satan and other demons in the present age, and the Last Judgment and the resurrection at the end of history. At this point, the book of Genesis was finalized, and Yahweh who was only a tribe deity concerning only the law of how his people should live was transformed into a Cosmic Destroyer.

Four hundred years after the Babylonian Exile, the book of Daniel appeared, and it was just one such apocalyptic work that pretended to predict the catastrophic events that in fact were happening in the author's own lifetime. At the same time, he predicted that the Son of Man, whom God had appointed as Israel's protector in God's sight, will be the coming savior. In the later apocalyptic works, the characteristics and the qualification of this Son of Man were clearly defined. First, he was thought to have existed even before the creation. Second, he must be descended from King David. Third, the end of time shall last one thousand two hundred and ninety days. Fourth, an eschatological prophet named Elias must come before the Son of Man. Fifth, the notion of resurrection was introduced by Daniel as the reward of the just at the end of time. Sixth, the Son of Man will die and be risen three days after his death.

VI

While Pharisees were waiting the coming of a Davidic messiah, the Essenes, a Zadokite sect of Judaism, came to expect two eschatological messiahs, one a high priest descended from Aaron and the other a world-emperor descended from David. They also practiced two religious rites. They celebrated the eschatological meal of bread and wine in anticipation of the coming messianic banquet (the pre-Eucharistical meal). They also practiced baptism by carrying out their own ablutions. With this background, in the year of 28 C.E., a person named John performed the similar ritual by washing not himself but his follower and so earned the title "the Baptist".

The original apocalyptic promise was the salvation for Jews and the destruction for all Gentile Kingdoms, but John preached that the eschatological judgment was directed against Jews, not Gentiles. He declared that ritual observance and cultic sacrifice were no guarantee against the final judgment. God's fire can burn through such externals. Only the change of heart through 'repentance' can provide salvation. John's call to personal responsibility changed the role of Yahweh from a cosmic avenger of Israel to the Lord of those who repent.

Whereas John had emphasized the woes of impending judgment, Jesus preached the joy of the already dawning kingdom of God. He said, "The kingdom of God has come upon you.... Blessed are the eyes which see what you see. For I tell you that many prophets and kings desired to see what you see, and did not see it, and to hear what you hear and did not hear it." Luke 11:20, 10:23-24. For Jesus, God is not coming but is already here. For Jesus, God is not a Creator, nor a lawgiver, nor history maker but a father, Abba. Jesus spent an inordinate amount of time at the dinner table and preached about the kingdom of God in terms of a great banquet. For a short time (a few months), Jesus' simple message drew great crowds in Galilee but soon he was rejected not only by the religious establishment but by the common people as well. Some even tried to kill him. "...that they might cast him [Jesus] down headlong. But he passing through the midst of them went his way." Luke 4:29-30.

No doubt, Jesus' teaching was the most advanced of his time. The Pharisees and the Sadducees were still worshipping the God of Law. The John Baptist were worshipping the apocalyptic God. Jesus was living with Abba in the kingdom of God although he did not have the slightest understanding of what the essence of God is, but he knew Abba loves mankind. Lacking the true understanding of what the essence of God is, Jesus was elected by his followers to take the title of God after his crucifixion. Since no one, including their master, can comprehend who and what God is, they thus can give out the title of God at their choosing. The process of giving Jesus the title of God by his follows is not a mystery but a history.

Although the gospels are fabricated history, we can very easily separate the history from the fiction. In fact, the desperate attempts to deify Jesus become the guiding light for finding the truth. In Jesus' time, Judaism was the way of life for the Jews. There was no 'faith' involved. Faith is quite different from belief. Belief springs out from culture ideology. Every Jew had to live according to the Law given by God with or without faith. Nonetheless, there was expectation and hope. They expected and hoped the coming of the Son of Man. The resurrection is also a commonly accepted notion and no reference to divinity. There was a rumor that Jesus was John the Baptist come back to life, and Herod Antipas who killed John not only believed but also prepared to take additional action. "Now Herod the tetrarch heard of all that was done, and he was perplexed, because it was said by some that John had been raised from the dead, by some that Elijah had appeared, and by others that one of the old prophets had risen. Herod said, 'John I beheaded. But who is this about whom I hear such things?' And he sought to see him." Luke 9:7-9.

This is why Mary Magdalene and the other Mary did not sense any joy after they had learned that Jesus was risen, according to the gospel of Mark. The resurrection of Jesus had no religious significance for those two Mary. In fact, the term of resurrection is an over used phrase in those days without any religious connotation. "And the graves were opened; and many bodies of the saints which slept 'arose,' and came out of the graves after his resurrection, and went into the holy city, and appeared unto many." Matthew 28:52-53. Long before Jesus' resurrection, many bodies arose from graves.

The transformation of this common notion of resurrection into a vehicle to divinity was done by Saint Paul after he had invented the Pauline Trilogy. Being a Pharisee, why did Paul became a member of the Jesus-movement? All Christian exegetes attribute the Pauline kerygma to be sprung up from his experience on the road to Damascus. No doubt, the road side experience played a small role, but the major reason is that he believed that only Jesus fit the description as the Son of Man, outlined by earlier eschatologists. He wrote, "...Christ died for our sins 'according to the scriptures';... he rose again the third day 'according to the scriptures.'"

According to gospels, Jesus did claim to be the Messiah on many occasions, and these self proclamations were the basis for his later enthronement. Many historians disagree with the gospels on this account and showed concrete evidence to support their claim. However, this is not an important issue whether Jesus indeed proclaimed himself to be the Messiah or not. The fact is that He was officially 'identified' as Christ twenty years after his death, in accordance with the Scriptures. At this point, no faith was involved in giving Jesus the title of Christ, the Son of Man. He simply was identified to be the Christ in accordance with the Scriptures.

Although the Pauline Trilogy was officially invented by Paul, the idea was an ancient one, such as the Greek myth of Perseus. The apocalyptic scenario — the predicted period of eschatological woes (a time of sufferings), the end of the world, the coming of the Son of Man, the divine judgment and reward — were also known to Jesus' disciples and Paul. Thus, this newly invented Trilogy must somehow be reconciled with Jesus' own teaching in order to become a legitimate doctrine of the Jesus-movement. In fact, three doctrines — the apocalyptic expectation of John the Baptist, the love of Abba in the kingdom of God, and the Pauline Trilogy — are unified into one, the hope of parousia (the second coming). At this point, Christianity was officially born, but at the same time the true Jesus was lost forever. Jesus abandoned John the Baptist's doctrine of apocalyptic expectation soon after he broke away from John, and He did not invent any Trilogy.

The original parousia Christology was only identifying Jesus to be a deputy of God and only to be sitting at the right hand of God. Furthermore, the original idea of parousia was not an indefinitely long wait but was only meant to be shorter than one life time; thus Jesus' original followers could witness his seconding coming.

When Jesus' second coming was indefinitely delayed, the Christian communities (especial the Hellenistic Christian group) entered a state of 'doubt.' At this point, two 'things' came alive. The first is faith. Parousia was no longer an expectation but must be supported with faith. The second is a process of transforming the Jesus of Nazareth from a crucified prophet to a divine ruler of the cosmos, God Himself. By enhancing the status of Jesus, the faith thus can grow. On the other hand, this increased status can only be supported with faith because it can no longer be identified or understood with old Scriptures or common sense. At this point, the Christian faith was born.

VII

After the Christian faith came alive, the only barrier of promoting the deputy of God to God is the monotheistic doctrine of Judaism. The way out was two actions. First, the Hellenistic Christian group formulated the theory of Trinity by borrowing the pagan belief of polytheism. Second, at this point they had to break away from Judaism although Jesus' teaching was intended to be only a reformation inside of Judaism.

Christian faith was forced into life because of the long delayed parousia. The only way to keep Christian faith alive was to heighten Jesus' status. The higher the status, the higher the absurdity, thus the stronger faith is needed. The stronger the faith, the higher the absurdity is not only acceptable but becomes a must. These two processes feed on each other, and Jesus was transformed from a common Jew to Messiah (Son of Man), then to Lord Jesus Christ, then to God-man (the Savior) and finally to God Himself.

The growth of faith takes time. It took 70 years to reach its maturity. Thus, the status of Jesus in the early version of the gospels was much lower than in the later ones. The later gospels were desperately inventing stories, which are absent from the early gospels, to justify the heightened status of Jesus. In Paul's Epistles (50 C.E.), the common notion of resurrection was transformed into a Trilogy that Jesus' death was only a part of God's cosmic plan for human salvation. For Saint Paul, Jesus became Lord Christ at the point of resurrection. Twenty years later (at 70 C.E.), Mark decided that Jesus was adopted as Lord Christ at the point of his baptism. The book of Mark starts from Jesus' baptism which is in fact the beginning of his religious career. Mark did not bother to talk about Jesus' early life. Fifteen more years later (at 85 C.E.), when Jesus' status was elevated from an adopted Christ at baptism to a begotten Savior at conception, thus both Matthew and Luke had to invent a virgin birth story. Ten more years later (at 95 C.E.), when Jesus became the eternal God Himself preexisting even before creation, Saint John invented the final Christian equation, that Jesus is equal to 'Word' which was with God and is God.

There is absolutely no mystery of how Jesus became God. This is a process not intended and not foreseen by Jesus Himself but was executed by his followers. This process not only destroyed Jesus' teaching completely but mutilated His human dignity. The virgin birth process is God's way of reproduction for cold blooded low lives. At least half of mankind viewed Mary as a whore and Jesus as an illegitimate because of this stupid virgin birth story. For Jesus' and Mary's sake, we shall drop this stupid virgin birth story, thus restore their dignity. Jesus became the Savior of mankind because of his teaching and because of his sacrifice. Simon, Paul and Mark worshiped Jesus without the virgin birth story, and we can do the same.

VIII

After a long search, I finally found the true Jesus. I finally can worship Him without feeling to be a hypocrite or a heretic. In fact, I have made Jesus' second coming complete. He was dead. He was risen, and now He is here.

Yahweh was only a God of Law for a desert tribe at the time of Moses. After the Babylonian Exile, Yahweh became an apocalyptic avenger of Israel. John the Baptist transformed Him to be an apocalyptic Judge of mankind; anyone who repents will be saved. Jesus preached that God is

Abba and that He is now among you. Everyone can see God's presence by loving God and his neighbor.

After Jesus' crucifixion and by yearning His presence, His teaching of the dawning of the kingdom of God was partially forgotten, and the hope of parousia came alive in Simon Peter. Simon 'identified" Jesus as the Son of Man after his Easter experience. Then Apostle Paul invented the Pauline Trilogy. At this point, twenty years after His crucifixion, Jesus was enthroned as the Lord Jesus Christ.

The 'identification' and the 'enthronement' did not require the work of 'faith'. For Simon and Paul, Jesus simply fit the description of the apocalyptic prophecy. But the long delayed parousia created 'doubt'. The only way to ward off any doubt is by creating 'faith'. At this point, Christian faith was born.

Belief usually springs up from culture ideology and is not faith. Both belief and hope can only give birth to faith but cannot sustain it. The only way to sustain faith is to heighten the stakes, the status of Jesus. The higher status demands greater wonders. Thus, Paul's epistles, which were written before the Gospels, mention no miracles at all. The miracles became necessary after faith cannot be sustained by belief and hope any more. In the first Gospel, Mark, the miracles were only healing and exorcism. Then the miracle legends began to inflate on both the quality and the number in the later gospels. In Mark (5:23), a girl who was described as 'at the point of death' was described as 'my daughter is even now dead' in Matthew (9:18) which was written 15 years after Mark.

On the one hand, miracles sustain faith; on the other hand, they create doubt because of its absurd nature. The only way to counter absurdness is by higher absurdity. Thus absurdity and faith fed on each other. Soon, it reached the highest absurdity, God Himself. God's nature is indeed the highest absurdity.

Since the beginning of mankind, humans are astonished by the mystery of existence, of nonexistence, of suchness and of the creation of the world and even of the creation of the godhead itself. The ancients developed animism, symbolism (mythology) and finally absurdism. God is indeed the highest absurdity. For two thousand years, God can only be embraced with the madness of blind faith. The madness of faith, the hope of parousia and the love taught by Jesus became the 2nd Christian Trilogy (Faith, Hope, and

Love). Jesus' teaching of love ranks the last in this new trilogy. Both Faith and Hope are products invented after Jesus' death.

The process described above created Christianity. There is no mystery in this process. This process does reach the domain of God because God's essence is indeed the highest absurdity that He is the union of the highest opposites (nothingness, infinity and chaos). By knowing this, we can thus truly and sincerely worship Jesus with all our heart, not with the madness of blind faith.

IX

On the one hand, I had found the true and undistorted Jesus and had made His second coming complete. On the other hand, the process of moving from His understanding of God (a loving Abba) to mine (a union of nothingness, infinity, and chaos) is not yet all clear. Why did science spring out from Christianity but not from Taoism?

The term of Dark Age was coined after the Renaissance, and it stretches from the fourth to fifteenth centuries. I was taught that the Christian Church was the only small candle light during this long 1200 years. Soon, I discovered two coincidences. The Dark Age began in the fourth century when Teodosius I prohibited Pagan teaching and ended at the Renaissance when pagan teaching came back alive. In short, pagan philosophy was murdered by Christianity in the fourth century, and the modern science, which was born by Christianity, is the reincarnation of the pagan teaching. At any rate, Christianity is the mother of modern science.

In fact, this Christian child (science) is conceived by the mother herself, that the absurdity impregnated the absurdity, a virgin birth. Furthermore, science was even brought up by the absurdity. Without the absurdness, there is no reason or strong motive to find what is behind this absurdity. In Taoism and Buddhism, there are superstitions but no absurdity; thus they did not and could not give birth to science. Only Christianity teaches mankind that the absurdity is the highest truth, the Almighty God Himself. The absurdity of Christianity is created by God for revealing Himself. Without the Christianity, science could not have been born. This is the grand detour for the birth of science.

With hindsight, I know that I could never reach the final enlightenment by studying Taoism or Buddhism. They contain too much truth. Those fuzzy truths will trap every genius in them eternally, and it was the fate of all the Chinese who lived one hundred years ago.

On the other hand, science being a child of absurdity demands reason and reason only. Thus, science was and still is unable to tackle the essence of the absurdity which is God.

I, being a Chinese, learned fuzzy methodology from Chinese knowledge, learned scientific facts from science and learned the absurd essence of God from Christian Church; thus I am the only one who is able to reveal the true God. The mystery of God and of Jesus can only be revealed by the person from the East; thus East and West can be united. This is the grand detour for humanity.

Chapter XIV
Book of Worship,
The Holy Communion

A professor of philosophy wrote me, "Mathematicians understand mathematics but do not worship it. Why shall we worship God simply because we finally understand Him?"

Only by understanding Him, do we truly know His omnipotence and omniscience. Only by truly knowing His infinite power, do we know that God is the Creator, the Sustainer and the Governor. Only by truly knowing His infinite compassion, we know His providence. Only with the understanding of God's essence, we know the way of Holy communion with God. The God of creation, of judgement, of history, of cosmic process, of abstract, of providence, is the one and only "living" God. We understand, therefore, we worship.

In God's likeness, man and the universe reside in three realms — physical, psychological and spiritual. The physical realm is ruled by physics laws. Either biochemistry or electronics must obey physics laws. On the other hand, the psychological realm is not controlled by traditional physics laws. Our reasoning ability and intuition, that discovered those physics laws, are not governed by traditional physics laws. In short, the Son cannot govern the Father.

The emotions — joy, anger, love and grief — are attributes of "self". In TOE (Theory of Everything), self can be expressed in terms of infinity in mathematics and of the exclusion principle in physics; it can also be expressed in terms of seven colors. No doubt, these three realms — physical, psychological and spiritual — are only three subsets of the Oneness. Nonetheless, I will define them in such a way so that we can discuss each of them separately.

The physical realm is defined by traditional physics laws. The psychological realm is defined with "self". So, delight at solving a mathematical problem, anger after being manipulated, joy at seeing someone you love after a long absence, peace after forgiving someone, a sense of creativity, an awareness of having made a commitment and a sense of courage in standing up for one of your rights are all psychological phenomena. Although those feelings could be shared with others, they are

201

primarily subjective feelings and belong to a self. On the contrary, the spiritual self transcends the physical and psychological self and craves to unite with the eternal Self — the Almighty God. Thus, the spiritual realm can be reached only with a series of activities to achieve that goal — the union with God, but the spiritual realm itself does not contain those activities. Since God Himself is also having three manifestations, our spiritual activities must align with all three of God's manifestations in order to reach a true union. Many religions that emphasize one alignment over the other are simply not knowing what God is and what spiritual means.

II

God's first manifestation is the Cosmos and the cosmic laws. Indeed, all life on earth is supported by the energy of the sun. The activities of sun spots greatly affect the weather system on earth. The moon not only causes tidal cycles but also affects many lives. Many farmers believe that cosmic force will effect the plant growth and plant downward-growing root crops when the moon is waning and upward-growing grain crops when the moon is waxing.

In the West, science discovers many cosmic laws, and technology is developed by aligning with those cosmic laws. This kind of technological alignment has indeed improved the quality of human life immensely. Nonetheless, this kind of alignment does not assure the alignment between our body and the evolving cosmic forces.

Mencius said, "In the cycle of the day or year, certain forces appear to be present. These life-renewing forces are especially strong before day break, and they are particularly active after a person is in a deep relaxed state. For only in such deep relaxation is a person sufficiently dissociated to absorb cosmic forces." In the state of relaxation and dissociation one is able to absorb cosmic life forces. The relaxed state can only be reached by means of correct exercise.

In order to align with the cosmic life force, first we must be in touch with our own soul. Our soul contains not only our present body but all the history and life-experience of our existence. Furthermore, our soul is the link between our body, mind and the Almighty God. Thus, our present body and present mind, being a finite part of an infinity, cannot comprehend and be in touch with our own soul. A concentrated attention is needed in order to be in touch with our own soul.

Our attention is subordinate to our will. It is up to us to direct our attention to the point at which we want it to be directed. But, such an act of the will needs an infinite amount of energy for a prolonged period of time; thus, the power to fix our attention does not come easily to our will. On the other hand, undirected attention does not use up any energy; thus, the fixing of attention must be guided independently of our mind and will but with our soul. Although the life energy that flows in our body follows God's will, our mind and will is in general not aware of this flow. Only our soul is able to know God's will.

Where is our soul then? Our soul is the link between our body, mind and the Almighty God. Thus, our soul is both inside and outside of our body. No doubt, our mind can venture outside of our body. First, I am reading a book. Then, I am aware of myself reading a book. I can also see myself reading that book. I can even go one step further; I can watch myself seeing myself reading that book. As for mind, the difference between subject and object vanishes; the object is also the subject and vice versa. Thus, the mind is not bound by the body, and soul is not bound by the mind. Although soul is not bound by the body and mind, it does dwell in the body. A simple way to tell what part of our body our soul calls home is to see how we react to a shocking news. Do we respond with our intellect and try to find a solution? Do we respond with our heart and express emotions? Do we respond with our gut and clench up? Once we notice where in our body our soul comes to rest, our mind can then be consciously in touch with it. After we are in touch with our soul, we then are able to know God's will because our soul is the only linkage between us and the Almighty God.

Although the resting place for soul is different from person to person, we can build a home for our soul by practicing the contemplative breathing. With a permanent home for our soul, we can get in touch with it anytime at our will. The contemplative breathing aligns our life force with the cosmic life force. As I have discussed before, life is as a donut. The cosmic life force flows into life from one opening and circulates inside and then exits from the opposite opening. Water, food and air are part of this cosmic force. The most important life force is controlled by breathing — chee. By condensing chee toward the center of our body, we will retain more life force inside of our body. After many years of practice, we will be not only able to align our own life force with the cosmic life force but are able to direct our internal life energy with our will. Thus, we will be able to adjust the balance of our internal organs at our will. Furthermore, this personal internal life energy can even be transmitted to another person to cure the other person's illness. But, most importantly, we can settle our soul at a fixed location — the chee center, the Dan-Tien. After we have reached this level, to contact our soul requires no effort any more. The dhyana of Buddhism and the Chee-Kong of Taoism are teachings of this kind — concentrating the life force (chee) and centering our soul. Here, I will only give a very brief instruction of what is condensing and contemplative breathing.

1) Relax the entire body to be sure that there is no physical tension at all so that our mind and will can be in touch with our soul.

2) Listen to our breath and feel the body's natural rhythm, which shall follow God's rhythm.

3) Imagine God's hand is pulling our crown point (top of the head) from above. Gradually apply deeper breathing and inhale directly into the Dan-Tien (a spot located approximately three inches below the navel and two inches inward).

After weeks or months of practice, we may sense a feeling that flows with the rhythm of our breathing. As we progress, this feeling grows stronger, and we can begin to control the flow of this energy without the assistance of deep breathing and use our mind to guide this chee to travel inside our body. However, without any further training, the chee in our body will offer no greater benefits than a heightened awareness of our own body.

Although chee is the guide to lead us to our soul, our mind cannot be in touch with our own soul unless it reaches the plane in which our soul resides. Our soul resides in the plane of nothingness. Thus, we must struggle to reach that plane. During the condensing breathing, we must contemplate the reality of nothingness by first trying to sense and to locate our bone structure while ignoring the existence of the surrounding muscles. As we inhale, imagine that our breath forces the bone to condense inward toward the bone marrow. After successfully practicing condensing breathing in both arms, apply the same technique to other areas of the body, spinal column, head, legs, etc. Finally, we will reach the plane of nothingness. In addition to this contemplative breathing, we shall also fellow the science of Feng Shui. At this point, not only is our mind constantly in touch with our soul but our body has aligned with the cosmic force, and the foundation has been built for aligning our psyche with God's.

III

God's will is neither goodness nor evil but is intelligence. God's intelligence is a self-cause which creates being and nonbeing at the same time. The intelligence creates, distinguishes and separates. God's will is creation, creating many selves. In short, God's will is embodiment. God manifests Himself in embodiment. Every self, being or nonbeing, is the center of God Space. As for nonbeing, its psyche is expressed in terms of the 2nd law of thermodynamics. As for humans, our psychic is expressed in terms of ego.

The human psyche moves toward nurturing and satisfying the needs of the ego. The first is the will to live and it consists of physiological needs — such as food, shelter, etc. — and of safety and security needs. The second is the will to grow — starting from the growth of the body, then the growth of self-esteem and finally the craving of immortality. This craving of immortality becomes the highest human need, the spiritual need.

Thus, human psyche is neither a state nor a quality but a process, starting from an ego-self to the growth of body, mind, self-esteem and self-actualization. After the completion of this ego-self development, it moves to unite with others. With the union of love, it reaches immortality through offsprings. Then, it craves immortal truths. After the realization of the immortal truths, it craves for the union with the Almighty God Himself.

By definition, the will to live and the will to grow belong to the psychological realm, and it shall align with God's psyche — love and intelligence. Intelligence creates and distinguishes. Thus, we shall shape and create our own life and make a difference in this world. Furthermore, this psychic realm is also the stepping stone for the spiritual realm. In this psychic level, we first build up the ego-wall by growth then try to break it down with love.

Love in the psychic realm is quite different from the compassion in the spiritual domain. Love is neither a feeling, a state nor a quality but a process. Love is a series of willful acts, expressed in conscious ego choices, and it calls for effort, patience and discipline. When a person reaches out to others and others with love, it is often an extension of his self-boundary in a process of ego-evolution or ego-expansion rather than a process of breaking down the ego-wall. Thus, by definition, love is conditional. Mother loves her children because they are her offsprings. Father loves his children because they win his approval. Church loves it followers because they believe in its dogma. Jesus teaches us to love our neighbor as ourselves, that is, to love ourselves first of all, and only if we know how to love ourselves first, then are we able to love our neighbor. Love does not really break down the ego-wall, but it is the first step for reaching the egoless compassion.

Although love is not a substance, it is still confined in physical and psychological realms. Love can only be transmitted through communication. Communication is quite different from communion. Communication always depends upon physical or psychological means, such as an act, a deed, a word, a gesture or a loving glance.

With communication, the subjective worlds are united, and this is the psychological mutual in-dwelling. With communication, we are not only seeing and knowing other people's subjective universe but indeed live in them. Although communication requires physical or psychological means, it can indeed break the barriers of time and space. Confucius, during the time of his greatest loneliness, lived in fellowship with the Duke of Chou, although he was separated from the Duke in time by five centuries.

In short, the psyche of god is love and intelligence in fellowship. Intelligence creates and distinguishes; love unites them in fellowship. Completeness of life is possible only in fellowship. In fellowship, there are intelligence, love, communication and mutual in-dwelling. With intelligence not with dogmatic faith, we learn God's words. With love and communication, we dwell in one another. The second alignment to God is accomplished only with love and intelligence in fellowship.

IV

The psychological realm exists in between the mortal physical world and the immortal spiritual domain. The psyche, on the one hand, depends upon the physical and psychological acts; on the other hand, it is not controlled by physics laws. On the contrary, the spiritual world resides entirely in the immortal sphere.

In the psychic realm, we can subjectively summon other people's spirit to be present in our subjective world. We can see the vivid presence of our deceased relative or friends. We can enjoy fellowship with Confucius, Buddha and Jesus. Nonetheless, these are only subjective psychological events.

Can our spirit be present in other people's spirit at our will? Can I send my spirit to be present in front of my friend's spirit while we are thousands of miles apart? Can I send my spirit to be present in front of Confucius or

Jesus while we are separated in time by many thousands of years? The answer must be "yes" if there is a spiritual world. Nonetheless, the spiritual communion with others can only be accomplished by first attaining Holy Communion with God.

Then, how to align our spirit with God's? What is God's spirit? You shall know what God's spirit is when you have studied the previous Chapters of this book in detail. Traditionally, many religions use the contemplative meditation as a way of recognizing God's spirit. The Intellectual understanding sometimes can be quite superficial. The contemplative meditation is not only an intellectual act but also an act of living; it is the homework for spiritual learning. Thus, I am listing a few examples from both Buddhist's contemplative meditation and Christian's contemplative prayer.

In Zen Buddhism, koan is an anecdote about the dialogue between master and disciples, and it is used as a subject for contemplative meditation because it is a real experience of searching for God's spirit by someone. It tries to express the imageless God with concrete thoughts or acts. It tries to reconcile the irreconcilable paradox not with reason but with life. It tries to grasp the formless spirit of God with daily life experience. Thus, koan cannot be understood or reasoned but must be contemplated.

1) A disciple asked, "If there is no bit of cloud in the sky for ten thousand miles, what do you do about it?" Master replied, "I do." "What is that?" asked the disciple. Master answered, "It is."

2) A disciple asked, "When the old creak of Zen dries out and there is not a drop of 'water' left, what can I see there?" Master answered, "water." "How can one drink that water?" again asked the disciple. "Drink," answered master.

3) A disciple asked, "How does an enlightened person return to the world of delusion?" Master replied, "As a shattered mirror."

4) A disciple asked, "In my house there is a stone. I intend to carve it as a Buddha. Can I do it?" "Yes, you can," said master. "Can I not do it?" asked the disciple. Master answered, "No, you cannot do it."

5) A disciple asked, "Is there any phrase which is neither right nor wrong?" Master said, "A piece of white cloud does not show any ugliness."

6) A disciple saw a turtle walking in the garden and asked, "Most of beings cover their bones with flesh and skin. Why does this being cover its

flesh and skin with bones?" The master took off his sandal and covered the turtle with it.

7) The cook monk was always punctual in serving morning meals. One day master asked, "What makes you keep the time so accurately?" "I watch the stars and the moon," he answered. "What if it rains or is foggy?" master again asked. "I watch rains and fog," he answered.

8) A visiting monk asked, "What is Zen?" Master whispered, "We do not speak in the meditation room." As they went into the library, master whispered, "We only read book here in silence." When master opened the door, he said "Good-bye" to the visitor.

9) Buddha's efforts to save all sentient beings are no better than the blossoming flowers of spring. The southern branch owns the whole spring, as also does the northern branch. Each branch has the perfect color of spring. Bees and butterflies encircle the bloom with pleasure. Do the three monks discuss the real or the painted flower?

10) From scribe to scribe the letters change, and likewise does the teaching evolve from hand to hand. But no matter how the Yellow River bends and turns, its water comes from the source in Kun-lun Mountain. What is the highest Buddhism? It is not Buddha. Zen is like the full moon.

With reasoning, these koans are only some meaningless stories. With contemplative meditation, God's spirit can be reached with the hint of these koans. For Christians, the contemplative praying is the way to meet God face to face.

All contemplative prayers must consist of three parts. The first is the purifying of the heart, which is a total acceptance of ourselves and of our situation as willed by God. Only with an unconditional and totally humble surrender to God, can we then embrace God's will in its naked and impenetrable mystery. In purification, we must undergo an emptying process to reach our true self, and only in this complete emptiness and nakedness do we no longer know ourselves apart from God. Surprisingly, this Christian purification process reaches the same spiritual state (the emptiness) as Buddhist does in Buddhism.

The second is building the faith in God. Our intuitive faith in God comes from God's embodiment. But, we cannot grasp God's spirit with only intuitive faith. Only transcendental faith can comprehend the impenetrable mystery of God. This transcendental faith is based on concrete truths, and they are obtained with scientific and philosophical methodologies which are processes of the interplay between doubting and verifying. Thus, we must doubt our faith first then can we build it. Descartes found himself (the Cogito) by first doubting his own existence. Thus, only contemplative prayer can guide us to attain the true spiritual experience of being apparently without faith in order to really grow in faith.

The third is seeing the grace of God. God is both nothingness and infinity. Thus, God has neither image nor form. But, we can see God through His providential grace and through His decree on cosmic laws. From these, we can also see His infinite compassion.

Compassion is different from love; it is unconditional love. God's essence is an impenetrable mystery because it is an infinite possibility, but God's spirit is touchable compassion. With contemplative meditation or prayer, we can align our spirit with God's compassion.

V

The Holy Communion with God can be reached only if all three realms are aligned with God. Our body must align with cosmic forces and laws because the Cosmos is God's body, and so we have good health to serve God. Our psyche must develop intelligence and love through communication in fellowship because God's psyche is intelligence and love in fellowship. Our spirit must also be filled with compassion, gained by contemplative meditation, because God's spirit is infinite compassion.

These three alignments can also be done in the form of liturgy. Since God's essence is the union of nothingness and infinity, God's essence is formless and imageless. But, God's body is the Cosmos which is form and image. God's psyche is love and intelligence and is not controlled by physics laws, but they must be transmitted with physical or psychological means, such as an act, a word or a thought.

Thus, worshipping God with forms and images is the necessary first step in order to reach God's formless and imageless essence. Anyone who denounces the worshipping of image not only lacks the understanding that all images are God's body and no image can be outside of God or be not of God, but they definitely have no chance to grasp God's imageless spirit. Every image, either as a statue of Buddha or as Jesus on a cross, is God's manifestation through different religions.

Liturgy is a process of worshipping God by using both forms (rites) and images. In fact, all forms and rites are images. The scene of Baptism is an image. The scene of sacramental communion is an image. All religious services paint an image of God's three bodies. There are many bodies gathering in worship. There is love flowing between worshipers. There are devotions to God in worship.

Any form of liturgical rites is accepted by God. Nonetheless, one particular form can be much more effective or much better than the others because it aligns with God's three bodies completely. This new liturgical rite consists of three parts — comprehending God's three bodies by reciting creeds, in-dwelling in God's psyche through sacraments and fellowship, and uniting with God's spirit through contemplative meditation and prayers. There are three creeds — Essence creed, Devotion creed and Unity creed.

Essence creed — God is an infinite possibility. His essence is formless and imageless. His psyche is love and intelligence in fellowship. His body is the Cosmos. His imageless and formless spirit is the infinite compassion. His intelligence and love creates the universe and rules it with providential grace. God is the union of both nothingness and infinity, of both utmost order and utmost chaos, of both Goodness and evil, and of both transcendent and immanent. God manifests Himself in forms of paradox, but He is the only reconciling force for all paradoxes. God is embodied in everything, we are in Him. We can never comprehend God because He is an infinite possibility. We can worship Him because He is in us and us in Him. Thus, we pray.

Devotion Creed — God is our Creator. We are part of Him. He gives us life in order to complete His eternal life. Thus, our life is not suffering, not sinful, but is filled with purpose. Our life is a destiny given by God. To love our destiny is faith. To fulfill our destiny is the devotion to God. Life is not suffering but a struggle to fulfill our destiny. Life has no sin but is sometimes sinned because of ignorance. Being ignorant, we may not know the will of God, thus commit sins. Being ignorant, we may not fulfill our destiny, thus commit sins. we are permanently confined in God; thus God gives us the free will. With our free will we can either align ourselves with God's three bodies or be ignorant and thus commit sins. We must recite and contemplate the Essence Creed daily in order to rid of our ignorance. We must fulfill our destiny with faith and devotion. To fulfill our destiny given by God is our devotion to God. Thus, we pray.

Unity creed — God is the absolute Totality. Nothing can be outside of God. Confucius was and still is in God. Buddha was and still is in God.

Jesus was and still is in God. We can worship God in different rites with different images, but we all worship the same God. The Body of Buddha and the Body of Christ are both in the same God. The sacramental communion and idol worship are both worshipping the same God. God is the absolute Totality. Nothing can be outside of God. We are all in the same God. We must try to comprehend God's infinite compassion and to love each other and to respect the difference between each other. Thus, we pray.

In addition to the three creeds, two sacraments shall be part of our life. Sacrament is form, image, symbol and act. Because God's spirit is imageless, we must contemplate to comprehend God's essence. We must act to give God our devotion. By acting, we grasp the imageless spirit of God with images and rites.

We have no choice whether to be born or not; God decides that. After our birth, we align with God's will when our body obeys the cosmic laws. In fact, our body must obey God's laws in order to live whether we recognize God's providential care or not. Baptism is a rite to awake and to enlighten us about God's providential care. God provides us with air, water and food for our life. Traditionally, both East and West have used water as the symbol of God's providence. Besides to be a substance of life, water also symbolizes God's spirit and essence. Laotse wrote, "There is nothing weaker than water. But none is superior to it in overcoming the hard. That the yielding conquers the strong, and the soft conquers the hard." In I-Ching, 28 out of 64 hexagrams describe the action, interaction or reaction of water as God's actions. The 63rd hexagram is fire below, water above and symbolizes a state settled in completion. Water is important to life and soul, and that the fire of the spirit must penetrate this water in order to reach completeness. John the Baptist said, "I indeed baptize you with water unto repentance. ... He shall baptize you with the Holy Ghost, and with fire." Matthew 3:11.

In Holy Baptism, we show our appreciation for God's infinite mercy and his infinite providential care. In the waters of Baptism, we accept our life and destiny from God. By water and the Holy Spirit we devote our life to God. By receiving the Sacrament of Holy Baptism, we proclaim our obedience to the will of God.

The second sacrament is the Sacramental Communion. We are permanently confined in God, and our life is supported only by God's infinite mercy and infinite providential care. It is the body of God nurturing our life. It is the spirit of God enlightening our soul. In Sacramental Communion, we acknowledge to both God and ourselves that we are permanently confined in God and show our appreciation for the daily bread given by God —the body of God, giving to us; the spirit of God, shining on us.

VI

The liturgical rite is a form, an image and an act. The liturgical rite uses the physical realm, the bodies of worshipers, as the foundation, then transcends this physical realm and enters the psychological realm — God's love in fellowship. Although the psyche is not controlled by physics laws; it still depends upon the physical and psychological realms to transmit its force. The love that flows between the members during a liturgical rite is not controlled by physics laws, but it is part of the rite which consists of physical bodies, things and psychological communication, and which is confined in space and time. On the other hand, the spiritual communion does not depend upon the physical or psychological means — an act, a rite or a thought. Nonetheless, we can never reach a true spiritual communion with God without a good solid spiritual foundation. This spiritual foundation is deeply rooted in the physical and psychological realms. Three steps are needed to build this spiritual foundation — centering our soul with contemplative breathing, understanding and grasping God's essence by studying this book and the aligning of our soul with God's spirit (dwelling in God spiritually) with contemplative meditation.

Centering our soul is not a easy task. Today, too many psychologists mistake it as easy as to count 1, 2 and 3. They said, "Close your eyes and visualize 3 three times, then visualize 2 three times, then 1 three times. And, the center there is." No doubt, this can be the beginning, but it will take years of practice to find your true center. You must practice the condensing and contemplative breathing to condense the cosmic chee into your Dan-Tien, and make it as a resting place for your soul. Your soul is both nothingness and infinity. It cannot be located by your mind but it is in general resting inside of your body. By intentionally building a resting place (Dan-Tien) for it, you can be in touch with your soul much easier. Only after you have built a Dan-Tien for your soul, can you get centered anytime at your will.

Going to church or temple, receiving sacraments or praying to God will help you to keep in touch with God's psyche, but it will not help you to understand the essence and the spirit of God. You must read this book over and over. You must contemplate each paragraph of this book over and over. Without understanding the essence of God, we are building churches or temples not to praise God but to establish more firmly the social structures and benefits that we presently enjoy. Without the true understanding the essence of God, religions will be reduced to being the servants of cynical and worldly power, no matter how hard their faithful may protest that they are fighting for the Kingdom of God. Only by understanding the essence of God, are you then able to understand God's infinite power, infinite mercy and infinite providence. Only by understanding God's providential care, you will then understand the destiny of your life. Only by understanding the destiny of your life, you will then be able to make meaning out of your life. Only by understanding the meaning of your life, you will then understand God's infinite compassion. Only by understanding God's infinite compassion, will you then be able to love your enemies. Only when your are able to love your enemies, will your spirit be ready to enter the spiritual communion with God.

The spiritual communion is quite different from the psychic one. The Bible is the best teacher on the psychic communion. "I am the vine, ye are the branches: He that abideth in me, and I in him, the same bringeth forth much fruit: for without me ye can do nothing. If a man abide not in me, he is cast forth as a branch, and is withered; and men gather them, and cast them into the fire, and they are burned. If ye abide in me, and my words abide in you, ye shall ask what ye will, and it shall be done unto you." John 15:5-7.

These verses are the foundation for the reality of a Christ-Body, but most important of all, they show the way of mutual in-dwelling. Nonetheless, it is not a spiritual communion but is a psychic one because it first depends upon Christ's "words" and because it is a conditional communion, that one will be cast into the fire if he abides not in Christ.

No one has the choice of abiding not in God. Nonetheless, God has infinite compassion. God will not cast us into fire because of our ignorance of not aligning our spirit with His. Physically, psychologically and spiritually, we are always in God and God in us. There is no escape. Nonetheless, we can be in God but not align with His will. When our body does not follow God's laws, we will get sick. When our psyche does not follow God's will, we will be doing evil things and will surely get punishment. When our spirit does not follow God's spirit, we lose the meaning of our life.

Thus, defining and finding the meaning of our life is the key to the door of God's spirit. After we have centered our soul, dwelled with love in fellowship, understood the essence of God and found the meaning of our life, we are in Holy Communion with God.

Université de Montréal
Faculté des arts et des sciences
Département de philosophie

Montreal, October 28, 1991

Dr. Jeh-Tween Gong
P.O. Box 1753
Bristol, VA 24203
U.S.A.

Dear Jeh-Tween,

I am in receipt of your card of last September 4 for which I thank you. You may have believed that I had forgotten you but that was not the case at all. I was waiting for copies of my text to be printed of which I forward you one with great pleasure.

I enjoyed your lecture last August and was happy to make your acquaintance. I hope all is well with you, and your research both scientific and philosophical, is progressing well.

It will be a pleasure to meet you again in the near future.

Yours sincerely,

Georges Hélal

GH/sl

"Truth, Faith, and Life" does present a
unified theory of science and art, of east
and west. It is a welcomed addition to the
literature dealing with these issues and it
laid foundation and direction for further
study and inquiry. I believe all readers from
college up can understand the book with
different degree of comprehension.

Anthony Yueh-shan Wei, Ph.D.
Professor of Philosophy
Governors State University
Illinois

Gong has no trouble with the limitations
of science which acknowledges that no
absolute truth can be found, but constant
observation and experiment allow statements
to be made about the world and nature which
serve to give us a workable and predictable
truth which is ever subject to modification.
He sees science as a kind of errant but
sincere junior partner which is forced to
admit its faults by higher aspirants to the
"real" or "higher" truth.

Vic Lloyd
Editor, The Rationalist News
Australia